iPad and iPad Pro

for **dummies**®

A Wiley Brand

iPad and iPad Pro

2024–2025 Edition

by Paul McFedries

iPad and iPad Pro For Dummies®, 2024–2025 Edition

Published by: **John Wiley & Sons, Inc.,** 111 River Street, Hoboken, NJ 07030-5774, www.wiley.com

Copyright © 2024 by John Wiley & Sons, Inc., Hoboken, New Jersey

Published simultaneously in Canada

For general information on our other products and services, please contact our Customer Care Department within the U.S. at 877-762-2974, outside the U.S. at 317-572-3993, or fax 317-572-4002. For technical support, please visit https://hub.wiley.com/community/support/dummies.

Wiley publishes in a variety of print and electronic formats and by print-on-demand. Some material included with standard print versions of this book may not be included in e-books or in print-on-demand. If this book refers to media such as a CD or DVD that is not included in the version you purchased, you may download this material at http://booksupport.wiley.com. For more information about Wiley products, visit www.wiley.com.

Library of Congress Control Number: 2024930676

ISBN 978-1-394-24128-6 (pbk); 978-1-394-24130-9 (ebk); 978-1-394-24129-3 (ebk)

SKY10067061_021424

Contents at a Glance

Table of Contents

Introduction

One of the nice things about an iPad is that you can start using one a few minutes after liberating the device from its box. After traipsing through a mercifully brief setup routine, you end up on the iPad's Home screen and you're good to go. Even if you'd never used an iPad before, you probably figured out lickety-split that tapping the screen makes things happen and running your finger across the screen scrolls things here and there.

The iPad basics are intuitive and not hard to master, but you might also have learned a hard iPad lesson: Once you've got the easy stuff down, the rest of the iPad is less intuitive. How do you make the screen brighter? How do you get that app that all the cool people are using? How do you set up your email? How do you take amazing photos and videos?

These are all great questions, but they probably only scratch the surface of what you want to know, iPad-wise. Not only that, but the iPad is a wonderfully complex device with hidden depths that enable the tablet to perform tasks you've likely never thought of. How do you get your iPad questions answered and how do you explore your iPad's depths?

I thought you'd never ask.

About This Book

Welcome, therefore, to *iPad and iPad Pro For Dummies*, 2024-2025 Edition. This book is designed to take you beyond the basics of your iPad and show you what your tablet can do. iPads aren't cheap, so you owe it to yourself to get the most out of your investment by learning not only the iPad's ABCs but also its XYZs. From mail to messaging, from Siri to settings, from contacts to calendars, this book covers all major iPad and iPadOS features (and quite a few minor ones, too).

I need to get one thing out of the way from the get-go. I think you're pretty darn smart for buying a *Dummies* book. To me, that says you have the confidence and intelligence to know what you don't know. The *Dummies* franchise is built on the core notion that everyone feels insecure about certain topics when tackling them for the first time, especially when those topics have to do with technology. The iPad is no exception.

This book is chock-full of useful tips, advice, and other nuggets that should make your iPad experience more pleasurable. I'll even go so far as to say you won't find some of these nuggets anywhere else. So, keep this book nearby and consult it often.

Foolish Assumptions

Although I know what happens when one makes assumptions, I've made a few anyway. First, I assume that you, gentle reader, know nothing about using an iPad or iPadOS, that you want to understand your iPad and its operating system without digesting an incomprehensible technical manual, and that you made the right choice by selecting this book.

I do my best to explain each new concept in full and loving detail. Perhaps that's foolish, but . . . oh, well.

One last thing: I also assume that you can read. If you can't, please ignore this paragraph.

Icons Used in This Book

Little round pictures (or *icons*) appear in the left margin throughout this book. Consider these icons as miniature road signs, telling you something extra about the topic at hand or hammering a point home. Here's what the icons in this book look like and mean.

These juicy morsels, shortcuts, and recommendations might make the task at hand faster or easier.

This icon emphasizes the stuff I think you ought to retain. You may even jot down a note to yourself on the iPad.

TECHNICAL STUFF

Put on your propeller beanie hat and insert your pocket protector; this text includes truly geeky stuff. You can safely ignore this material, but if it weren't interesting or informative, I wouldn't have bothered to write it.

WARNING

You wouldn't intentionally run a stop sign, would you? In the same fashion, ignoring warnings might be hazardous to your iPad and (by extension) your wallet. There, you now know how these warning icons work, for you have just received your very first warning!

Beyond the Book

I wrote a bunch of things that just didn't fit in the print version of this book. Rather than leave them on the cutting room floor, I've posted the most useful bits online in a cheat sheet for your enjoyment and edification.

To find them, go to www.dummies.com and type *iPad and iPad Pro For Dummies cheat sheet* in the Search field. Here's what you'll find: info on using the iPad's buttons and icons, tips for mastering multitouch, and where to find additional help if your iPad is acting contrary.

Where to Go from Here

Why, go straight to Chapter 1, of course (without passing Go).

Note: At the time I wrote this book, all the information it contained was accurate for all Wi-Fi and Wi-Fi + Cellular iPads that support iPadOS. The book is also based on version 17 of the iPadOS operating system. Apple is likely to introduce new iPad models and new versions of iPadOS between book editions, so if the hardware or user interface on your new iPad looks a little different, be sure to check out what Apple has to say at www.apple.com/ipad. You'll no doubt find updates on the company's latest releases.

1

Getting to Know Your iPad

Chapter **1**

Unveiling the iPad

Are you familiar with the old proverb that says, "Well begun is half done"? Some say it comes from Aristotle, so if you mumbled to yourself that the phrase is "Greek to me," you'd be spot on! The proverb's meaning is straightforward enough: If you start a project well, the rest of it will proceed so swimmingly that it'll feel like you need to expend only half the effort to get it done.

This chapter is your chance to get your relationship with your iPad off to such a good start. Sure, you can dive right in and start tapping and scrolling stuff willy-nilly. If that's your style, go for it; I won't judge. However, one thing I've learned over the years is that if you approach a new piece of technology slowly and curiously, you'll end up with a solid grounding in the basics that will pay back your initial time investment manyfold.

To that end, in this chapter, I offer a gentle introduction to all the pieces that make up your iPad, plus an overview of its most useful hardware features and a few software features that come with iPadOS.

REMEMBER

iPadOS is the software that runs behind the scenes to control just about everything that happens on your iPad. The *OS* part of *iPadOS* is short for *operating system*, which tells you that iPadOS is the iPad equivalent of macOS on a Mac or even Windows on a PC.

In this book, I cover all iPad models that can run iPadOS 17:

>> iPad sixth generation (2018) and later

>> iPad Pro 11-inch first generation (2018) and later; iPad Pro 12.9-inch second generation (2017) and later

>> iPad Air third generation (2019) and later

>> iPad mini fifth generation (2019) and later

TIP

To figure out which generation iPad you have, open the Settings app, tap General, tap About, and then read the model name, which will be something like *iPad (10th generation)*.

The iPad: A Bird's-Eye View

The iPad has many interesting and useful features, but perhaps its most notable feature is something that it *doesn't* have: a physical keyboard or mouse. Instead, every iPad is designed so that you can control it with a device that you're intimately familiar with: your finger.

The iPad also ships with a boatload of built-in sensors. It has an accelerometer that detects when you rotate the device from portrait to landscape mode — and instantly adjusts what's on the display. A light sensor adjusts the display's brightness in response to the current ambient lighting conditions. Then there's a three-axis gyro that works with the accelerometer and built-in compass. And all iPadOS-capable models also include Apple's Touch ID sensor or Face ID. These features let you unlock your iPad with your fingerprint (Touch ID) or just by looking at it (Face ID)! I talk about both in detail later.

Last, but definitely not least, all iPads include Siri, a voice-controlled personal assistant happy to do almost anything you ask.

In the following sections, it's time to take a brief look at the rest of the iPad's features, broken down by product category.

The iPad as a media player

The iPad's built-in speakers and sharp, clear display mean you can enjoy all your favorite media — music, audiobooks, audio and video podcasts, music videos, YouTube cat videos, television shows, and movies — from the comfort of your favorite armchair.

If you can get a media file — be it video, audio, or whatever — on your iPad, you can watch or listen to it on your iPad. And, of course, you can always buy or rent content on your iPad in the iTunes Store. You can also watch streaming content from Netflix, Hulu, Apple's own Apple TV+ streaming service, and a host of others through apps.

An *app* (it's short for *application*) is a program you can run on your iPad. For example, you browse the web with the Safari app, exchange email with the Mail app, and customize your iPad with the Settings app.

The iPad as an internet device

The iPad is a full-featured internet device. For example, your iPad comes with the Safari app, which is a no-compromise web browser that makes navigating web pages intuitive and even fun. Check out Chapter 4 to learn how to surf the web using Safari.

Many other iPad web browsers are available, including Google Chrome, Mozilla Firefox, and Microsoft Edge, but I don't talk about them in this book. If you use the desktop equivalent of one of these browsers, you might want to try out the iPadOS version.

The iPad also comes with an email app (called, somewhat boringly, Mail) that's compatible with most mail services. For more on using your iPad for email, see Chapter 5.

If you're more into text messaging, your iPad has you covered with the Messages app. The details are in Chapter 6.

Another major internet feature is Maps, a mapping app that not only lets you see where things are located but also can provide directions to get from here to there. For the full scoop on Maps, see Chapter 13.

The iPad as an e-book reader

Open your iPad's free Books app or install any of the excellent (and also free) third-party e-book readers such as the Kindle app from Amazon, and you'll discover a new way of finding and reading books. The Apple Book Store and News app (covered in Chapter 7) are chock-full of good reading at prices that are lower than what you'd pay for a printed copy.

Sure, you and I both know that there's nothing better than reading a printed book. Still, when you read an e-book, at least you can say you're helping the environment and saving trees. Interestingly, some titles include audio, video, or graphical content that's not available in the printed edition. Plus, tons of e-books are free; sure, the quality of most of these is suspect, at best, but there are all kinds of classic reads available for zero dollars. And it's kind of cool to know that you can carry an entire library in one hand.

The iPad as a multimedia powerhouse

Your iPad has built-in speakers and support for connecting external headphones or speakers (directly or via Bluetooth), so if you want to listen to some tunes, your iPad is happy to help, as I show in Chapter 7.

All iPads also come with a couple of cameras, so you can use your tablet as a (slightly bulky) video camera (see Chapter 8) or still camera (see Chapter 9).

The Retina display on all iPads since the third generation makes the experience of watching video a pleasure. You can use AirPlay to send your video out to Apple TV, too, and your iPad turns into a superb device for watching video on a TV, with support for output resolutions up to 4K. Chapter 8 talks about watching video on your iPad.

You can also use the iPad cameras and the FaceTime app to video-chat with family and friends. Chapter 8 gets you started with FaceTime.

The iPad as a platform for third-party apps

Your iPad comes with quite a few apps, but you can always get more from the App Store. How many more? Lots: Literally *millions* of apps are available in the App Store, in categories such as games, business, education, entertainment, healthcare and fitness, music, photography, productivity, travel, and sports. The cool thing is that most of them, even ones designed for the iPhone, also run on the iPad (although, it must be said, they look a tad weird on the larger screen). And more than a million are designed *specifically* for the iPad's larger screen. Chapter 10 helps you fill your iPad with all the cool apps your heart desires.

The iPad as a multitasking content production device

Apple has made the iPad more and more of a device for creating content as opposed to only consuming it. Writing, taking and editing photos, recording and editing music or videos, and even putting together full-scale presentations — all these tasks are doable with iPadOS, especially on the iPad Pro. Split-screen views, support for the Files app, and a fast processor give the iPad more than enough power to handle most tasks you throw at it. I talk more about multitasking in Chapter 2.

What do you need to use an iPad?

To *use* your iPad, only a few simple things are required. Here's a list of everything you need:

>> An iPad (duh)

>> An Apple ID (assuming that you want to acquire content such as apps, TV shows and movies, music, books, and podcasts, which you almost certainly do)

>> Internet access — broadband wireless internet access is recommended

Several years ago, you needed a computer with iTunes to sync your iPad. That's no longer true; these days you can activate, set up, update, back up, and restore an iPad wirelessly without ever introducing it to a computer.

If you do decide to introduce your iPad to your computer (and I think you should), you need one of the following for syncing (which I discuss at length in Chapter 3):

>> A Mac with a USB 2.0, 3.0, or USB-C port, macOS version 10.8.5 or later, and iTunes 12.7 or later (for macOS Mojave and earlier) or Finder (macOS Catalina or later)

>> A PC with a USB 2.0 or 3.0 port, Windows 7 or later, and iTunes 12.7 or later

iTunes is a free download, available via the Microsoft Store if you're running Windows 10 or 11.

Touring the iPad Exterior

The iPad's exterior is sleek and smooth, but it's not feature-free. In fact, it's no exaggeration to say that the exterior doohickeys are some of the most important features of the iPad. Therefore, you need to know your way around the outside of your iPad, which is the job of this section.

Checking out the top

What's on the top edge of your iPad depends on which model and which generation of that model you're using. First, Figure 1-1 shows the top edge of the four current iPad models (current as I write this, anyway) and point out the salient features.

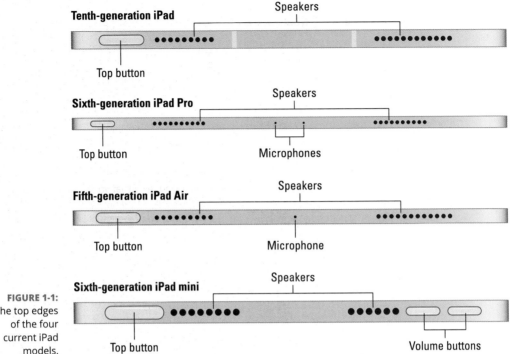

FIGURE 1-1:
The top edges
of the four
current iPad
models.

Here's a summary of the features mentioned in Figure 1-1:

REMEMBER

>> **Top button:** This is one of the crucial features I mention earlier because this deceptively simple button can do a ton:

- *Sleep and wake your iPad:* To put your iPad to sleep, just press the top button. The screen turns off and your iPad goes into low-power mode to save the battery. To wake up a sleeping iPad, either press the top button once again or just tap the screen.

  Your iPad's battery will run down faster when your iPad is awake, so it's a good idea to get into the habit of putting your tablet to sleep when you're not using it. In Chapter 14, you learn how to make your iPad go to sleep automatically after a period of inactivity.

- *Turn the iPad on and off:* To shut your iPad down completely, press and hold down both the top button and one of your iPad's volume buttons for a few seconds. When you see the Slide to Power Off control, slide your finger from left to right across the control to shut down your tablet. (Refer to "Exploring the right side" for the location of the volume buttons.) To restart the device, press and hold the top button until you see the Apple logo on the screen.

- *Verify that it's you:* On some iPad models, you also use the top button as a fingerprint sensor for the Touch ID security feature (covered in Chapter 17).

>> **Microphone(s):** Each tiny dot represents a microphone.

>> **Speakers:** These grilles cover two of the iPad's four speakers. The other two are on the bottom.

>> **Volume buttons (iPad mini only):** I talk about the volume buttons a bit later (refer to "Exploring the right side").

Perusing the bottom

What's on the bottom edge of your iPad? That depends on which iPad model and which generation of that model you're using. Figure 1-2 shows the bottom edge of the four iPad models that are the latest generations as I write this.

Here's a summary of the features pointed out in Figure 1-2 (they apply to all four models):

>> **USB-C connector:** This connector has three purposes:

- *Recharge your iPad's battery:* Connect one end of the cable that came with your iPad to the iPad's USB-C port and the other end to the charging brick, which then connects to a power outlet. Alternatively, if you have a multiport wall charger that includes a USB-C port, you can disconnect the other end of your iPad's cable from the charging brick and insert the cable into the wall charger's USB-C port.

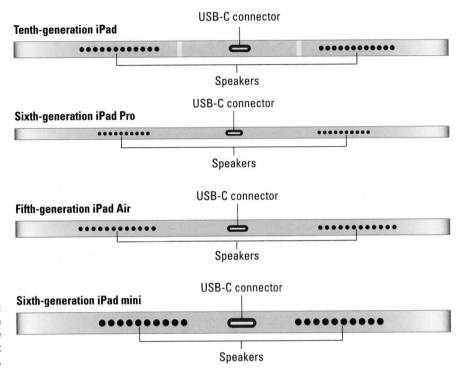

Tenth-generation iPad
USB-C connector
Speakers

Sixth-generation iPad Pro
USB-C connector
Speakers

Fifth-generation iPad Air
USB-C connector
Speakers

Sixth-generation iPad mini
USB-C connector
Speakers

FIGURE 1-2:
The bottom edges of the four current iPad models.

- *Synchronize your iPad:* Connect one end of the iPad cable to the iPad's USB-C connector and the other end (once you've removed it from the charging brick) to a Thunderbolt, USB4, or USB-C port on your computer.

- *Connect your iPad to an external device:* For devices such as headphones, cameras, or televisions, connect the device's cable to your iPad's USB-C connector. For some devices, you might need to use an adapter that enables the device's cable to plug into your iPad's USB-C connector.

REMEMBER

Instead of a USB-C connector, the iPad Pro has a Thunderbolt/USB4 connector. The connector type is the same, but an iPad Pro can connect to not only USB-C devices but also Thunderbolt and USB4 devices.

REMEMBER

If you connect your iPad to a port and get a *Not Charging* message, the port doesn't have enough power. Generally speaking, USB-C-compatible ports built into recent Macs and PCs, on powered hubs, or (of course) on the charging brick that came with your iPad will charge your iPad properly. Any USB-C-compatible data port connected to your Mac or PC will allow you to sync your iPad, whether or not it's charging.

>> **Speakers:** These grilles cover two of the iPad's four speakers. The other two are on the top.

Exploring the right side

The first question you might be asking yourself is, "How do I know which side is the right side?" Great question! To make sure we're talking about the same thing here, maneuver your iPad so that the screen is facing you and the top button is at the top. The side of the iPad that's now to your right is the one I'm talking about in this section.

REMEMBER

When you've turned your iPad so that the shorter edges are on the top and bottom and the longer edges are on the left and right, your iPad is said to be in *portrait orientation*. If you were to rotate your iPad 90 degrees either way so that the shorter edges are now on the left and right and the longer edges are now on the top and bottom, your iPad would now be in *landscape orientation*.

The knickknack population of your iPad's right side depends on which iPad model and which generation of that model you're using. Figure 1-3 shows the right edge of the four iPad models that are the latest generations as I write this.

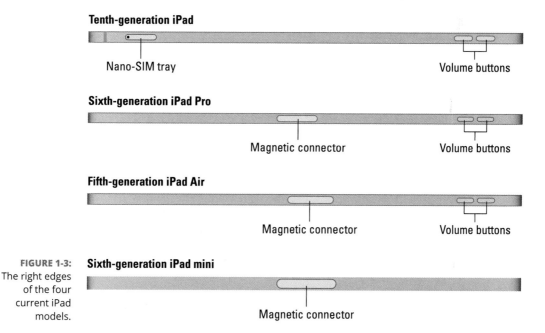

Tenth-generation iPad

Nano-SIM tray   Volume buttons

Sixth-generation iPad Pro

Magnetic connector   Volume buttons

Fifth-generation iPad Air

Magnetic connector   Volume buttons

FIGURE 1-3: The right edges of the four current iPad models.

Sixth-generation iPad mini

Magnetic connector

Here's a summary of the features pointed out in Figure 1-3:

>> **Volume buttons:** You use these buttons mostly to control the volume. Press the upper button (the right button on the top of the iPad mini) to increase the volume; press the lower button (the left button on the top of the iPad mini) to

decrease the volume. I wrote *mostly* because there are a few other uses for the volume buttons:

- *Shutting down the iPad:* As I describe earlier in the "Checking out the top" section, you can shut off your iPad by pressing and holding the top button and any volume button.

- *Taking a photo or video:* In the Camera app (check out Chapter 9), you can use either volume button to take a photo. You can also use either volume button to start and stop video recording (check out Chapter 8).

- *Capturing a screen shot:* Quickly press and release both the top button and any volume button to capture the current iPad screen.

TIP

The latest iPad models support *dynamic* volume buttons, which means that the volume buttons adjust as you rotate the iPad. In other words, if the iPad is in portrait orientation, the topmost volume button always increases the volume. Even when you rotate the device 180 degrees, the volume button that's now on top is the one that increases the volume.

» **Magnetic connector:** This strip is magnetized, which enables certain accessories — notably the Apple Smart Cover or Smart Folio or the Apple Pencil — to attach magnetically to the iPad. Note that for the iPad model simply called iPad, the magnetic connector is on the left side of the tablet.

» **Nano-SIM tray (cellular models only):** On iPads with cellular capabilities, this tray is where you insert the Nano-SIM card given to you by your cellular provider. Wi-Fi-only models don't have a SIM card tray.

TIP

Apple used to include a SIM card eject tool with iPads and iPhones. If you don't have one lying around, you can straighten a paper clip and use it as an ersatz SIM card eject tool. Just insert the tip of the straightened paper clip into the small hole near the edge of the tray and then press until the tray ejects slightly. Make sure you use a paper clip with a relatively light gauge wire so that the tip will fit into the hole.

Getting to know the back

On the back of your iPad, all the action is in the top-left corner (assuming your tablet is in portrait orientation with the top button at the top). What you see up there depends on your iPad model and generation. Figure 1-4 shows the back of the four iPad models that are the latest generations as I write this.

Tenth-generation iPad

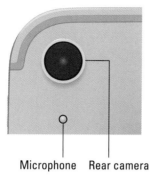

Microphone   Rear camera

Sixth-generation iPad Pro

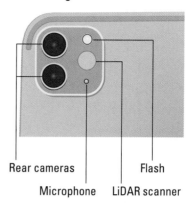

Rear cameras   Flash

Microphone   LiDAR scanner

Fifth-generation iPad Air

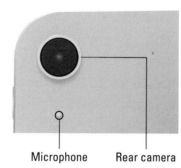

Microphone   Rear camera

Sixth-generation iPad mini

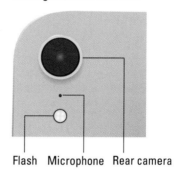

Flash Microphone Rear camera

FIGURE 1-4:
The backs of the latest iPad models.

Here's a summary of the features pointed out in Figure 1-4:

>> **Rear camera(s):** The workhorse camera for taking photos and capturing video. The iPad Pro's rear camera array includes two cameras: Wide and Ultra-Wide. Check out Chapters 8 and 9 to learn more about the rear camera and how it works.

>> **Microphone:** All iPad models except the iPad Pro have an extra microphone just below the rear camera. For the iPad Pro, the extra microphone is part of the rear camera array.

>> **Flash:** A device that produces a brief burst of light to illuminate a scene, which enables you to take photos in very low light conditions, even complete darkness.

>> **LiDAR scanner:** This light detection and ranging scanner helps you take sharper pictures in low-light conditions.

REMEMBER

Both the iPad Pro and the iPad Air have an extra connector. To see it, flip the tablet so you can see the back, and then look in the center, near the bottom. See those three horizontal dots? That's called the Smart Connector, and it's used to connect and provide power to Apple's Smart Keyboard (as well as some third-party keyboards).

Becoming familiar with the front

The current generations of all the iPad models have fronts that look essentially the same, just with different size screens. On the front of most iPad models, you'll find the following (labeled in Figure 1-5):

>> **Touchscreen:** This is where all the iPad action happens. I describe how to use the iPad's touchscreen in Chapter 2.

>> **Front (FaceTime) camera:** You use the front camera for FaceTime video chats (refer to Chapter 8) and taking selfies (check out Chapter 9). Note that the tenth-generation iPad has the front camera on the right bezel, in the center.

Figure 1-5 also points out a microphone, which comes with the iPad Pro and iPad. In both cases, the microphone sits beside the front camera but, again, for the tenth-generation iPad, the front camera is on the right bezel, and that's where you'll find the microphone (it's just below the camera).

FIGURE 1-5:
The front of an iPad Pro.

Exploring the Home Screen and Dock

The iPad *Home screen* refers to the screen you see when your iPad is unlocked and you're not working in an app. The Home screen is divided into multiple pages; you scroll to the next page by swiping your finger to the left on the screen and you scroll to the previous page by swiping right. (I describe what *swiping* is in Chapter 2.) Each Home screen page can hold up to 30 icons, with each icon representing a different built-in app or function.

Each Home screen page also displays the *dock,* which is a strip that runs along the bottom of the page. The dock can store up to 15 app icons, depending on your iPad model.

If your iPad is asleep, press the top button or tap the screen to display the unlock screen. Now use a finger to swipe up from the bottom edge of the screen. With your iPad unlocked, you see the app or page that was displayed when the tablet went into sleep mode. To get to the Home screen (if it's not displayed already, that is), swipe up from the bottom of the screen again.

REMEMBER

When you unlock your iPad, you might have to enter a passcode. To learn more about passcodes, see Chapter 17.

In the following sections, I tell you briefly about the icons preloaded on your iPad's Home screen pages, as well as the icons you find on the dock. Because the rest of the book covers most of these babies in full and loving detail, I provide only brief descriptions here.

Interpreting the status bar

The status bar, which is at the top of the screen, displays tiny icons that provide a variety of information about the current state of your iPad:

>> **Airplane mode:** Airplane mode should be enabled when you fly. It turns off all wireless features of your iPad — the cellular, 5G, 4G, LTE, 3G, GPRS, and EDGE networks; GPS; Wi-Fi; and Bluetooth — so you can enjoy music, video, games, photos, or any app that doesn't require an internet connection while you're in the air.

Tap the Settings app and then tap the airplane mode switch on (so green is displayed). The icon shown in the margin appears on the left side of your status bar when airplane mode is enabled. You can also pull Control Center down from the top-right corner and tap the airplane mode icon to turn airplane mode on (the icon turns orange). Check out Chapter 15 to learn more about airplane mode.

Disable airplane mode when the plane is at the gate before takeoff or after landing so you can send or receive email and iMessages.

To use Wi-Fi in flight, first enable airplane mode and then reenable Wi-Fi.

>> **Wi-Fi:** If you see the Wi-Fi icon, your iPad is connected to a Wi-Fi network. The more semicircular lines that are lit (up to three), the stronger the Wi-Fi signal. If your iPad has only one or two semicircles of Wi-Fi strength, try moving around a bit. If you don't see the Wi-Fi icon on the status bar, Wi-Fi is not currently available.

>> **Personal Hotspot:** You see this icon when you're sharing your internet connection with computers or other devices over Wi-Fi, USB, or Bluetooth. Personal Hotspot is available for every cellular-enabled iPad but may not be available in all areas or from all carriers. Additional fees may apply. Contact your wireless carrier for more information.

>> **Syncing:** This icon appears on the status bar when your iPad is syncing with your Mac or PC.

>> **Activity:** This icon tells you that some network or other activity is occurring, such as over-the-air synchronization, the sending or receiving of email, or the loading of a web page. Some third-party apps use this icon to indicate network or other activity.

>> **VPN:** This icon shows that you're currently connected to a virtual private network (VPN).

>> **Lock:** This icon tells you when your iPad is locked. See Chapter 2 for information on locking and unlocking your iPad.

>> **Screen orientation lock:** This icon appears when the screen orientation lock is engaged.

>> **Location Services:** This icon appears when an app (such as Maps; see Chapter 13 for more about the Maps app) is using Location Services (such as GPS) to establish the location of your iPad.

>> **Do not disturb:** This icon appears whenever do not disturb is enabled, silencing alerts and incoming FaceTime calls. See Chapter 14 for details on do not disturb.

>> **Play:** This icon informs you that a song is currently playing. You find out more about playing songs in Chapter 7.

>> **Bluetooth:** This icon indicates the current state of your iPad's Bluetooth connection. If you see this icon on the status bar, Bluetooth is on and a device (such as a wireless headset or keyboard) is connected. If the icon is gray, Bluetooth is turned on but no device is connected. If the icon is white, Bluetooth is on and one (or more) devices are connected. If you don't see a Bluetooth icon, Bluetooth is turned off. Chapter 14 goes into more detail about Bluetooth.

» Bluetooth battery: This icon displays the battery level of supported Bluetooth devices (while connected). Only certain devices — mostly headsets and speakers — support this feature. If you see this icon in your status bar, it's telling you the approximate battery level of whichever supported device is currently connected with your iPad.

» Battery: This icon shows the level of your battery's charge and also indicates when your device is connected to a power source. It's completely filled when your device isn't connected to a power source and is fully charged. It then empties as the battery becomes depleted. You see an onscreen message when the charge drops to 20 percent or below, and another when it reaches 10 percent.

Exploring the Home screen

As shown in Figure 1-6, the first page of the iPad Home screen is divided into three sections:

» Widgets: These items appear in the top half of the screen in landscape mode and include the following default widgets: Clock, Notes, Calendar, Photos, and Weather. See Chapter 10 to learn how to customize your widgets.

» App icons: These items represent (mostly) apps that you can launch with a tap of your finger.

» Dock: This area also contains (mostly) app icons, but the dock appears on every Home screen page, so you always have quick access to these apps.

If you haven't rearranged your icons, you see the following apps on the first Home screen page, starting on the left side of the first row of apps:

» FaceTime: Participate in FaceTime video chats, as you discover in Chapter 8.

» Files: View and work with the files you've saved to your iCloud Drive. Apple apps as well as many third-party apps know how to use the Files app to store documents.

» Reminders: Display alerts that remind you to perform some task. You can think of Reminders as a kind of fancy-schmancy to-do list. If you ask Siri to remind you, it's added as a reminder in this app, too. You can do both location- and time-based reminders, which will be synced to your other Apple devices. Learn more about reminders in Chapter 12.

» Maps: View street maps, satellite imagery, transit information, and more for locations around the globe. Or ask for directions, traffic conditions, or the location of a nearby pizza joint. I show you more about Maps in Chapter 13.

Widgets

Dock   Apps

FIGURE 1-6:
The iPad's
first Home
screen page.

>> **Home:** Access and control your HomeKit smart home devices. Almost like a sci-fi movie, you can control lights, appliances, and surveillance cameras from an app or with your voice using Siri. You'll read much more about this great app, but you have to wait until Chapter 12.

>> **Camera:** Shoot pictures or videos with your iPad's front- or rear-facing camera. You find out more in Chapters 8 (videos) and 9 (photos).

>> **App Store:** Search for iPad apps you can purchase or download for free. Chapter 10 is your guide to buying and using apps from the App Store.

>> **Books:** Read e-books, which you can buy in the Book Store. I discuss the Books app more deeply in Chapter 7.

>> **Podcasts:** Subscribe and listen to your favorite podcasts.

>> **TV:** Watch and manage your movies, TV shows, and music videos. You add videos via Finder in recent versions of macOS or iTunes on older Macs or on PCs or by purchasing them directly in the TV app or the iTunes Store app. Check out Chapter 8 to find out more.

>> **News:** Read the latest news from magazines, newspapers, and websites, and subscribe to Apple News+ for access to paid content from many mainstream sources. You read more about News in Chapter 7.

>> **Settings:** Customize your iPad and apps by modifying their settings. With so many options in the Settings app, you'll be happy to hear that Chapter 14 is dedicated exclusively to Settings.

The second Home screen page (swipe your finger left on the screen to get there) contains the following default apps:

>> **Clock:** Check the current time (locally as well as from anywhere in the world) and set alarms and timers. You hear more about this nifty app in Chapter 12.

>> **Weather:** Get current conditions and forecasts for your location and just about any other place on Earth.

>> **Stocks:** Track stocks. You can also get news articles about the companies you're following.

>> **Find My:** Locate a lost iPad (or iPhone, AirPods, or Mac). I look more closely at Find My in Chapter 14.

>> **iTunes Store:** Buy or rent music, movies, TV shows, audiobooks, and more. You find more info about iTunes Store in Chapter 7.

>> **Contacts:** Store information about the people you know. Chapter 11 explains how to use the Contacts app.

>> **Translate:** Translate a word or phrase in one language (entered by typing or speaking) into another language. See Chapter 12 for the details.

>> **Shortcuts:** Combine two or more actions — such as taking a photo and sending it via text message to someone — into a single script that you run by tapping an icon.

>> **Voice Memos:** Record everything you speak into your iPad's microphone. For more about the Voice Memos app, turn to Chapter 12.

>> **Measure:** Measure distances in the real world by using the iPad's rear camera. Seriously, try it! Turn to Chapter 12 for more on the Measure app.

>> **Magnifier:** Using the iPad's rear camera, zoom in on real-world objects that are too small to see clearly. Chapter 12 shows you how the Magnifier app does its job.

>> **Photo Booth:** Take fun selfies with your iPad's front camera. Chapter 9 explains how.

- >> **Freeform:** Create freeform drawings using your finger or a stylus such as the Apple Pencil.
- >> **Tips:** Get tips for using your iPad.
- >> **Health:** Store health-related data and track medications, activities, sleep and more.

Depending on your iPad model, the second page of the Home screen might also house a few other Apple apps, such as Pages (word processor), Keynote (presentations), Numbers (spreadsheet), Apple Store (buy Apple stuff), iMovie (create digital movies), Clips (create short video clips), and GarageBand (record and edit music).

Getting to know the dock

At the bottom of every iPad Home screen page, you see a special shelflike area called the dock. By default, the dock includes the following:

- >> **Messages:** Exchange free, unlimited text or multimedia messages with any other device running iOS 5 or later or Mac OS X Mountain Lion or later. Find out more about Messages in Chapter 6.
- >> **Safari:** Navigate sites and pages on the web. Chapter 4 shows you how to start using Safari on your iPad.
- >> **Music:** Listen to music or podcasts. You discover how the Music app works in Chapter 7.
- >> **Mail:** Send and receive email with most email systems. Chapter 5 helps you start emailing from your iPad everyone you know.
- >> **Calendar:** Create and manage appointments. You learn more about Calendar in Chapter 11.
- >> **Photos:** View, edit, and manage the photos in your iPad library. To get started, see Chapter 9.
- >> **Notes:** Type to-do lists, ideas, reminders, inspirations, and other notes. For help using Notes, flip to Chapter 11.
- >> **Suggested and Recent Apps:** Get quick access to three apps you've used recently and that iPadOS suggests for you.
- >> **App Library:** Get quick access to all your apps organized by category. I explain more in Chapter 10.

Feel free to add icons to or remove icons from the dock to suit the way you work or play. To add or remove dock icons, press and hold down on any icon and tap Edit Home Screen on the menu that appears. Your app icons will begin wiggling. Tap and drag a wiggling app icon to move it to or from the dock. Tap and drag an existing dock icon to change its position. When you're satisfied, tap Done in the upper-right corner of the Home screen (or just tap any empty part of the screen) to exit wiggly mode and save your arrangement.

Depending on your iPad model, you have between 11 and 15 app icons on the dock. If you find you don't use App Library all that much, choose Settings ⇨ Home Screen & App Library and tap the Show App Library in Dock switch to off (that is, from a green background to a light gray background). You can now add an extra app icon to the dock.

Two last points:

» *Notifications* are messages from iPadOS and your apps that tell you about recent activity on your tablet. I wanted to mention them even though they don't have an icon of their own. You hear much more about notifications in Chapter 12. To see them now (I know you can't wait), swipe from the middle-top of your screen to the middle to make them appear. Then swipe from the bottom to put them away again.

This gesture works anytime — even when your iPad is locked. If it's locked, you'll see your most recent notifications when you swipe down. Then swipe up to see older notifications.

» I'd be remiss not to mention the useful Control Center, with controls for Wi-Fi, Bluetooth, audio playback, and much more, all available from any screen in any app. You discover much more about Control Center in Chapter 14, but if you can't stand the suspense, put your finger in the top-right corner of your iPad screen and swipe down to open Control Center (and then tap some other part of the screen to put it away).

IN THIS CHAPTER

» **Getting your iPad ready for action**

» **Mastering multitouch**

» **Cutting, copying, and pasting**

» **Multitasking with your iPad**

» **Getting comfortable with the keyboard**

Chapter **2**

Basic Training

E verybody and their sister say that you can do useful — perhaps even amazing — things with an iPad "right out of the box." Everybody and their brother say that an iPad "just works." I have a couple of problems with these pronouncements. First, it's not true that you can start using an iPad immediately after removing the shrink wrap, nor is it in any way obvious how you're supposed to interact with a screen that lacks buttons and switches and any other bell or whistle. Second, the notion that the iPad is both easy and intuitive can make the rest of us feel like real dummies when we can't figure out how to get our iPad to do something useful, or when we end up in a weird iPad place and can't figure any way to get out of it.

The iPad *is* awesome and fun, but it's not without a learning curve. Happily, it's not a steep learning curve, so as long as you master a few basics, you'll be in a position to make the most out of your device.

This chapter is where you learn those basics. In the pages that follow you learn how to get through the initial setup procedure; operate the iPad's screen; perform essential tasks such as copying and pasting stuff and searching; and use the iPad's onscreen keyboard. Consider this your iPad boot camp, albeit one where no buzz-cut is required and no tough-as-nails sergeant will yell at you.

d. *After the camera captures the blob of dots, tap Set Up for Me on the other device.* Your other device will say *Finish on New iPad,* while your new iPad asks you to *Enter Passcode of Your Other Device.*

e. *On your new iPad, enter the passcode from your other device.* This passcode is now the one for your iPad, too. (You can change it later, as detailed in Chapter 17.) As soon as you enter the passcode successfully, your iPad automatically displays the Touch ID screen (for iPads with Touch ID) or the Face ID screen (for iPad Pro models with Face ID).

f. I tell you how to set up Touch ID and Face ID in Chapter 17, so if you want, you can tap either Set Up Touch ID Later or Set Up Face ID Later, and then skip to Step 5.

FIGURE 2-1:
Maneuvering an iPad to pair with an existing iOS or iPadOS device for automatic setup.

3. **Set up Touch ID or Face ID:**

To set up Touch ID on iPad models that support it:

a. *Tap Continue.*

b. *Place your finger on the top button (or the Home button, if your iPad has one) each time you're asked.* With each touch, sensors comprehensively map your fingerprint.

c. *When the Adjust Your Grip screen appears, tap Continue, and continue the process until the Complete screen appears.*

To set up Face ID on iPad Pro models that support it:

a. *Tap Continue.* The front camera activates.

b. *When asked, turn your head in different directions until your entire face is scanned.*

c. *After completing one scan, complete a second scan when asked.*

4. **On the Complete screen, tap Continue.**

The screen displays *Setting Up Your Apple ID* while your other device and your iPad exchange information, including Contacts, Calendar, and Keychain passwords. Your other device also copies over all your Wi-Fi settings, even passwords, so your iPad automatically joins your network. This process could take a few minutes. When it's finished, the Make This Your New iPad screen appears.

5. **Tap Customize.**

The Apps & Data screen appears.

6. **Choose how to set up your iPad by tapping one of the options and following the onscreen prompts.**

Your five choices are From iCloud Backup, From Another iPad, From Mac or PC, From Android, and Don't Transfer Anything.

When the process is complete, you're returned to the Make This Your New iPad screen.

7. **Tap Continue.**

The Terms and Conditions screen appears.

8. **Tap Agree to accept the terms and conditions, and then tap Agree again on the pop-up dialog that appears.**

9. **Tap Continue.**

The Apple Pay screen appears.

10. **Confirm or set up Apple Pay.**

If Apple Pay is set up on your other device, confirm each credit card you've set up. Otherwise, you can now add credit cards one at a time or set up Apple Pay later by tapping the Set Up Later in Settings button. (Learn more about Apple Pay in Chapter 6.)

11. **Tap Continue.**

If you already have an Apple Card set up on your other device, the Get Daily Cash Every Time screen appears.

12. **If you have an Apple Card, tap Set as Preferred Card and follow the onscreen instructions.**

You can make your Apple Card the default credit card for Apple Pay transactions. You can also set up Apple Cash on your iPad.

13. **Decide whether to share your analytic data with developers.**

In Step 8, you chose whether to share analytics data with Apple. Now you're asked if you want to share analytics with developers. If you agree to share with developers, you're not just trusting Apple; you're trusting all those developers, too.

14. **Tap Continue to cycle through a series of screens highlighting new features of iPadOS specific to your iPad model.**

At the end, the Get Started screen appears.

15. **Tap Get Started.**

You are taken to the Home screen! That's it! You're now ready to use your iPad.

If you ever need to restore your iPad to factory condition, follow the preceding steps to set it up again.

Manual setup

If you've already gone through the automatic setup process, skip this section. If you want to know how to manually set up your iPad, however, you're in the right place. In the interest of space, I won't repeat details for instructions that are identical to what I explained in the "Automatic setup" section. Also, depending on the choices you make during the setup process, some of these steps may be different:

1. **Begin the setup process:**

   a. *Press and hold down the top button on the upper-right edge.* The Apple logo appears, followed by the word *hello* and similar greetings in a bunch of other languages.

   b. *When the* Swipe Up to Open *message appears (in English or another language), do so.* The language screen appears.

   c. *Tap to choose your language, followed by your country or region preferences.* The Quick Start screen appears, along with a blue Set Up Manually button.

2. **Tap the Set Up Manually button.**

3. **Tap to choose an available Wi-Fi network, provide a password (if necessary), tap the Join button, and then, after the connection is complete, tap the Next button.**

   Certain iPad models may allow you to choose a cellular network, if available, and set up or change your Wi-Fi network later. (Refer to Chapter 15 for setting up Wi-Fi in Settings.) After you tap Next, your iPad automatically advances to the Data & Privacy screen.

4. **Tap Continue to acknowledge the Data & Privacy icon and its meaning.**

   Apple takes your privacy seriously, calling privacy a human right! The icon at the top of this screen appears whenever your iPad asks to use your personal information.

   You advance to the Set Up Touch ID or Set Up Face ID screen, depending on your iPad model.

5. **Set up Touch ID or Face ID:**

   If your iPad model supports Touch ID but you don't want to set up Touch ID now, tap Set Up Touch ID Later (check out Chapter 17 for the details), tap Don't Use, and then skip to Step 7. Otherwise, follow these steps to set up Touch ID:

   a. *Tap Continue.*

b. *Place a finger on the top button (or the Home button, if your iPad has one) each time you're asked.* With each touch, sensors comprehensively map your fingerprint.

c. *When asked, tap Continue to adjust your grip, and continue the process until the Complete screen appears.*

If your iPad model supports Face ID but you don't want to set up Face ID now, tap Set Up Face ID Later (refer to Chapter 17 for the details), tap Don't Use, and then skip to Step 7. Otherwise, follow these steps to set up Face ID:

a. *Tap Continue.* The front camera activates.

b. *When asked, turn your head in different directions until your entire face is scanned.*

c. *After completing one scan, complete a second scan when asked.*

6. **Tap Continue.**

Your iPad prompts you to create a passcode.

7. **Type a 6-digit passcode to unlock your iPad. When the Re-enter Your Passcode screen appears, type your passcode again.**

The Apps & Data screen appears.

8. **Choose how to set up your iPad by tapping one of the options and following the onscreen prompts.**

Your five choices are Restore from iCloud Backup, Restore from Mac or PC, Transfer Directly from iPad, Move Data from Android, and Don't Transfer Apps & Data. When the process is complete, the Apple ID screen appears.

9. **If you don't have an Apple ID or you've forgotten it:**

a. *Tap the Forgot Password or Apple ID? button.*

b. *Set up a new account or bypass this step until later by choosing Settings ⇨ Apple ID.*

The Terms and Conditions screen appears.

10. **If you have an Apple ID:**

a. *Enter your Apple ID email address, click Next, enter your Apple ID password, and click Next.*

b. *If you have activated two-factor authentication (sometimes called 2FA), approve this login on one of your other Apple devices, and then enter the passcode displayed on that device.*

    c. *If you use a different Apple ID for iCloud than you do for iTunes, enter both by tapping the Use Different Apple IDs for iCloud & iTunes? button and entering your credentials for both.*

When your Apple ID has been set up, the Terms and Conditions screen appears.

11. **Tap Agree to accept the terms and conditions.**

12. **Tap Continue.**

The Siri screen appears.

13. **Tap Continue to activate Siri.**

Siri is activated by default. Although you can turn Siri off in Settings, I strongly recommend that you keep this feature on and use it. Siri is a good voice assistant, and Apple is improving it steadily.

Your iPad prompts you to say a few phrases to set up the Hey Siri feature.

14. **Say the phrases as each is offered to you.**

When Hey Siri is set up, the Improve Siri & Dictation screen appears.

15. **Tap Share Audio Recordings.**

The iPad Analytics screen appears.

16. **Tap Share with Apple.**

The Welcome to iPad screen appears.

17. **Tap Get Started.**

You are taken to the Home screen! You're now ready to use your iPad.

REMEMBER

If you ever need to restore your iPad to factory condition, follow the preceding steps to set it up again.

Mastering the Touchscreen

The iPad doesn't come with an external mouse, trackpad, or keyboard. So how are you supposed to make anything happen? The key is that the iPad's innocuous-looking screen has a secret superpower: It responds to the touch of a finger, which is why it's called a *touchscreen*. As you soon learn, the iPad screen can also respond to actions performed by two or more fingers at once, which is why nerds also refer to the screen as a *multitouch interface*. (Yes, nerds are very bad at naming things!)

In the following sections, you discover how to use your fingers to make the touchscreen do your bidding.

Training your digits

The way your make your iPad do something useful is by placing one or more fingers on the touchscreen and then performing certain actions — known in the trade as *gestures* — that let the iPad know your intentions. Here's a quick look at the most important gestures:

>> **Tap:** Use any finger to lightly press on the iPad screen and then immediately release. A tap on a touchscreen is the equivalent of clicking a mouse on a Mac or PC screen.

>> **Double-tap:** Tap the screen twice in rapid succession. This action usually has the effect of zooming into (or out of) what's on the screen (such as a web page, map, or email). Double-tapping is similar to double-clicking a mouse.

>> **Long-press:** Place a finger on a screen object and leave your finger there until the desired action occurs (such as a menu of options appearing). This gesture is also called *press and hold* or *tap and hold*.

>> **Flick:** Quickly swipe a finger along the screen. Flicking lets you scroll through lists of songs, emails, and picture thumbnails. Tap the screen to stop scrolling, or wait for the scrolling list to stop.

>> **Pinch/spread:** Place two fingers on the screen and pinch them together to zoom out of images, web pages, text, videos, and more. Or spread the fingers apart to zoom in on things. These gestures will quickly become second nature!

>> **Drag:** Place a finger on a screen object and then move the finger along the screen. The object moves along with your finger.

>> **Swipe down from the top center of the screen:** This special gesture displays notifications. Place your finger at the very top of the screen and drag down.

>> **Swipe down from the top right of the screen:** This time, you're calling up Control Center (shown in Figure 2-2), a handy repository for quite a few important iPad features. You learn the details of this incredibly useful tool in Chapter 14.

Swipe down from the top-right corner to display Control Center

FIGURE 2-2:
Swipe down from the top-right corner of the iPad screen to reveal the handy Control Center.

- » **Swipe down in the middle of any screen:** Display the search feature, a discussion for later in this chapter.

- » **Swipe from left to right on the first Home screen page:** Summon the Today screen, which shows the appointments and reminders you have coming up, app suggestions and News stories, and the search feature. The today view is available on the lock screen and the Home screens.

- » **Swipe from right to left on the lock screen:** Summon the iPad's camera app.

- » **Swipe up from the bottom of the screen:** Open App Switcher, which enables you to quickly switch among or view running apps (check out the later section, "Running Multiple Apps"). You can also use App Switcher to quit an app by dragging the app's thumbnail above the top of the screen.

Navigating beyond the main Home screen page

As I discuss in Chapter 1, by default your iPad comes with two Home screen pages, indicated by the row of two tiny dots that appear just above the dock. After you start adding apps from the App Store (refer to Chapter 10), that row might expand to three or more dots. Each dot denotes a Home screen page, each of which can contain 30 additional icons, not counting the additional icons on your iPad's dock. You can have up to 15 Home screen pages. You can also have more or fewer icons on your dock, but I can't think of a decent reason why you'd want to ditch any of them. In any case, more on these in a moment.

Here's what you need to know about navigating among the Home screen pages:

- » To navigate between pages, flick from right to left or left to right across the middle of the screen. The number of dots represents the current number of Home screen pages on your iPad. The white dot denotes the page you're currently viewing. Flicking from left to right from the first Home screen page brings up the aforementioned Today screen.

- » Make sure you flick and not just tap, or you'll probably open one of the apps on the current screen instead of switching pages.

- » To jump back to the first Home screen, swipe up from the bottom of the screen. Alternatively, pinch the screen using four or five fingers.

>> You can put as many as 15 apps and as few as none on the dock. The dock also shows the three most recently opened apps on the right side of the divider line, making for a quick return to an app. (If the recent apps don't appear on the dock, launch Settings, tap Home Screen & App Library, and then tap the Show Suggested and Recent Apps in Dock switch to on.) You can access the dock from an open app by swiping up a short way from the bottom of your screen.

Select, cut, copy, and paste

You can select and copy (or cut) content from one place on the iPad and then paste it elsewhere, just like you can with a Mac or PC. You might copy text or a URL from the web and paste it into an email or a note. Or you might copy a bunch of pictures or a video into an email.

Here's how you to exploit the copy-and-paste feature:

1. **Select what you want to copy:**

   - If the text isn't editable (such as text on a web page), select a word by long-pressing it.

   - If the text is editable, select a word by long-pressing it and then tapping Select in the Edit menu that appears.

   - If the text is editable, select the entire text by long-pressing anywhere within the text and then tapping Select All in the Edit menu that appears.

   iPadOS selects the text and displays a different Edit menu just above the selection. If the Edit menu doesn't appear, tap the selection.

2. **Drag the *grab points* (also called *grab handles*) to select a larger or smaller block of text.**

   The grab points, which are vertical lines connected to circles, appear to the left and right of the selected text, as shown in Figure 2-3. The tininess of the grab points means that dragging them may take a little practice. Note, too, that as you drag a grab handle, iPadOS displays a bubble that displays a magnified version of the text you're selecting.

FIGURE 2-3:
Drag the grab handles to select text.

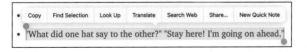

3. **Tap Copy.**

If you have the virtual keyboard displayed, you can alternatively tap the copy icon, shown in the margin.

If you were removing text from a document you created, instead of copying it, you would tap Cut instead. If you have the virtual keyboard displayed, you can alternatively tap the cut icon, shown in the margin.

4. **Open the app into which you want to paste the copied text.**

5. **Position the cursor where you want to insert the text you just copied, and then tap the cursor.**

Up pops the Edit menu, a version of which is shown in Figure 2-4. (The commands that appear vary by app.)

6. **Tap Paste to paste the text into the document.**

If you have the virtual keyboard displayed, you can alternatively tap the paste icon, shown in the margin.

FIGURE 2-4:
Tap Paste
and your
copied text
will appear.

To err is human, to undo divine

TIP

If you make a mistake when cutting, pasting, or typing, you can reverse your most recent action as follows:

» If the virtual keyboard is onscreen, tap the undo icon, shown in the margin.

» Shake the iPad and then tap the Undo option that appears.

» Double-tap the screen with three fingers.

» Place three fingers on the screen and then drag them a little to the left.

If you change your mind, you can redo the action either by tapping the redo icon (shown in the margin) on the virtual keyboard (if it's displayed) or by placing three fingers on the screen and then dragging them a little to the right.

TAKING ADVANTAGE OF THE UNIVERSAL CLIPBOARD

If you have a Mac (running macOS 10.12 or later), iPhone (with iOS 10 or later), or another iPad (with iPadOS 13 or later), and if that device uses the same Apple ID as your current iPad, and if both devices have turned on Wi-Fi (Settings ⇨ Wi-Fi), Bluetooth (Settings ⇨ Bluetooth), and Handoff (Settings ⇨ General ⇨ AirDrop & Handoff), you can use the Universal Clipboard to copy and paste data between the two devices. Cut or copy data on one device, bring the two devices near each other (within 33 feet, or about 10 meters), then paste the data on the other device. Note that copied data is saved in the Universal Clipboard for only a few minutes, so be sure to paste the data on the destination device sooner rather than later.

Running Multiple Apps

Through *multitasking*, you can run two or more apps simultaneously and switch from one app to another. The following examples illustrate what multitasking enables you to do on your iPad:

›› A media app, such as Music, can continue to play while you do something else, such as surf the web, peruse photos, or check email. Without multitasking, the media app would pause the moment you opened another app.

›› A navigation app can update your position while you're listening to, say, a podcast. From time to time, the navigation app will pipe in with turn-by-turn directions, lowering the volume of the podcast so you can hear the instructions.

›› If you're uploading images to a photo website and the process is taking longer than you want, you can switch to another app, confident that the images will continue to upload behind the scenes.

Switching between running apps

If you have multiple apps on the go, how do you switch from one to another? One way is to swipe up from the bottom of your screen to display App Switcher, as shown in Figure 2-5. You get thumbnail versions of your open apps. Scroll to the left to access more apps. Tap the thumbnail for the app you want to switch to; the app remembers where you left off.

To remove an app from App Switcher, drag the app's thumbnail up and beyond the top of the screen. Poof — it's gone.

TIP

Another way to switch between running apps is to place four or five fingers on the screen (now *that* is what I call multitouch!) and then drag left or right to bring the previous or next app into view.

You'll use the App Switcher a lot, but your iPad has some other tricks that make multitasking even more powerful by exploiting all that screen real estate to get multiple apps to share the screen.

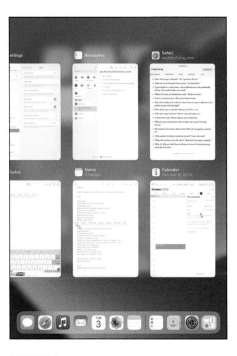

FIGURE 2-5:
App Switcher shows you the apps you've recently used or are still running.

Sharing the screen with split view

Your iPad comes with a feature called split view, which enables you to display two app windows onscreen at the same time, with each app getting half the screen. Here's how it works:

1. **Launch the first app you want to use.**

2. **Tap the multitasking icon: the three dots in the top center of the screen (labeled in Figure 2-6).**

   This step displays the multitasking menu, a version of which is pointed out in Figure 2-6.

3. **Tap Split View.**

   iPadOS prompts you to choose another app.

4. **Tap the icon of other app you want onscreen.**

   Now the second app is running side by side with your first app. Nice!

Split view mode is shown in Figure 2-6. Drag the gray resizer bar between the two apps to resize them.

Multitasking

Resizer

The split view feature works with most of Apple's own apps and some third-party apps. If the multitasking icon doesn't appear, it means the app doesn't support split view.

TIP

In Safari, you have two ways to open in split view. The first way is to long-press a link on a web page, which opens several options, including a preview of the link. Tap the Open in Split View command to open the linked page in split view. The second way requires you to have at least two tabs open in the Safari app. You can then drag a tab to the left or right edge of the screen and release, and a new split view is created.

I bet you can think of all sorts of reasons to run two apps at the same time. Maybe you're composing a message to a friend in the Mail app while scrolling through Safari in the smaller panel to find a place to have lunch. Or perhaps you're sketching in one app while using a photo in another as a reference point.

When you're finished with split view, tap the multitasking icon in the app you want to use and then tap Full Screen.

Sharing the screen with slide over

Another way to get two apps to share the screen at the same time is the slide over feature. Instead of running side by side, as in split view, with slide over one app runs full screen and a second app runs in a window that takes up about a third of the screen width. This second window is in slide over mode, which means it runs on top of the full-screen app and can be dragged to the left or right side of the screen, as needed.

To give slide over a whirl, first launch the app that you want to run in slide over mode. Tap the app's multitasking icon (labeled in Figure 2-6) to display the multitasking menu, and then tap Slide Over. iPadOS shrinks the app window and displays the Home screen. Tap the icon of the app that you want to run full screen. This second app opens normally and the slide over app remains onscreen on top of the full-screen app.

When you're finished with slide over, tap the multitasking icon in the slide over app and then tap Full Screen.

The slide over feature works with most of Apple's own apps and quite a few third-party apps. If the multitasking icon doesn't appear, it means the app doesn't support slide over.

All the iPad's a stage: Multitasking with Stage Manager

If you have an 11-inch iPad Pro, a 12.9-inch iPad Pro (third generation or later), or an iPad Air (fifth generation or later), you can take advantage of a powerful multitasking feature called Stage Manager. This feature is a replacement for the split view and slide over features that I talk about in the previous two sections. Stage Manager enables you to resize windows, move windows around, overlap windows, combine multiple app windows into a group, and more.

Your first task is to turn on Stage Manager, which you can do by opening the Settings app, tapping Multitasking & Gestures, and then selecting the Stage Manager option.

With Stage Manager on, you can use the following techniques to manage your app windows:

>> **Resize a window:** Look for the corner that contains a black arc (usually either the bottom-right or bottom-left), and then drag that corner until the window is the size you want.

» **Move a window:** Drag the top of the window until the window is in the position you want.

» **Switch to a recently used app:** Tap the app thumbnail in the recent apps list on the left side of the iPad screen. If the recent apps aren't onscreen, swipe right from the left edge of the screen.

» **Move a window to the recent apps list:** Tap the multitasking icon (. . .) in the top center of the window, and then tap Minimize.

» **Maximize a window:** Tap the multitasking icon (. . .) in the top center of the window, and then tap Enter Full Screen.

» **Create a group of app windows:** Open or switch to the first app you want to include in the group. Tap the multitasking icon (. . .) in the top center of the window, tap Add Another Window, and then tap the thumbnail or icon for the app you to include in the group. Within your group, you can move, resize, and overlap app windows, as shown in Figure 2-7.

Drag the top to move a window

Drag this icon to resize a window

FIGURE 2-7:
An app window group created using Stage Manager.

Sharing the screen with picture-in-picture

There's a good possibility that your television at home has a picture-in-picture feature that enables you to watch one channel in the main portion of the TV screen while checking out a second channel in a small window on the screen. You don't really want to miss any of the action in the big game now, do you?

Your iPad has the same feature. The picture-in-picture feature on the iPad works when you're on a FaceTime video call, watching a video stored on your iPad, or streaming a video from one of the many streaming video services. These topics are reserved for Chapter 8.

To give picture-in-picture a whirl, start a video and then either swipe up from the bottom of the screen all the way to the top or, in the video app, tap the picture-in-picture icon, shown in the margin. The video picture shrinks into a small window hanging out in the lower-left corner of the display.

 You can pause the video or shut it down by tapping the controls that appear in this diminutive video window. (Tap the window if the controls don't appear.) If you want the video to take over the entire iPad screen, tap the restore icon (shown in the margin) inside the video window.

Meanwhile, if the video window is blocking a portion of the screen that you want to work with, you can drag the video window to another position.

Organizing Icons into Folders

Finding the single app that you want to use among apps spread out over 15 screens may seem like a daunting task. But Apple felt your pain and added a handy organizational tool: folders. The Folders feature lets you create folder icons, and within each of those icons you can store a selection of related apps. This technique reduces Home screen clutter and organizes related apps together for easy access.

To create a folder, follow these steps:

1. **Long-press any Home screen icon until the shortcut menu appears, then tap Edit Home Screen.**

   All the icons on the screen start wiggling.

2. **Pick the first two apps you want to move to a folder, and then drag the icon for the first app on top of the second app.**

   The two apps now share living quarters inside a newly created folder. Apple names the folder according to the categories of two apps inside the folder.

3. **(Optional) Change the folder name by tapping the X on the bar where the folder name appears and then typing a new name.**

4. **Tap outside the folder.**

5. **To add more apps to the folder, long-press any Home screen icon until the shortcut menu appears, tap Edit Home Screen, drag each app icon on top of the folder icon, then tap Done.**

   You can have multiple pages of apps with a single folder, so feel free to add as many apps as needed to your new folder.

To launch an app inside a folder, tap that folder's icon and then tap the icon for the app that you want to open.

When you drag all the apps from a folder, the folder automatically disappears.

Printing

iPadOS's AirPrint feature allows you to print wirelessly from the iPad to an AirPrint-capable printer, available from all major printer manufacturers.

AirPrint works with Mail, Photos, Safari, and Books (PDF files). You can also print from apps in Apple's iWork software suite, as well as third-party apps with built-in printing.

REMEMBER

An AirPrint printer doesn't need any special software, but it does have to be connected to the same Wi-Fi network as the iPad.

To print, follow these steps:

1. **Tap the share icon, and then tap the Print command.**

   In the Mail app, open the message you want to print, tap the reply icon in the lower-right corner, and then tap Print.

   The share icon is shown in the margin.

2. **In the Print Options dialog that appears, tap Select Printer to select a printer, which the iPad locates in short order.**

3. **Depending on the printer, specify the number of copies you want to print, the number of double-sided copies, and a range of pages to print.**

   A graphic indicating how much ink is left in the printer might even appear.

4. **When you're happy with your settings, tap Print.**

Searching Your iPad

You can search for just about anything across your iPad and in specific apps, using a combination of the search feature and Siri. I show you how to search in apps in the various chapters dedicated to Mail, Contacts, Calendar, and Music.

The search feature can find news and trending topics, local restaurants, movie times, and content in Apple's own iTunes Store, App Store, and Book Store. Moreover, with Siri teaming up with the search feature, you'll also get circled icons representing the contacts you engage with the most, the people you are next scheduled to meet, as well as eateries, shops, and other places of possible interest nearby.

Searches are also proactive, meaning that the device gets to know you over time and makes suggestions accordingly. It attempts to read your mind. The tablet might surface the News app, for example, if it learns that you turn to it every morning (while enjoying your coffee). Or if you're in a particular area, you may get the news that's trending in your location.

Here's how the search feature works:

1. **Swipe down from the center of any Home screen page to access Search.**

   The Search dialog slides into view at the top of the screen.

2. **Tap the Search text box and use the virtual keyboard to enter your search text.**

   The iPad spits out results the moment you type a single character; the list narrows as you type additional characters.

   The results are pretty darn thorough. Say that you entered *Ring* as your search term. Contacts whose last names have *Ring* in them show up, along with friends who might have done a trapeze act in the Ringling Bros. circus. All the songs on your iPad by Ringo Starr show up too, as do such song titles as "Ring-A-Ling," from the Black-Eyed Peas if that happens to be in your library. The same goes for apps, videos, audiobooks, events, and notes with the word *Ring*. You'll get web and App Store references as well.

3. **Tap any listing to jump to the contact, ditty, or app you seek.**

TIP

At the bottom of the search results list, you get several commands for running your search query in specific apps, such as Contacts, Messages, and Maps.

You can prevent specific apps and their content from appearing in the search results by choosing Settings ⇨ Siri & Search. In the list of apps, tap an app and then tap the Show App in Search switch to off to prevent the app from appearing in your search results. To also prevent the app's content from appearing in your search results, tap the Show Content in Search switch to off.

Getting to Know the iPad's Onscreen Keyboard

You use your finger as a handy (pun intended) substitute for an external mouse or trackpad to control things on your iPad's touchscreen. But your iPad also doesn't come with an external keyboard, so how are you supposed to type things like email messages, texts, and web addresses?

Ah, don't put your fingers away just yet, friend, because their work isn't done. Whenever you have to type something into an app, your iPad realizes this and calls for the onscreen keyboard, which slides up from the bottom of the screen. For example, if you tap inside the To box of the Mail app, iPadOS automatically surfaces the keyboard shown in Figure 2-8.

FIGURE 2-8: Tap inside a box that requires typing and the onscreen keyboard pops up automatically.

You have a choice of several English-language or (depending on what you chose during setup) foreign-language keyboard layouts, including variations on the alphabetical keyboard, the numeric and punctuation keyboard, the more punctuation and symbols keyboard, and the emoji keyboard.

REMEMBER

Note that you don't get the identical keyboard every time because an app might display a version of the keyboard suitable to the task at hand. In Figure 2-8, for example, when you tap in the To box of the Mail app, note the @ key that appears to the right of the *m* key. All email addresses include the @ character, so Mail puts that key within easy reach for you.

TIP

Note the little gray letters and numbers at the top of most keys in Figure 2-8? If you swipe down on one of these keys instead of tapping it, you'll get that second character instead of the main one. Try it!

Before you consider how to *use* the keyboard, I want to share a bit of the philosophy behind its so-called *intelligence.* Knowing what makes this keyboard smart can help you make it even smarter when you use it. The keyboard

» Has a built-in English dictionary that includes words from today's popular culture. Apple uses machine learning to quickly identify new trending words, too. Dictionaries in other languages are automatically activated when you use a given international keyboard, as described in the sidebar "A KEYBOARD FOR ALL BORDERS," later in this chapter.

» Adds your contacts to its dictionary automatically.

» Uses complex analysis algorithms to predict the word you're trying to type.

» Suggests corrections as you type. It then offers you the suggested word just below the misspelled word. When you decline a suggestion and the word you typed is *not* in the iPad dictionary, the iPad adds that word to its dictionary and offers it as a suggestion if you mistype a similar word in the future.

TIP

If the term you typed is correct, tell your iPad to accept it as-is by tapping the term, which appears in quotation marks to the left of the suggested corrections. This helps train your intelligent keyboard.

» Reduces the number of mistakes you make as you type by intelligently and dynamically resizing the touch zones for certain keys. The iPad increases the zones for keys it predicts might come next and decreases the zones for keys that are unlikely or impossible to come next. Thanks!

A KEYBOARD FOR ALL BORDERS

Apple expanded the iPad's reach globally with international keyboard layouts for dozens of languages. To access a keyboard that isn't customized for Americanized English, tap Settings ⇨ General ⇨ Keyboard ⇨ Keyboards ⇨ Add New Keyboard. Then flick through the list to select the keyboard you want to use. Have a multilingual household? You can select as many of these international keyboards as you might need by tapping the language in the list.

When you're in an app that summons a keyboard, long-press the emoji key (the one with a smiley face shown in the margin) or the international key (the globe icon also shown in the margin) to display a list of keyboards, and then tap the keyboard you want to use.

To remove a keyboard that you've already added to your list, tap the Edit button in the upper-right corner of the Keyboard settings screen displaying your enabled keyboards and then tap the red circle with the white horizontal line that appears next to the language to which you want to say "adiós," and then tap Delete.

Meanwhile, your iPad keyboard is even more fluent with iPadOS. You can now type in two languages at once, without switching keyboards. You can type with any pair of the following languages: English, French, German, Italian, Portuguese, and Spanish. This multilingual typing feature is also supported for English and Chinese.

Anticipating what comes next

The keyboard takes an educated stab at the next word you mean to type and presents what it surmises to be the best possible word choices front and center. Say you're in the Messages app and the last message you received was an invitation to lunch or dinner. Above the row of keys on the iPad keyboard, you'd get buttons with three word suggestions: *Dinner, Lunch,* and *Not sure.* If one of those was the appropriate response, you could tap the button to insert its text into your reply.

If you wanted to respond with something different than the three options presented by Apple, you'd just type your response with the regular QWERTY keys. As you type additional letters and words, the three suggested word choices above the keyboard change in real time. For instance, if you start by typing *That's a* in your message, the new trio of word choice buttons that show up might be *great, good,* and *very.*

To exploit the predictive text feature, make sure the Predictive setting is turned on (as it is by default). Go to Settings ⇨ General ⇨ Keyboards and slide the Predictive switch to on.

Discovering the special-use keys

The iPad keyboard contains several keys that don't type a character. Here's the scoop on each of these keys:

>> **Caps Lock:** If you're using the alphabetical keyboard, press Caps Lock to lock the uppercase letters. This enables you to type a long stretch of uppercase without having to constantly press the Shift key, discussed next. (To enable Caps Lock on the iPad mini, you need to double-tap the Shift key.)

- **Shift:** If you're using the alphabetical keyboard, the Shift key switches between uppercase and lowercase letters. You can tap the key to change the case or hold down Shift and slide to the letter you want to be capitalized.

- **Keyboard:** Tap the key with the keyboard graphic (shown in the margin) to hide the keyboard. Alternatively, long-press the keyboard key and then tap Floating to shrink your keyboard to a smaller version that you can then drag. Tap and drag the gray bar at the bottom of the floating keyboard to drag it where you want it; if you drag to the bottom of the screen, you dock the keyboard and expand it to its full size.

- **.?123:** Tap this key to switch to a keyboard that shows only numbers and symbols. The traditional Shift key is replaced with a key labeled #+=. Pressing that key displays a keyboard with more symbols.

- **Emoji:** Tap the key with the smiley face (shown in the margin) and you can punctuate your words by adding smiley faces and other emojis.

- **Delete:** Tapping this key (otherwise known as the backspace key) erases the character immediately to the left of the cursor.

- **Return:** This key moves the cursor to the beginning of the next line. You might find this key labeled Go or Search, depending on the app you're using.

- **Dictation:** Tap the key with the microphone icon (shown in the margin) and start talking. The iPad listens to what you have to say. You can use this dictation feature in many of the instances in which you can summon the keyboard, including the built-in Notes and Mail apps, as well as many third-party apps. Refer to Chapter 14 for more on dictation. When you're done, tap the key again to tell your iPad to stop listening.

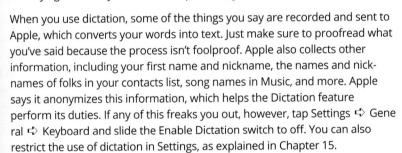

WARNING

When you use dictation, some of the things you say are recorded and sent to Apple, which converts your words into text. Just make sure to proofread what you've said because the process isn't foolproof. Apple also collects other information, including your first name and nickname, the names and nick-names of folks in your contacts list, song names in Music, and more. Apple says it anonymizes this information, which helps the Dictation feature perform its duties. If any of this freaks you out, however, tap Settings ➪ General ➪ Keyboard and slide the Enable Dictation switch to off. You can also restrict the use of dictation in Settings, as explained in Chapter 15.

On the top row of the keyboards that pop up in certain apps — Mail and Notes, for instance — tap Aa to find **B**, *I*, U̲, and S̲ formatting keys. These permit you to bold, italicize, underline, or strikethrough selected text, respectively. Other formatting options, depending on the app you're using, might include paragraph alignment, ordered and unordered lists, font colors, and more.

To the left of the three alternative word suggestions on various keyboards are icons for undoing or redoing your last steps, plus a third icon that pastes the last selected word or passage that you copied or cut. Refer to the section "To err is human, to undo divine," earlier in this chapter. You might get different icons depending on the app you're using.

Finger-typing on the virtual keyboards

The virtual keyboards in Apple's multitouch interface might be considered a stroke of genius. Or they might drive you nuts. If you're patient and trusting, in a week or so, you'll get the hang of finger-typing — which is vital to moving forward because you have to rely on a virtual keyboard to tap a text field, enter notes, type the names of new contacts, and so on.

Apple has built intelligence into its virtual keyboard, so it can correct typing mistakes on the fly or provide helpful word choices by predicting what you're about to type next. The keyboard isn't exactly Nostradamus, but it does an excellent job of coming up with the words you have in mind. Apple is also increasingly relying on deep neural network technology to improve accuracy even more.

TIP

As you start typing on the virtual keyboard, I think you'll find the following additional tips helpful:

>> **Know what letter you're typing.** As you press your finger against a letter or number on the screen, the individual key you press darkens until you lift your finger. That way, you know that you struck the correct letter or number.

>> **Slide to the correct letter if you tap the wrong one.** No need to worry if you touched the wrong key. You can slide your finger to the correct key because the letter isn't recorded until you lift your finger.

>> **Long-press to access special accent marks, alternative punctuation, or URL endings.** Sending a message to an overseas pal? Keep your finger pressed against a letter, and a panel of keys showing variations on the character for foreign alphabets pops up. This panel lets you add the appropriate accent mark. Just slide your finger until you're pressing the key with the relevant accent mark and then lift your finger.

Meanwhile, if you long-press the .? key while typing an address in Safari, it offers you the choice of .us, .org, .edu, .com, or .net with additional options if you also use international keyboards.

Chapter **3**

Synchronicity: Getting Stuff to and from Your iPad

I have good news and . . . more good news. The good news is you can easily set up your iPad so your contacts, appointments, reminders, events, mail settings, bookmarks, books, music, movies, TV shows, podcasts, and photos are synchronized between your computer and your iPad (or other iDevices). And the more good news is that after you set up your iPad, your contacts, appointments, events, and everything else just mentioned can be kept up to date automatically on all of those devices.

This communication between your iPad and computer is called *syncing* (short for *synchronizing*). Don't worry: It's easy, and I walk you through the entire process in this chapter.

Another form of syncing is moving files to and from your iPad and other iDevices or to and from a Mac or PC. You can do it using Finder in macOS Catalina and later, or you can do so via iTunes with macOS Mojave and earlier or with Windows.

In this chapter, you find out how to sync all the digital data your iPad can handle, right after a short interlude about Apple's iCloud service.

A Brief iCloud Primer

Apple's iCloud is a complete online data synchronization and storage service. In a nutshell, iCloud stores and manages your digital stuff — music, photos, contacts, events, and more — and makes it available over the internet to all your computers and iDevices automatically.

iCloud pushes information such as email, calendars, contacts, reminders, and bookmarks to and from your computer and to and from your iPad and other iDevices, and then keeps those items updated on all devices without any effort on your part. iCloud also includes nonsynchronizing options, such as Photo Stream and iCloud photo sharing (see Chapter 9) and email (see Chapter 5).

Your free iCloud account includes 5GB of storage, which is all many users will need. If you have several devices (including Macs and PCs) or like saving data in the cloud, you'll probably need more storage by subscribing to an iCloud+ plan; 50GB ($0.99 per month), 200GB ($2.99 per month), 2TB ($9.99 per month), 6TB ($29.99 per month), and 12TB ($59.99 per month) upgrades are available (all prices in US dollars).

A nice touch is that music, apps, periodicals, movies, and TV shows purchased from the iTunes Store, as well as your photo stream and iTunes Match content (see Chapter 7), don't count against your 5GB of free storage. E-books don't count against your 5GB either, but audiobooks do. You'll find that the things that do count — such as mail, documents, account information, settings, and other app data — don't use much space, so 5GB might last a long time.

Conversely, if you use iCloud Photos and take a lot of photos and videos with your iDevice cameras, you're going to fill up your free 5GB pretty fast.

REMEMBER

If you're not using iCloud Photos (lovingly described in Chapter 9), you might want to sync your iPad photos with a computer every so often and then delete the photos from the iPad. Otherwise, over time, those photos will take up a lot of space and eventually fill up your iPad.

If you plan to go PC-free, as described in Chapter 2, but still want to have your email, calendars, contacts, and bookmarks automatically synchronized between your computers and other iDevices (and believe me, you do), here's how to enable iCloud syncing on your iPad:

1. **On your Home screen, tap Settings.**

2. **At the top of the Settings list, tap your name.**

3. **Tap iCloud.**

The iCloud screen appears, which includes a list of apps in the Apps Using iCloud section.

4. **Tap Show All.**

Settings displays the complete list of apps that can sync with iCloud.

5. **Depending on the app, use one of the following methods to toggle iCloud syncing:**

   - *The app doesn't display a switch:* Tap the app and then tap the app's Sync This iPad switch on or off to enable or disable iCloud sync. This method applies to the following apps: Photos, iCloud Drive, iCloud Mail, Passwords and Keychain, Notes, Messages, Health, and iCloud Calendar.

   - *The app displays a switch:* Tap the switch on or off to enable or disable iCloud sync.

REMEMBER

Apple's Keychain service keeps passwords and credit card information you save up to date on all devices you approve. The info is encrypted and can't be read by Apple (or, thankfully, by anyone else).

TIP

Near the top of the iCloud screen, tap Manage Account Storage to open the Manage Account Storage screen and check your iCloud storage or upgrade your storage plan. Tap Share with Family — or Family Usage, if you've already set up Family Sharing — to add or remove family members and shared payment methods from your Family Sharing plan.

You find out much more about iCloud in the rest of this chapter and several other chapters, so let's move on to syncing your iPad.

Getting in Sync

You can sync your calendars, reminders, bookmarks, and other data and documents among your iDevices and computers via iCloud, iTunes (macOS Mojave or earlier and Windows), Finder (macOS Catalina or later), or a combination of the three.

WARNING

While I'm talking about syncing, it's important to remember that although you can back up your iPad to iCloud, you'll need to sync it with a Mac or PC to have a local backup, too. I strongly believe that a single backup is never enough. The best practice is to maintain at least two different backups: one in iCloud and another stored locally on your Mac or PC.

Sync prep 101

Synchronizing your iPad with your computer isn't difficult, as the following steps show:

1. **Start by connecting your iPad to your computer with the USB-C cable that came with your iPad.**

2. **If this is the first time you've introduced your iPad to iTunes or Finder:**

   a. *When you see an alert on your PC that says "Select to choose what happens with this device," click the alert and then click Take No Action. When you see an alert on your Mac that asks "Allow this accessory to connect?" click Allow.*

   b. *On your iPad screen, when you see an alert asking, "Trust this computer?" tap Trust. Enter your passcode if requested, put down the iPad, and go back to iTunes or Finder on your computer.*

   When you connect your iPad to your computer, iTunes (or Finder in macOS Catalina or later) should launch automatically. For Windows or macOS Mojave and earlier, if iTunes doesn't launch automatically, try launching it manually. In macOS Catalina or later, click Finder to open a Finder window.

3. **If you see an alert on your Mac or PC asking whether you want iTunes to open automatically when you connect this iPad, click Yes or No, depending on your preference.**

   You can change this setting later, so don't give it too much thought.

4. **Click the iPad icon, shown in the margin and near the top left of the iTunes window (refer to Figure 3-1) or in the left sidebar of a Finder window. If you see a message asking whether to trust this iPad, click Trust.**

iPad icon

FIGURE 3-1:
In iTunes, click the iPad icon.

   If you don't see the iPad icon and you're positive it's connected to a USB port *on your computer* (not the keyboard, monitor, or hub), try restarting your computer.

TIP

   If you're using a Mac running macOS Catalina or later, skip to Step 6.

5. **For Windows PCs and for Macs running macOS Mojave or earlier, if you've connected more than one iDevice with this computer, select your iPad in the drop-down list of all your devices that appears when you click the iPad icon.**

   The iPad screen appears.

6. **If you're not using iTunes, click the General tab, as shown in Figure 3-2. If you're using iTunes, click the Summary pane.**

   This takes you to some useful basic options, which I get into next.

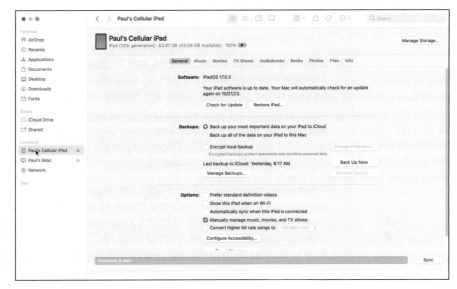

FIGURE 3-2:
The General
tab for a
connected
iPad Pro.

On the General tab (Finder) or the Summary tab (iTunes), you can set any options you want from the Options area:

WARNING

>> **Prefer Standard Definition Videos:** If you want high-definition videos you import to be automatically converted into smaller standard-definition video files when you transfer them to your iPad, select this check box.

   Standard-definition video files are significantly smaller than high-definition video files. You'll likely notice the poorer quality when you watch the video on your iPad, but you can have more video files on your iPad because they take up less space.

   The conversion from HD to standard definition takes a *long* time, so be prepared for very long sync times when you sync new HD video and have this option selected.

   If you plan to use Apple's digital AV adapter or Apple TV to display movies on an HDTV, consider going with high definition. Although the files will be bigger and your iPad will hold fewer videos, the HD versions look spectacular on a big-screen TV.

Syncing icon

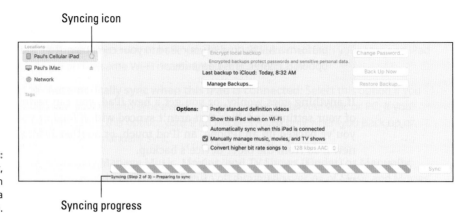

Syncing progress

When the sync is finished, the syncing icon stops spinning and morphs back into the eject icon, and the message at the top of the window disappears.

Synchronizing Your Data

Your next order of business is to tell iTunes what data you want to synchronize between your iPad and your computer. To get started, click the Info tab. Here's the general procedure to follow:

1. **In the Info tab, choose the data you want to sync between your iPad and your computer.**

    The sections that follow provide the details.

2. **Click Apply to put the settings into effect.**

3. **If your computer asks you to confirm, click Sync and Replace.**

    Finder or iTunes synchronizes your selected data.

REMEMBER

If you're using iCloud to sync contacts, calendars, and bookmarks, you won't be able to enable these items in Finder or iTunes. Turn off iCloud syncing on your iPad (open Settings, tap your Apple ID, tap iCloud, and then tap Show All) for items you want to sync with your Mac or PC.

In both Finder and iTunes, the Info pane has a section for syncing contacts, a section for syncing calendars, and a section with advanced options. The iTunes Info pane also has a section for syncing bookmarks.

REMEMBER

To use your iPad with a Google or Yahoo! account, you must sign in with the appropriate account on your iPad, as described in Chapter 5. After you've added the account to your iPad, you can enable contact or calendar syncing with that account in the Settings app under Mail, Contacts, and Calendars.

WARNING

In iTunes, when you enable syncing for either contacts or calendars (as I describe in the next two sections), you see the dialog shown in Figure 3-4. The message in the dialog means that Apple will one day disable synchronizing contacts and calendars between your iPad and your computer. No one knows when this will

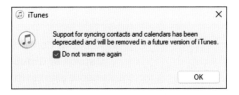

FIGURE 3-4:
Syncing contacts and calendars is going away.

happen, so proceed if you must, but be aware that eventually Apple wants everyone syncing this info via iCloud. If you're on a Windows PC, you can use iCloud for Windows (available from the Microsoft Store) to sync your contacts and calendars.

Syncing contacts

The syncing contacts section of the Info pane determines how synchronization is handled for your contacts and contact groups. The iPad syncs with the following address book programs:

>> **Mac:** Contacts and other address books that sync with Contacts, such as Microsoft Outlook

>> **PC:** Windows Contacts, Microsoft Outlook, and Microsoft Outlook Express

>> **Mac and PC:** Yahoo! Address Book and Google Contacts

You can sync contacts with multiple apps.

To enable synchronization of contacts between your iPad and your computer, do one of the following:

>> **iTunes:** Select the Sync Contacts With check box, and then select a contacts app from the pop-up menu.

>> **Finder:** Select the Sync Contacts Onto *iPad*, where *iPad* is the name of your iPad.

With contacts syncing activated, the contacts section enables the following options:

- **All Groups (Finder) or All Contacts (iTunes):** Synchronize all your contacts.

- **Selected Groups:** Synchronize only the contact groups that you select in the list of groups.

- **Add New Contacts from This iPad To (Finder) or Add Contacts Created Outside of Groups on This iPad To (iTunes):** Select this check box and then choose a group from the pop-up menu. New contacts created on this iPad will belong to the group you select.

Syncing calendars

The syncing calendars section of the Info pane determines how synchronization is handled for your appointments, events, and reminders. The iPad syncs with the following calendar programs:

- **Mac:** Calendar

- **PC:** Microsoft Exchange and Outlook 2003, 2007, 2010, and later

- **Mac and PC:** Google Calendar and Yahoo! Calendar

To enable synchronization of calendars between your iPad and your computer, do one of the following:

- **iTunes:** Select the Sync Calendars With check box, and then select a calendar app from the pop-up menu.

- **Finder:** Select the Sync Calendars Onto *iPad*, where *iPad* is the name of your iPad.

With calendar syncing activated, the calendar section enables the following options:

- **All Calendars:** Synchronize all your calendars.

- **Selected Groups:** Synchronize only calendars that you select in the list of calendars.

- **Do Not Sync Events Older Than *X* Days:** Select this check box and then enter a number in the text box to specify the oldest an event can be (in days) before it will be synchronized.

Syncing bookmarks

In the Windows version of iTunes, the Info tab includes a section named Other that contains only the Sync Bookmarks With check box. Selecting this check box activates a pop-up menu that contains just one item: Internet Explorer! Since barely anyone uses Internet Explorer anymore, this is not a useful setting, to say the least. If you want to sync your iPad bookmarks with a modern browser (such as Chrome, Firefox, or Edge), you need to use iCloud for Windows (available for free from the Microsoft Store).

Advanced syncing

Every so often, the contacts and calendars on your iPad get so messed up that the easiest way to fix things is to erase that information from your iPad and replace it with information from your computer.

If that's the case, go to the Advanced section of the Info pane and click to select the Contacts or Calendars check box (or both). (In Finder, the check boxes are Replace Contacts and Replace Calendars.) Then, the next time you sync, that information on your iPad will be replaced with the contacts or calendars from your computer.

Synchronizing Your Media

If you chose to let iTunes manage synchronizing your data automatically, welcome. This section looks at how you get your media — your music, podcasts, videos, and photos — from your computer to your iPad. Here's the general procedure to follow:

1. **Use the Finder or iTunes tabs to choose the media you want to sync between your iPad and your computer.**

   The sections that follow provide the details.

2. **Click Apply to put the settings into effect.**

3. **If your computer asks you to confirm, click Sync and Replace.**

   Finder or iTunes synchronizes your selected media.

REMEMBER

Podcasts and videos from your computer are synced only one way: from your computer to your iPad. If you delete a podcast or a video that got onto your iPad via syncing, the podcast or video will not be deleted from your computer when you sync.

That said, if you buy or download any of the following items from the iTunes Store, Book Store, or App Store *on your iPad,* the item *will* be copied back to your computer automatically when you sync:

>> Songs

>> Podcasts

>> Videos

>> E-books and audiobooks from the Book Store

>> Playlists you created on your iPad

And if you save pictures from email messages, the iPad camera, web pages, or screen shots, these too can be synced.

You use the Music, Movies, TV Shows, and Photos panes to specify the media you want to copy from your computer to your iPad. The following sections explain the options you find in each pane.

To view any of these panes, make sure your iPad is still selected and then click the appropriate tab in the Settings list on the left (iTunes) or across the top of the screen (Finder).

The following sections focus only on syncing. If you need help acquiring apps, music, movies, podcasts, or anything else for your iPad, just flip to the most applicable chapter for help.

WARNING

Music, podcasts, and videos are notorious for using massive amounts of storage space on your iPad. If you try to sync too much media content, you see lots of error messages. Forewarned is forearmed. One solution is to create one or more iPad-specific playlists and sync only those. You might also listen to podcasts with the Podcasts app, which can stream episodes (in addition to letting you download them). Streamed episodes don't take up storage on your iPad!

Syncing music, music videos, and voice memos

REMEMBER

Before you can sync music between your iPad and your computer, you must disable iCloud Music syncing on your iPad. Choose Settings ➪ Music, tap the Sync Library switch off, and then tap Turn Off when Settings asks you to confirm. You'll need to disconnect your iPad from your computer and then reconnect to put the new setting into effect.

To transfer music to your iPad, select the Sync Music check box in the Music pane. You can then select the Entire Music Library option or the Selected Playlists, Artists, Albums, and Genres option. If you choose the latter, select the check boxes next to particular playlists, artists, albums, and genres you want to transfer. You also can choose to include music videos or voice memos or both by selecting the appropriate check boxes near the top of the pane.

WARNING

If you choose Entire Music Library and have more songs in your iTunes library than storage space on your iPad, the sync will fail and the capacity bar at the bottom of the screen will display your overage.

Finally, if you select the Automatically Fill Free Space with Songs check box (Finder only), the sync will fill any free space on your iPad with music. I strongly recommend against choosing this option because you can easily run out of space for pictures and videos you shoot or documents you save (to name just a few of the possible consequences of filling your iPad with songs outside your control).

Syncing movies

To transfer movies to your iPad, select the Movies tab. Next, select the Sync Movies check box and then, from the pop-up menu, choose an option for movies you want to include automatically. If you choose an option other than All, you can optionally select individual movies and playlists by selecting the boxes in appropriate sections.

Syncing TV shows

To sync TV shows, select the TV Shows tab and then select the Sync TV Shows check box. Leave the Automatically Include check box selected. Next, choose how many episodes to include from the pop-up menu and whether you want all shows or only selected shows from the second pop-up menu. If you want to also include individual episodes or episodes on playlists, select the appropriate check boxes in the lists provided.

Syncing audiobooks

To sync audiobooks (Finder only), select the Audiobooks tab. To sync everything, select the All Audiobooks option; otherwise, select the Selected Audiobooks option and then select the check box beside each audiobook you want to include in the sync.

Syncing books

To sync books (Finder only), select the Books tab. To sync everything, select the All Books option; otherwise, select the Selected Books option and then select the check box beside each book you want to include in the sync. You can also click the PDFs tab to add PDF files to the sync.

Syncing photos

REMEMBER

Before you can sync photos between your iPad and your computer, you must disable iCloud Photos syncing on your iPad. Choose Settings ⇨ Photos, tap the iCloud Photos switch off, and then tap what you want to do with your photos: Remove from iPad or Download Photos & Videos. You'll need to disconnect your iPad from your computer and then reconnect to put the new setting into effect.

Select the Photos tab, select the Sync Photos check box, and then choose an application or folder from the pop-up menu. Then you can select the All Folders option to sync everything, or you can select the Selected Folders option and then select the check box beside each folder you want to include in the sync.

2

The Internet iPad

Chapter **4**

Exploring the Web with Safari

R ecent years have seen the rise of a new pastime: *couch surfing*. This term refers to exploring the seemingly infinite realm of the web from the comfy and cozy confines of your couch. Sure, you might have a decent-sized screen connected to your desktop computer, but that means meandering from one site to another while sitting at your desk. Ugh. That plush sofa is much more inviting, but what device is best? Is it a laptop? Perhaps, but they can get awfully hot and lead to the ickily-named *toasted skin syndrome* (a skin rash caused by lengthy exposure to a heat source, such as laptop balanced on the thighs for an extended period). Your iPhone? Not bad, but even the most humungous iPhone screen is often too small to display many websites.

No, if you want a couch-surfing session that's both safe and satisfying, the clear winner here is your iPad. With its generous screen size, light weight, and never-hotter-than-warm temperature, it just might be the ideal web device. In this chapter, you discover the pleasures — and the few drawbacks — of navigating cyberspace on your iPad.

Introducing the Safari Web Browser

The app of choice when it comes to navigating the web on your iPad is the Safari web browser. Safari comes with every bell and every whistle you'll need to get around the web as well as a few you probably didn't know you needed.

Exploring the browser

You start your cyberexpedition with a quick tour of the Safari browser. To get Safari onscreen, tap the Safari icon (the compass) in the dock. The screen you see will look similar to the one shown in Figure 4-1, which points out the major features. Not all browser controls found on a Mac or a PC are present, but Safari on the iPad still has a familiar look and feel. I describe these controls and others throughout this chapter.

Blasting off into cyberspace

Most of the time, your web adventures begin with a web address, which you type in the Smart Search field (labeled in Figure 4-1). Why is it smart? Because you can use it to enter not only web search text but also web addresses.

TIP

When you tap inside the Smart Search field, your iPad parks its virtual keyboard at the bottom of the screen. When you're entering an address in the Smart Search field, here are a few tips for using the keyboard in Safari (see Chapter 2 for more help with using the virtual keyboard):

Safari sidebar · Previous page · Next page · Website settings · Smart Search field · Tabs · Add tab · Share · Reload

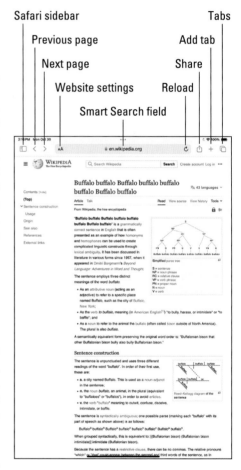

FIGURE 4-1:
The iPad's Safari browser.

>> Almost all website addresses these days begin with the characters *https://*. Safari knows this and will add these to the start of the address automatically, so you don't need to type them.

>> You usually don't need to type **www** to start a web address. For example, if you want to visit www.theonion.com, typing **theonion.com** is sufficient to transport you to the humor site. However, some sites (thankfully, very few) work only if the address includes *www*, so if your site fails to load, try adding **www.** to the address.

>> As you type, Safari displays a list of web addresses that match what you've entered so far. For example, when I typed *new* (as shown in Figure 4-2), I saw web listings for The New Yorker (newyorker.com) and CBC News (cbc.ca/news). You'll likely see other sites, but the point is that if you see the site you want, you can stop typing and just tap the site in the menu to go there directly.

>> Many web addresses end with one of the following suffixes: .us, .edu, .com, .net, or .org. Instead of typing one of these suffixes manually, long-press the .? key. iPadOS displays a menu that includes these five suffixes. Slide your finger up to the suffix you need and then lift your finger to add the suffix to the Smart Search field. Some options appear only if you've selected an international keyboard (as discussed in Chapter 2).

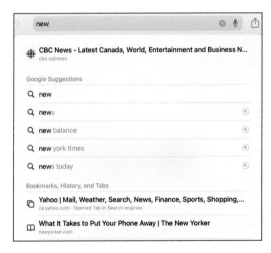

FIGURE 4-2:
Safari displays
web pages that
match what
you've typed
so far.

TIP

While you're entering a web address in the Smart Search field, the iPad uses three resources to determine which websites to suggest:

>> **Bookmarks:** The iPad suggests websites you've bookmarked in Safari (or synchronized from your other devices, as described in Chapter 3). More on bookmarks later in this chapter.

>> **History:** The iPad suggests sites from the history list — those cyberdestinations where you recently hung your hat, including websites you've visited on your other Apple devices. Because history repeats itself, I tackle that topic later in this chapter.

>> **Smart Search field:** When you type an address in the Smart Search field, you see icons for sites you frequent most often. You can tap any of those icons to jump immediately to the associated site.

So, here are the steps to follow to open a web page by entering its address:

1. **Tap the Safari icon docked at the bottom of the Home screen.**

2. **Tap in the Smart Search field (refer to Figure 4-1).**

3. **Begin typing the web address, or *URL* (which is short for *uniform resource locator*, if you must know), on the virtual keyboard that slides up from the bottom of the screen.**

4. **Do one of the following:**

   - *To accept one of the bookmarked (or other) sites that show up in the list, tap the name.* Safari automatically fills in the URL in the Smart Search field and takes you where you want to go.

   - *Keep tapping the required keyboard characters until you enter the complete web address for the page you have in mind, and then tap the Go key on the right side of the keyboard.*

Zooming in and out of a page

Most web pages are easily read on your iPad, but every now and then you come across a page where the type or images or both are too small to decipher. No problem: You can zoom in on the page to read and see the page content without ruining your eyesight.

Here are the techniques you can use:

>> **Rotate the iPad to its side.** This action reorients your tablet from portrait view to a widescreen landscape view. That wider screen often results in an increased size of the screen content, which might get the job done for you.

>> **Increase the text size.** Tap the ᴀA icon in the Smart Search field and then tap the A button to the right of the percentage value, as pointed out in Figure 4-3. As you tap, Safari increases the web page text, first to 115%, then 125%, and so on.

>> **Zoom the entire page.** Placing two fingers (usually your thumb and either your index finger or middle finger) on the screen and then spreading them apart zooms in on the page and makes the page's content bigger. Not all the content will fit on the screen, so you'll need to flick left and right and up and down to see more of the page. When you're done, you zoom back out to normal size by placing two fingers on the screen and pinching them together.

Reading clutter-free web pages with reader view

It's all too easy to get distracted reading web pages, what with ads, videos, and other clutter surrounding the stuff you want to take in. Reader view (shown in Figure 4-4, right) can remove most of those distractions, but you need to activate it first.

When you first pull up a new web page that has reader view available, the Smart Search field briefly displays *Reader Available*. To activate reader view, tap the Smart Search field's AA icon and then tap Show Reader. If Show Reader appears dimmed, reader view is not available on this page.

Decrease text size   Increase text size

FIGURE 4-3:
You can increase the text percentage to a value that makes the web page readable.

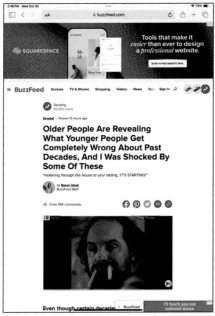
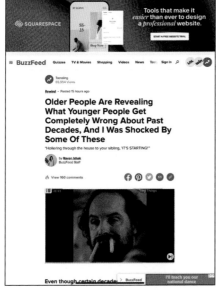

FIGURE 4-4:
Reducing web page clutter thanks to reader view.

Finding Your Way around the Web

In this section, I discuss ways to navigate the web on your iPad by using links and tabs.

Looking at links

Because Safari functions on the iPad in the same way browsers work on your Mac or PC, text links that transport you from one site to another typically are underlined, are shown in blue, red, or bold type, or appear as images or items in a list. Tap the link to go directly to the site or page.

Other types of links lead to different outcomes:

>> **Map location link:** Tap a real-world address and the iPad usually launches the Maps app and displays the location.

>> **Email address link:** Tap an email address and the iPad opens the Mail app (see Chapter 5), starts a new message, and populates the To field with that address. The virtual keyboard is also summoned so you can add other email addresses and compose a subject line and message. For this feature to work, your Mail app must be set up (see Chapter 5).

TIP

To see the URL for a link, long-press the link until a preview of the linked web page pops up, along with a list of options (see Figure 4-5). You can use this method also to preview where a linked image will take you. (If you don't see the preview, tap the Tap to Show Preview text.)

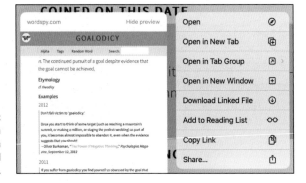

FIGURE 4-5:
Long-press a link to see a preview and other options.

As for the link options shown in Figure 4-5, here's what six of them do:

>> **Open:** Opens the link in the current tab

>> **Open in New Tab:** Opens the link in a new tab (see "Tabbed browsing," next)

>> **Open in Tab Group:** Opens the link in a new or existing tab group (see "Wrangling tabs into tab groups," later in this chapter)

>> **Open in New Window:** Opens the link in a separate Split View window (see Chapter 2)

>> **Copy Link:** Copies the link URL to your iPad's clipboard so you can paste it elsewhere

>> **Share:** Opens the same sharing options presented when you tap the share icon

Tabbed browsing

When I surf the web on a Mac or PC, I rarely go to a single web page and call it a day. In fact, I often have multiple web pages open at the same time. Sometimes I choose to hop around the web without closing the pages I visit. Sometimes a link automatically opens a new page without closing the old one, whether I want it to or not.

Safari on the iPad, like the desktop version of Safari (and other browsers), lets you open multiple pages, and each page is displayed in a separate browser area called a *tab*. After you have one page open, you have two ways to open additional web pages in Safari so they appear on the tab bar at the top of the screen (rather than replace the page you're currently viewing):

>> **Tap + (add tab) near the top-right corner of the Safari screen.** A tab named Start Page appears, as shown in Figure 4-6. Now type a URL, tap a bookmark or an icon for a favorite or frequently visited site, or initiate a search, and the result will appear on this tab.

>> **Hold your finger on a link until a list of options appears (refer to Figure 4-5), and then tap Open in New Tab.**

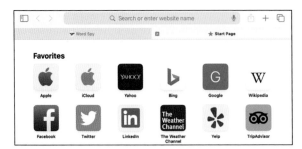

FIGURE 4-6:
A new tab, ready to display any page you choose.

To switch tabs, tap the tab you want to view. To close a tab, switch to that tab and then tap the gray *x-in-a-square* that appears near the left edge of the tab.

You can manage tabs in one other way. Tap the tabs icon in the top-right corner of the browser (labeled in Figure 4-1 and shown in the margin) to summon thumbnail views of your open web pages, as shown in Figure 4-7. (Alternatively, place three fingers on the iPad screen and pinch them together.) With the tab thumbnails displayed, you can perform any of the following tasks:

>> Tap a thumbnail to switch to that tab.

>> Tap + (add tab) to create a fresh tab.

>> Tap the X on any thumbnail to close the tab.

>> Go into private browsing mode (discussed later in this chapter).

>> Work with tab groups, the topic you dive into in the next section.

>> Tap Done to close the thumbnails and return to the tab you were viewing.

Wrangling tabs into tab groups

Most of the time, the tabs you have open in Safari will be unrelated to each other. However, sometimes you find yourself working with two or more tabs that are connected in some way. For example, if you're working on a special project for work, you might have a fistful of tabs open for web pages related to that project. If you then get a second project and also have a personal hobby you're researching, your tabs can get messy in a hurry.

The solution is to organize your related tabs into separate tab groups: one for each project, interest, or obsession that you currently have in your life. Safari gives you two methods to create and populate a tab group:

Tab groups

FIGURE 4-7:
A thumbnail
view of all your
open tabs.

 ❯❯ Open a tab for each page you want in your tab group and close any tabs you don't want in your group. Tap the tabs icon (shown in the margin), tap Tab Groups (labeled in Figure 4-7), and then tap New Tab Group with *X* Tabs, where *X* is the number of tabs you have open. In the New Tab Group dialog, type the tab group name and then tap Save.

❯❯ Tap the tabs icon, tap Tab Groups, and then tap New Empty Tab Group. In the New Tab Group dialog, type the tab group name and then tap Save. Safari creates a new tab for the group, which you can populate with a page. For subsequent pages, display each page in a new tab.

If you want to move a tab from one group to another, long-press the tab, tap Move to Tab Group, and then tap the group in the list that appears.

To switch from one tab group to another, tap the name of the current tab group in the upper-left corner of the Safari screen (just beside the Safari sidebar icon). Alternatively, tap the Sidebar icon (shown in the margin) to display the sidebar, which includes a list of your tab groups. Tap the name of the tab group you want to use.

Revisiting Web Pages

Surfing the web would be a lot less fun if you had to enter a URL every time you wanted to navigate from one page to another. To find those favorite websites in the future, the iPad provides bookmarks, web clips, the reading list, and the history list.

Bookmarking your favorite sites

In the same way that a bookmark helps you find a specific page in a physical book, a *bookmark* in Safari help you return to a specific page on the web. Follow these steps to create a bookmark for a web page that you want to save or visit often:

1. **Make sure the page you want to bookmark is front and center, and then tap the share icon (shown in the margin) at the top of the screen.**

    You have many options beyond bookmarking when you tap the share icon, as you discover later in this chapter.

2. **Tap Add Bookmark.**

    The Add Bookmark dialog opens with a default name for the bookmark, its web address, maybe a logo, and its folder location.

3. **To change the default bookmark name, tap the *x*-in-a-circle next to the name and then type the new title.**

4. **To change the location where the bookmark is saved, tap the Location field, which likely shows Favorites, and then tap the folder where you want the bookmark to be kept.**

    A check mark appears beside the folder.

5. **Tap Save.**

To open a bookmarked page after you set it up, tap the Safari sidebar icon (shown in the margin) to open the Safari sidebar, and then tap Bookmarks. If the bookmark you have in mind is buried inside a folder, tap the folder name first and then tap the bookmark you want.

Managing bookmarks

Once you have a bunch of bookmarks stuffed into Safari, you might need to make changes or even get rid of a bookmarked site that's no longer meaningful. Here are some techniques you can use:

>> **To display the Bookmarks list,** tap the Safari sidebar icon and then tap Bookmarks.

>> **To remove a bookmark (or folder),** display the bookmarks list and then tap Edit. Tap the red circle next to the bookmark (or custom folder) you want to toss off the list, and then tap Delete.

TIP

To remove a single bookmark or folder, you can also swipe its name from right to left and then tap the red Delete button.

>> **To change a bookmark name or location,** display the bookmarks list and then tap Edit at the bottom-right corner of the list. Tap the bookmark to open the Edit Bookmark pane with the name, URL, and location of the bookmark already filled in. Tap the fields you want to change. In the Name field, tap the gray *x*-in-a-circle and then use the keyboard to enter a new title. In the Location field, tap the location name and scroll up or down the list until you find a new home for your bookmark.

>> **To create a new folder for your bookmarks,** display the bookmarks list, tap Edit, and then tap New Folder. Enter the name of the new folder and then use the Location field to choose where to put the new folder.

>> **To move a bookmark up or down in a list,** display the bookmarks list, tap Edit, and then drag the three bars that appear to the right of the bookmark's name up or down to the bookmark's new resting place.

Saving a page to your reading list

When you visit a web page you'd like to read, but just not now, the reading list feature is sure to come in handy, including when you're offline. Here's how it works:

>> **Saving a page for later:** Tap the share icon and then tap Add to Reading List. Or, if you see a link to a page you'd like to read later, long-press the link until a list of options appears (refer to Figure 4-5) and then tap Add to Reading List. The first time you add an article to your reading list, you may be asked if you would like to automatically save reading list articles for offline viewing. Tap Save Automatically or Don't Save Automatically, as you want.

>> **Viewing your reading list:** Tap the Safari sidebar icon and then tap Reading List. Safari displays your saved pages, as shown in Figure 4-8.

>> **Reading a page on your reading list:** Open the reading list and then tap the page.

>> **Keeping track of what you've read:** Open the reading list and then tap Show Unread to display only those items you haven't read yet. Tap Show All to show all the items in the reading list.

>> **Marking an item as read or unread:** Open the reading list, swipe the item from left to right, and then tap its blue Mark Read or Mark Unread button.

>> **Removing an item from the Reading List:** Open the reading list, swipe the item from right to left, and then tap its red Delete button.

Finally, don't forget you can share your reading list (and bookmarks) among your computers and iDevices with iCloud.

FIGURE 4-8:
Tap a page in the reading list to read it.

Clipping a web page to the Home screen

You frequent lots of websites, some way more than others. For example, perhaps you consult the train schedule several times during the day. You could bookmark that page, but it would still require a few taps to open it. For a one-tap solution to any frequently visited page, add a Home screen icon for that page. Tapping that icon opens Safari and takes you directly to the page.

To create one of these so-called web clips, follow these steps:

1. **Open the web page in question and tap the share icon.**

2. **Tap Add to Home Screen.**

   Apple creates an icon out of the area of the page that was displayed when you saved the clip, unless the page has its own custom icon.

3. **Type a new name for your web clip or leave the one Apple suggests.**

4. **Tap Add.**

   The icon appears on your Home screen.

TIP

As with any icon, you can remove a web clip by long-pressing its icon until you see the shortcut menu. Tap Delete Bookmark, and then tap Delete.

Letting history repeat itself

Sometimes you want to revisit a site you failed to bookmark, but you can't remember the darn destination or what led you there in the first place. Good thing you can study the history books.

Safari records the pages you visit and keeps the logs on hand for several weeks. Here's how to access your history:

1. **Tap the Safari sidebar icon (shown in the margin) to open the Safari sidebar, and then tap History.**

   The history list appears.

2. **Scroll down to the day you think you hung out at the site.**

   Sites are listed under such headings as This Morning, Thursday Evening, or Thursday Morning, or segregated by a specific date.

3. **If the day's sites aren't displayed, tap the day to expand it.**

   If you're not sure when you visited the site, you can also use the Search History text box to type a word or two that describes the site. To display the Search History box, drag down the History pane until the box appears.

4. **When you find the page you want to revisit, tap it.**

   You're about to make your triumphant return.

TIP

To clear your history so no one can trace your steps, tap Clear in the bottom-right corner of the history list, tap what you want to clear — All History, Today and Yesterday, Today, or Last Hour — and then tap Clear History. Alternatively, starting on the Home screen, tap Settings ⇨ Safari ⇨ Clear History and Website Data, and then tap Clear History when Settings asks you to confirm.

WARNING

When you clear your history from settings, your history, cookies, and browsing data will be removed from all the devices signed into iCloud. If that was not your intention, tap Cancel.

Saving web pictures

You can capture most pictures you come across on a website — but be mindful of any potential copyright violations, depending on what you plan to do with the images. To copy an image from a website, follow these steps:

1. **Long-press the image.**

A preview of the image you have selected appears, along with a pop-up menu offering the following options: Share, Add to Photos, and Copy.

2. **Tap Save to Photos.**

Saved images end up in your Photos, where they can be synced back to a computer.

TIP

Tap Copy instead, and you can paste the image into an email or as a link in an app such as Notes. Tap Share to display the regular Sharing pane.

Sharing Your Web Experiences

When you find a great website you just must share, tap the share icon (shown in the margin) or tap Share after tapping and holding down on a link, and you find these sharing options:

>> **One Tap Suggestions:** Tap an icon in the top row of the Sharing pane, which contains people and places iPadOS thinks you're most likely to want to share with, such as nearby AirDrop devices, as described next, as well as a combination of your most-used and recent Messages contacts.

>> **AirDrop:** Share the page with other people who have compatible devices and AirDrop. You'll need to turn on AirDrop in Control Center (swipe down from the top-right corner of the screen). Then choose whether to make your iPad discoverable to everyone or only people in your contacts (refer to Chapter 12 for more about AirDrop).

>> **Messages:** Send a link to the web page in a text or an iMessage.

>> **Mail:** Open the Mail app, with a new message containing a link for the page and the name of the site or page in the Subject line.

>> **News:** Go to the Apple News version on the article you're viewing.

- » **Reminders:** Add to a new reminder a link to the web page you're viewing so you don't forget! If you tap Details, you can be reminded on a given day or location.

- » **Notes:** Open a pane that allows you to save the web page as an attachment in an existing or a new note. Tap Save to finish the process and return to Safari.

- » **Books:** Convert the web page you're viewing into a PDF that is then added to your Books library.

- » **Freeform:** Save the page info — title, URL, and sometimes the site's main image — as an object in a Freeform board.

- » **More:** Display other recent apps — including social networking apps such as X (formerly Twitter), Facebook, Tencent Weibo, and others.

Your list may not look exactly like the list just described, which was based on a clean iPad set up just for this book. If you've been using your iPad for a while, you'll see your frequently used apps.

- » **Copy:** Copy the address and title of the page.

- » **Add to Reading List:** See the "Saving a page to your reading list" section for details.

- » **Add Bookmark:** Bookmark the web page.

- » **Add to Favorites:** Add the web page you're viewing to this most-favored-nation-status grouping (which appears when you tap + to add a new tab).

- » **Add to Quick Note:** Add info (such as page title and URL) for the web page you're viewing to a Quick Note. (To see the quick note, open the Notes app, display the Folders sidebar, and then tap Quick Notes.)

- » **Find on Page:** Type a word you want to find. Matching words are highlighted; use the up and down arrows that appear to cycle through each mention. Tap Done when you're finished.

- » **Add to Home Screen:** This feature is described in the "Clipping a web page to the Home screen" section.

- » **Markup:** Convert the web page to a PDF you can then draw on! Use the brush palette that appears at the bottom of the screen to choose a color, a type of pen, and other markup controls. Tap Done to either save or delete the PDF.

- » **Print:** Print to an AirPrint printer. You can choose the number of copies you want. Tap Print to complete the job.

Launching a Mobile Search Mission

Apple combines the address bar and Search fields into a single, convenient, unified strip called the Smart Search field, following the path taken on most popular web browsers for PCs and Macs. Although you can certainly use the virtual keyboard to type google.com (or bing.com, or duckduckgo.com, or whatever search engine you prefer) in this field, Apple doesn't require that tedious effort. Instead, just type your search query directly in the box.

To conduct a web search on the iPad, tap the Smart Search field. You immediately see icons for your favorite web destinations. But when you start typing in the Smart Search field, a Google search mission commences, with live guesses shown at the top. (Google is your iPad's default search engine.)

TIP

To learn how to switch the search field from the current search engine to another search engine on your iPad, check out the "Smart Safari Settings" section, later in this chapter.

You see other search suggestions as you start tapping additional letters. Tap any search result that looks promising or tap Go on the keyboard to immediately land on the top hit. Or keep tapping out letters until you generate the search result you want.

TIP

You can also find your search word or phrase on the web page you have onscreen. If there's a match, you'll see an On This Page entry at the bottom of the Smart Search results. If you tap that result, the Smart Search pane vanishes, and the Find on Page pane comes up from the bottom of your screen.

Through the search engine suggestions and Safari suggestions features, you can get potentially useful information even if you don't explicitly search for it. If you search the name of a movie, for example, Safari will also provide showtimes at nearby theaters without being asked. If you're not comfortable with this feature, you can turn it off in Settings.

Private Browsing

Don't want to leave any tracks while you surf? Turn on private browsing for a "what happens in Safari stays in Safari" tool. Those truly bent on staying private will also want to tap Clear History, as mentioned earlier in this chapter.

To go incognito, you have two choices:

>> Tap the tabs icon (labeled in Figure 4-1 and shown in the margin), tap Tab Groups (labeled in Figure 4-7), and then tap Private.

>> Tap the Safari Sidebar icon (labeled in Figure 4-1 and shown in the margin) to display the Safari sidebar, and then tap Private.

After private browsing is on, any traces of your visit to shhhh.com (or wherever) are nowhere to be found. Your history is wiped clean, open tabs don't appear in iCloud tabs, and your autofill information is not stored anywhere. To remind you that you're browsing privately, the Smart Search field now shows white text on a dark gray background.

To come out of hiding, tap the tabs icon again or display the Safari sidebar and then tap a tab group.

The history of pages you've visited can be useful and a huge timesaver, so don't forget to disable private browsing when you're finished.

Be mindful of your settings on other machines. If you run Safari on both an iPad and a Mac, but choose to go private only on the tablet, your Mac browsing history will still show up in your history list on the iPad. Safari's Private tab group on the iPad will still bring in sites from iPhones or Macs via iCloud. Mark things private across all devices to keep things really private.

Smart Safari Settings

Safari works well in its default setup, but the app comes with a ton of settings that you can use to customize your Safari experience. To get started, tap the Settings icon on the Home screen and then tap Safari. The following settings enable you to create a bespoke version of Safari to suit your surfing style:

>> **Siri & Search:** Tap this setting to specify what Safari content you want accessible via Siri and the iPadOS search feature.

>> **Search Engine:** Tap the search engine you want Safari to use when you run queries from the Smart Search field: Google, Yahoo!, Bing, DuckDuckGo, Ecosia, or if you've enabled a Chinese keyboard, Baidu. Other settings found here let you determine whether the iPad can make search engine suggestions and Safari suggestions, features touched on earlier in this chapter.

>> **Quick Website Search:** When this setting is on, you can use website shortcuts when you're searching in a website. For example, you can type **wiki FDR** to show Wikipedia entries for Franklin Roosevelt.

>> **Preload Top Hit:** When this setting is on, Safari preloads the top search result in the background for speedier surfing.

>> **AutoFill:** Safari can automatically fill out web forms by using your personal contact information, usernames, and passwords, or information from your other contacts. Tap AutoFill and then use the following settings to customize AutoFill.

  ● Tap the Use Contact Info switch on if you're comfortable using the information found about your contacts.

  ● Tap My Info to select yourself in your contacts so that Safari knows which address, phone number, email address, and other information to use when it fills in a form.

  ● Tap the Credit Cards switch on if you're okay with allowing AutoFill to use your saved credit-card information. Tap Saved Credit Cards to view the cards you've saved on your iCloud devices or to add others.

WARNING

Turning on AutoFill can compromise your security if someone gets hold of your iPad. It can also affect security across all your iCloud-enabled devices. If you use AutoFill, be sure to protect your iPad as described in Chapter 17.

>> **Favorites:** Apple lets you quickly access favorite bookmarks when you enter an address, search, or create a tab. Tap the folder of sites for which you'd like to see icons (News, Business, Technology, whatever). A check mark appears next to your selection. Or leave the default Folder setting as Favorites.

>> **Show Favorites Bar:** If you enable this option, you'll see Safari's Favorites bar between the Smart Search field and tab bar. To get a bit more room on the favorites bar, you can tap Show Icons in Favorites Bar off to hide the site icons.

>> **Show Links on Hover:** If you're using an Apple Pencil, tap this switch on to view link addresses by hovering over a link.

>> **Block Pop-Ups:** *Pop-ups* are web pages that appear whether or not you want them to. Often, they're annoying advertisements. But on some sites, you welcome the appearance of pop-ups, so remember to turn off blocking under such circumstances.

>> **Extensions:** Enables you to manage any Safari extensions you've installed. An *extension* is a mini-app that extends the functionality of Safari in some small (but, I hope, useful) way.

>> **Downloads:** Tap through to decide where the files you download to your iPad will reside, in iCloud Drive or directly on your iPad. If you choose the iCloud

Drive option, the files will be available on all of your Apple devices signed into iCloud Drive.

» **Tabs:** You can choose either Separate Tab Bar (which appears under the Smart Search field) or Compact Tab Bar (which appears near the top-left corner of the Safari display).

» **Open New Tabs in Background:** If you enable this setting, new tabs that you open in Safari will load in a new tab, but you stay in the current tab.

» **When Using New Keyboard Shortcut:** Tap the command — Open Tab or Open Window — you want Safari to run when you press ⌘+N on a keyboard connected to your iPad.

» **Close Tabs:** Tap through to decide whether you want to close tabs manually — which I recommend — or have them closed automatically after one day, one week, or one month.

» **Profiles:** Set up different profiles to keep your Safari surfing sessions separate. For example, you might want one profile for personal browsing and a second profile for work-related stuff. Tap New Profile and then fill in the New Profile dialog to get started.

» **Prevent Cross-Site Tracking:** Apple is the tech leader in protecting your privacy, and no close second exists. The Prevent Cross-Site Tracking feature makes it difficult for Google, Facebook, and the myriad of advertising trackers on the internet to track you as you go from site to site. This feature is enabled by default, and I recommend you keep it enabled.

» **Hide IP Address:** When you set this option to From Trackers, Safari doesn't share your IP address with sites that are trying to track you across the web.

» **Require Passcode/Touch ID/Face ID to Unlock Private Browsing:** Tap this switch on to protect your Safari private browsing tabs with your iPad passcode or Face ID (both discussed in Chapter 17). If this switch is disabled, you haven't set up a passcode or Face ID.

» **Fraudulent Website Warning:** Safari can warn you when you land on a site whose producers have sinister intentions. The protection is better than nothing, but don't let down your guard because this feature isn't foolproof. The setting is on by default.

» **Clear History and Website Data:** You met this option earlier. Tap it to erase everything in Safari's history, leaving nary a trace of the pages you've visited.

» **Settings for Websites:** Use the settings here to configure the defaults you want Safari to use for every website you visit:

   • *Page Zoom:* Apple offers several settings for controlling what happens on every website, starting with Page Zoom. Tap Page Zoom to change the default setting for every website. You have options ranging from 50% to 300%, which is useful if you find yourself constantly adjusting the zoom level for new web pages.

- *Request Desktop Website:* Safari for iPadOS requests the desktop version of every website, rather than the mobile version. If you want to turn off this feature for some reason, tap Request Desktop Website and toggle the All Websites switch from green to white. Turning off this feature allows the server to decide whether you get the website's mobile version or desktop version.

- *Reader:* Tap the Reader category, and then tap the All Websites toggle to green if you want to view in reader mode every website you visit (or, at least, every website that supports reader mode).

- *Camera, Microphone, or Location:* You set up all three features in the same way. Tap through Camera, Microphone, or Location to control how websites request access to these features on your iPad. By default, they're all set to Ask, which means a website must ask for your permission before accessing one of these features.

» **Show Color in Compact Tab Bar:** When this setting is on, Safari changes the background color of the compact version of the tab bar to match the background color of the current web page.

» **Automatically Save Offline:** Tap the toggle for this setting to have your iPad automatically save to your iPad any web page you added to your reading list so you can read the page offline, without an internet connection.

» **Advanced:** The Advanced category has several settings most iPad users will never need to worry about. But because I love you, dear reader, I'm going to explain just in case! Tap Advanced to access the following additional settings.

- *Website Data:* Tap to view and manage the data cached by websites you've visited. They're listed in order by how much data they've saved, showing only the top ten by default. Tap Show All Sites to see the rest. If you tap and slide to the left on an individual website, you reveal a red Delete button. Tap Delete to remove that site's data. Tap and slide back to the left to hide the Delete button after you're finished with the site. Tap the Remove All Website Data to remove all cached data from every site at once.

- *Advanced Tracking and Fingerprinting Protection:* Prevents advertisers from tracking you across websites. This setting is turned on by default for private browsing, but you can also opt to use it for all your browsing. That sounds like a good idea, but this privacy feature might prevent some of your sites from displaying properly, so proceed with caution.

REMEMBER

- *Block All Cookies: Cookies* are tiny bits of information a website places on the iPad when you visit so that the site recognizes you when you return. You need not assume the worst; most cookies are benign.

  If this concept wigs you out, take action and block cookies from third parties and advertisers by tapping the Block All Cookies switch on.

  If you set the iPad so that it doesn't accept cookies, certain web pages won't load properly, and other sites such as Amazon won't recognize you or make any of your preferred settings or recommendations available.

- *Privacy Preserving Ad Measurement:* When this setting is on, Safari prevents websites from accessing your personal info to serve ads targeted at you.

- *Check for Apple Pay:* If you come to a website that accepts Apple Pay (Apple's mobile payments service), the site can check whether you have Apple Pay enabled on your tablet. If you're not comfortable with this idea, make sure this switch is off.

- *JavaScript:* Tap to toggle JavaScript on or off. JavaScript is a programming language that powers advanced and interactive features on all but the simplest websites, so it's unlikely you'll ever want to turn it off.

- *Web Inspector:* Tap to toggle to enable the capability to inspect different elements of a website. This feature is typically used by developers and isn't something the rest of us will ever need to think about.

- *Remote Automation:* This is another developer feature and I do not recommend that you enable it.

- *Feature Flags:* Tap to unveil a wealth of different things Apple is experimenting with in WebKit, the engine that powers Safari. I strongly recommend that you leave this entire section alone, unless you're a developer who needs to access these features to develop a website.

IN THIS CHAPTER

» **Setting up email accounts**

» **Reading and managing email messages**

» **Sending email messages**

» **Working with attachments**

» **Ensuring the swift completion of your email rounds**

Chapter **5**

The Email Must Get Through

lthough in this modern age lots of people prefer to communicate via text message (you get to that in Chapter 6), it's still impossible to imagine a world without email. Sure, we moan and complain about the sheer volume of messages that fill our inboxes every day, but many of us have jobs and relationships that rely on email and would be unthinkably more difficult without it.

Happily, your iPad knows all about this email business and can be configured to work with just about any email account. With your iPad set up to send and receive email, you're free to leave your desk and handle all your email tasks in a more comfortable place. Sure, you might be doing that already with your smartphone, but the iPad's big screen makes those email chores much easier and more pleasurable.

In this chapter, you learn the ins and outs of the Mail app. You begin by setting up and managing email accounts on your iPad. Then you move on to discovering the Mail app's many useful techniques for managing incoming email messages, including dealing with any file attachments that come your way. From there you investigate the Mail app's impressively long list of features related to sending emails. This chapter closes with a look at a few message and account settings that are sure to make your email tasks easier and more efficient.

Prep Work: Setting Up Your Accounts

First things first. To use Mail, you need an email address. You can get a free email account (for example, yourname@icloud.com) from Apple as part of iCloud. If you need to create a new iCloud account, go to Settings ⇨ Mail ⇨ Accounts ⇨ Add Account ⇨ iCloud. Then tap Create a New Apple ID and follow the onscreen directions.

If, for some reason, you don't want an iCloud account, you can also get a free from Google Gmail (https://gmail.com), Microsoft Outlook (https://outlook.live.com/), or numerous other service providers.

You can add as many accounts as you want to your mail or just stick with the one that comes with your iCloud account.

TIP

Many so-called free email providers add a bit of advertising to the end of your outgoing messages, or they sift through your email to add to their profile of you, which they then use to sell advertising. If you'd rather not be a billboard for your email provider, use an iCloud email, use the address that came with your broadband internet access (yourname@comcast.net or yourname@att.net, for example), or pay a few dollars a month for a premium email account.

Finally, while the rest of the chapter focuses on the Mail app, you can also use Safari to access most email systems via the web, if that's your preference. You can also install separate Gmail, Outlook, and other dedicated email apps from the App Store.

Getting started

If you're ready to roll with setting up an email account on your iPad, here's how you get started:

> **If you don't have an email account on your iPad:** The first time you launch Mail, you see the Welcome to Mail screen. Your choices are iCloud, Microsoft Exchange (business email), Google (Gmail), Yahoo!, AOL, Outlook.com, and Other.
>
> Tap the account type you want to add to the iPad and follow the steps in the upcoming "Setting up an account with another provider" or "Setting up corporate email" section.

>> **If you have one or more email accounts on your iPad and want to add a new account manually:** Tap Settings on the Home screen and then tap Mail ⇨ Accounts ⇨ Add Account.

You see an Add Account screen, shown in Figure 5-1, with the same account options that appear on the Welcome to Mail screen. Proceed to one of the next three sections, depending on the type of email account you selected.

FIGURE 5-1:
Tap a button to set up an account.

Setting up an email account with iCloud, Gmail, Yahoo!, AOL, or Microsoft Outlook

If the account you want to set up is with iCloud, Gmail (Google), Yahoo!, AOL, or Outlook, follow these steps:

1. **Tap the appropriate button on the Welcome to Mail screen (refer to Figure 5-1).**

   A dialog appears for the email service. Figure 5-2 shows the dialog that appears if you tap Google.

2. **If you already have an account with the service, sign in using your existing email address and password. Otherwise, to create an account with the service, tap Create Account.**

   Each service is different and wants different information from you. Most will ask for your name and other identifying information. Follow the onscreen instructions until the process is finished.

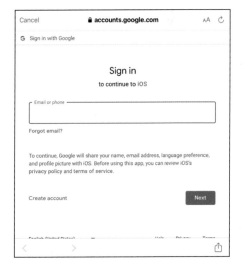

FIGURE 5-2:
The Create Account button is below the login option offered for people who already have accounts.

That's all there is to setting up your account. You can now proceed to "See Me, Read Me, File Me, Delete Me: Working with Messages."

Setting up an account with another provider

If your email account is with a provider other than iCloud, Microsoft Outlook, Gmail (Google), Yahoo!, or AOL, you have a bit more work ahead of you. You need a bunch of information about your email account you may not know or have handy.

I suggest you scan the following instructions, note the items you don't know, and go find the answers before you continue. To find the answers, look at the documentation you received when you signed up for your email account or visit the account provider's website and search there.

Here's how you set up an account:

1. **Starting at the Home screen, tap Settings ⇨ Mail ⇨ Accounts ⇨ Add Account ⇨ Other.**

2. **Tap Add Mail Account.**

3. **Fill in the name, address, password, and description in the appropriate fields, and then tap Next.**

   With any luck, that's all you'll have to do. The iPad will look up and retrieve your account settings. If that doesn't happen, continue with Step 4.

4. **Tap the button at the top of the screen that denotes the type of email server this account uses, IMAP or POP, as shown in Figure 5-3.**

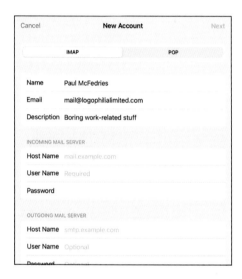

FIGURE 5-3:
If you set up an IMAP or a POP email account, you may have a few more fields to fill in before you can rock.

5. **Fill in the internet hostname for your incoming mail server, which looks something like mail.providername.com.**

6. **Fill in your username and password.**

7. **Enter the internet hostname for your outgoing mail server, which looks something like smtp.providername.com.**

8. **Enter your username and password in the appropriate fields.**

9. **Tap the Next button in the upper-right corner to create the account.**

   You're now ready to begin using your account. See the section "See Me, Read Me, File Me, Delete Me: Working with Messages."

TIP

Rarely, outgoing mail servers don't need your username and password. The fields for these items on your iPad note they're optional. Still, I suggest you fill them in anyway. Doing so saves you from having to add them later if your outgoing mail server does require an account name and a password, which almost all do these days.

Setting up corporate email

The iPad makes nice with the Microsoft Exchange servers that are a staple in large enterprises, as well as many smaller businesses.

What's more, if your company supports Microsoft Exchange ActiveSync, you can exploit push email so messages arrive pronto on the iPad, just as they do on your other computers. (To keep everything up to date, the iPad also supports push calendars and push contacts.) For push to work with Exchange Server, your company must support one of the last several iterations of Microsoft Exchange ActiveSync (most companies do). If you run into a problem, ask your company's IT or tech department.

Setting up Exchange email isn't particularly taxing, but you might have to consult your employer's techie-types for certain settings.

Start setting up your corporate email on your iPad by following these steps:

1. **Tap the Microsoft Exchange listing on the Welcome to Mail or Add Account screen.**

   Refer to Figure 5-1.

2. **Fill in your name and the description you want for your account. Then tap Next.**

3. **On the next screen, enter your name, email address, password, server, and domain, assuming the Microsoft Autodiscover service didn't already find it. Then tap Next.**

   You might need to contact your company's IT support to fill in any information you don't know.

4. **Choose which information you want to synchronize through Exchange by tapping the switch on beside each item you want.**

   You can choose Mail, Contacts, Calendars, Reminders, and Notes.

5. **Tap Save.**

WARNING

The company you work for doesn't want just anybody having access to your email — heaven forbid your iPad is lost or stolen — so your bosses may insist you change the passcode lock in Settings on your iPad. (The passcode lock is different than your email account password.) Now if your iPad ends up in the wrong hands, your company can wipe the contents clean remotely.

If you're moonlighting at a second job, you can configure more than one Exchange ActiveSync account on your iPad; there used to be a limit of just one such account per device.

See Me, Read Me, File Me, Delete Me: Working with Messages

Now that your email accounts are all set up, it's time to figure out how to receive and read the stuff. Fortunately, you did most of the heavy lifting when you set up your email accounts. Getting and reading your mail is a piece of cake.

You can tell when you have unread mail by looking at the Mail icon in the dock at the bottom of your Home screen. The cumulative number of unread messages across all your email inboxes appears in a little red badge in the upper right of the icon, as shown in Figure 5-4.

FIGURE 5-4:
When new mail arrives, the Mail icon displays a badge to let you know.

TIP

The badge display is the default behavior. If you don't care for it, turn it off by opening Settings ⇨ Notifications ⇨ Mail and tapping the Badges switch off.

In the following sections, you find out how to read messages and attached files and then send messages to the trash, or maybe a folder, when you've read them. Or, if you can't find a message, check out the section on searching your email messages.

Reading messages

To read your mail, tap the Mail icon on the Home screen to open the Mail app. What appears onscreen depends on whether you're holding the iPad in landscape or portrait mode, as well as what was on the screen the last time you opened the Mail app:

>> **Landscape:** With the iPad in landscape mode, you usually see your account's inbox folder and the currently selected message, as shown in Figure 5-5. Note all the little icons in the toolbar and elsewhere. You learn about all these features later in the chapter.

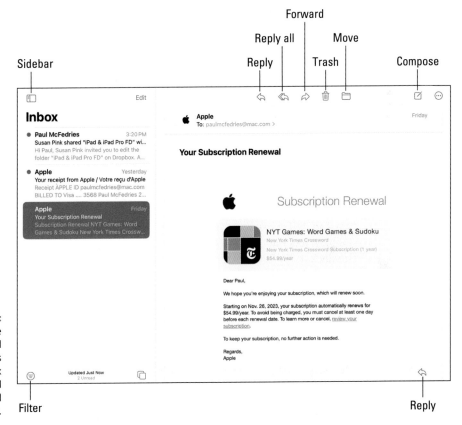

FIGURE 5-5:
In landscape mode, Mail displays your inbox folder and the selected message.

>> **Portrait:** When you hold the iPad in portrait mode, the last selected message fills the entire screen, as shown in Figure 5-6. Note that most of the toolbar icons are the same as those in Figure 5-5, with a couple of exceptions that

I point out in Figure 5-6. To see the current account folder (usually Inbox), tap the sidebar icon or swipe right from the left edge of the screen.

How do you change to a different account folder? That's one of the more confusing aspects of the Mail interface, so it's best to tackle it right off the bat. Again, it depends on whether your iPad is oriented in landscape mode or portrait mode:

>> **Landscape:** Tap the sidebar icon (labeled in Figure 5-6). Alternatively, swipe right from the left edge of the screen.

>> **Portrait:** Tap the sidebar icon (labeled in Figure 5-6), and then tap Mailboxes near the upper-left corner of the screen. Alternatively, swipe right from the left edge of the screen to display the current folder, and then keep swiping right until the Mailboxes pane appears.

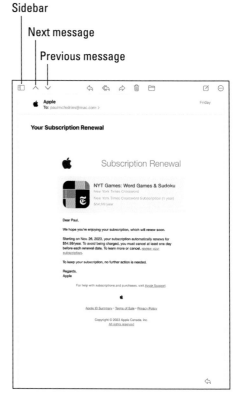

Sidebar

Next message

Previous message

FIGURE 5-6:
In portrait mode, Mail displays the selected message.

Whichever method you use, the Mailboxes pane appears. Figure 5-7 shows the Mailboxes pane in landscape mode with a single email account.

Mailboxes, as its name suggests, is a repository for all the messages across all your accounts. The number to the right of Inbox (2 in Figure 5-7), which matches the number on the Mail icon on your Home screen, is the cumulative tally of unread messages across all your accounts. If you have more than one email account set up, Inbox will instead say All Inboxes.

Below the Inbox or All Inboxes listing are the inboxes for your individual accounts. On the test device shown in Figure 5-7, I had just set up a new account, so it looks all clean and pretty. Depending on how you use email, yours might look considerably busier. Each individual inbox you have displays the number of unread messages for that one account.

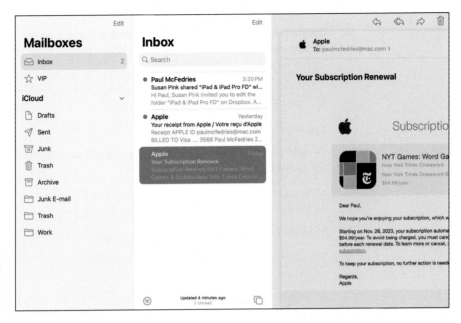

FIGURE 5-7:
The Mailboxes pane in landscape mode.

In this view, you can also see the available subfolders for your accounts (Drafts, Sent, Junk, Trash, and so on). If you have multiple accounts, tap through to each account to see its subfolders.

Check out the VIP mailbox, too. The VIP mailbox lists all messages from senders you deem most important. I tell you how to give someone VIP status in the later section, "More things you can do with messages."

REMEMBER

Depending on the last time the Mail app was open, you may see previews of the messages in your inbox. Previews display the name of the sender, the time the message arrived, the subject header, and the first two lines of the message. (In Settings ➪ Mail ➪ Preview, you can change the number of lines shown in the preview from one line to five, or even to no preview lines.)

Messages are displayed in *threads*, or conversations, making them easy to follow, but you can still view messages individually. To read your email:

1. **(Optional) To check for new messages, drag down the Mailboxes panel that lists your accounts or mailboxes and immediately release.**

   If you see a spinning gear, the iPad is searching for new mail. If a blue dot appears next to a message, the message hasn't been read.

2. **If the email mailbox you want to see isn't front and center, display the Mailboxes list and then tap the mailbox you want.**

   If you have multiple email accounts set up, tap All Inboxes, instead, to view the unified inbox (that is, all the messages from all your account inboxes in one handy location).

3. **Tap a message to read it.**

4. **To read the next message in the current mailbox, use one of the following techniques:**

   - *In landscape mode:* In the list of messages on the left side of the screen, tap the next message.

   - *In portrait mode:* Tap the next message icon (pointed out in Figure 5-6).

5. **To read the preceding message in the current mailbox, use one of the following techniques:**

   - *In landscape mode:* In the list of messages on the left side of the screen, tap the preceding message.

   - *In portrait* mode: Tap the previous message icon (pointed out in Figure 5-6).

6. **Repeat Steps 2 through 5 until you've read all the messages you want to view in this session.**

Threading messages

Apple lets you display related messages as *threads*. The beauty of this arrangement is you can easily trace an email conversation. When you organize messages by thread, the related messages appear as a single entry in the preview pane mailbox, with a right–pointing arrow in a circle to indicate that the message is indeed part of a larger ongoing exchange. When you tap that listing, all messages that make up the threaded conversation appear in the larger pane on the right, though you may have to scroll up or down to see them all.

If you tap an individual message from the thread in the pane on the right, you can swipe to quickly reply to the message, forward it, or mark it unread. These are the same options you see when you swipe a preview in the message list.

When you look at a message that's part of a thread, the number at the top of the screen tells you how many individual messages make up the entire conversation.

To customize threading, go to the Home screen and tap Settings ➪ Mail. In the Threading section, you have the following settings:

>> **Organize by Thread:** Toggles threading on (the default) or off.

>> **Collapse Read Messages:** Mail displays a minimal version of thread messages you've already read, which makes it easier to navigate the thread.

>> **Most Recent Message on Top:** Mail displays the most recent message in a thread on top.

>> **Complete Threads:** Mail always displays all the messages in the conversation, even if you've previously moved some messages to other mailboxes.

>> **Muted Thread Action:** Determines the action that Mail takes when you mute a thread. The default is Mark as Read, but you can also choose Archive or Delete.

Managing messages

Managing messages typically involves either moving the messages to a folder or deleting them. To herd your messages into folders, you have the following options:

>> **To create a folder to organize messages you want to keep:** Open the Mail app, display the Mailboxes pane, and then tap Edit. Tap New Mailbox at the bottom to open the New Mailbox dialog. Type a name for the mailbox, choose a location for it, and then tap Save.

>> **To file a message in another folder:** Tap the move icon (refer to Figure 5-5). When the list of mailboxes appears, tap the folder where you want to file the message.

>> **To read a message you've filed:** Display the Mailboxes pane, tap the folder where the message now resides, and then tap the message.

>> **To delete, move, or mark multiple messages:** In the account folder pane (such as Inbox), tap Edit. Tap each message you want to select so that a check mark appears, or tap Select All to work with every message. You use the following icons at the bottom of the pane to manage the selected messages:

●   *Mark:* Displays a list of actions you can apply to the selected messages: Move to Junk (moves the messages to the Junk folder); Mark as Read (marks unread messages as read); Mark as Unread (marks read messages as unread); Flag (adds a flag icon to the messages); or Unflag (removes the flag icon from the messages).

●   *Move:* Displays a list of folders to which you can move the selected messages. Tap the new location to move the messages.

●   *Trash:* Deletes the selected messages (that is, it moves the selected messages to the account's Trash folder).

TIP

» **To delete a single message:** Display the message and then tap the trash icon (refer to Figure 5-5) in that open message.

If you find yourself often deleting a message by mistake, you can configure Mail to confirm each deletion. Choose Settings ➪ Mail, and then tap the Ask Before Deleting switch on.

» **To delete a single message without opening it:** Swipe left across the message in the mailbox list, and then tap the red Trash button that appears to the right of the message. You'll also see a Flag option and a More button. Tapping More gives you, well, more options: reply, forward, mark it as unread, move it to junk or elsewhere, or have the iPad send a notification when someone replies to the message or thread.

TIP

In certain Mail accounts, Gmail being one, the Trash option may be replaced by an Archive option, depending on your preference. That means you're not getting rid of a message but stashing it or, to be precise, saving the message in your All Mail folder. If the Archive option does present itself, you can turn the feature on or off in Settings ➪ Mail.

Searching emails

With the search feature, you can quickly search through a bunch of messages to find the one you want to read. In any mailbox, if you don't see the Search field, drag down in the list to display it. Now you can use the Search box to type whichever search term seems relevant. Mail immediately runs the search on all your mailboxes. If you'd prefer to restrict the search to just the mailbox that's open, tap the Current Mailbox tab.

What's more, Apple has helpfully organized the search results, so if you search for *dummies,* senders who have that word as part of their name are separated from the subject headings of email messages that include the search term.

Search in the Mail app is powerful. For example, you can search by time frame by typing something along the lines of *March meetings.* You can also search to find just flagged messages from your VIPs (*flag unread VIP*).

TIP

Siri can also find emails on your behalf. For example, ask Siri to find all the emails from a particular person in a particular month, or have Siri run a text search.

If you're using Exchange, iCloud, or certain IMAP-type email accounts, you may even be able to search messages stored on the server.

Dealing with attachments

Your iPad's file viewer can work with attachments in a wide variety of popular file formats. Which file formats does the iPad support? Glad you asked:

- **Images:** .jpg, .tiff, .gif, .png
- **Microsoft Word:** .doc, .docx
- **Microsoft PowerPoint:** .ppt, .pptx
- **Microsoft Excel:** .xls, .xlsx
- **Web pages:** .htm, .html
- **Apple Keynote:** .key
- **Apple Numbers:** .numbers
- **Apple Pages:** .pages
- **Preview and Adobe Acrobat:** .pdf
- **Rich Text:** .rtf
- **Text:** .txt
- **Contact information:** .vcf

WARNING

If the attachment is a file format the iPad doesn't support (for example, an Adobe Photoshop .psd file), you see the name of the file in your email, but you can't open it on your iPad, at least not without an assist from a third-party app you may have installed.

Here's how to read a supported attachment:

1. **Open the email that contains the attachment, which you can identify by a little paper clip icon.**

   Another option is to conduct a search for *Messages with Attachments.*

2. **Tap the attachment.**

   The attachment typically appears at the bottom of the message, so you might need to scroll down to see it.

   In some cases, the attachment downloads to your iPad and opens automatically. In other instances, you may have to tap the button representing the attachment to download it.

3. **Read or (in the case of a picture) eyeball the attachment.**

   Tap the attachment (in the case of a document), and you can likely read it immediately. Tap Done to return to the message text.

Alternatively, long-press the attachment in the email and then tap the app from the presented options. Among the possible choices: Tap Quick Look for a quick peek at the attachment or tap Markup and Reply to add your comments to a document before whisking it back to the sender. You can also add the attachment to iCloud Drive or Notes or import it to Apple's Pages word processor should that app resides on your tablet. Third-party apps you added to your iPad may also become available as a destination for said attachment.

More things you can do with messages

Wait! You can do even more with your incoming email messages:

>> **To reply to, flag, or delete a message:** Swipe left on the message in the message list to reveal the More, Flag, and Trash buttons. Tap More and then tap Reply, Reply All, or Forward to respond to the message. Tap Flag to flag the message so it will turn up in any search for flagged messages. Tap Trash to quickly delete the message.

>> **To see all recipients of a message:** Assuming you can't see all the names of the people receiving the message, tap the triangle to the right of the recipient. That name expands to show everyone to whom the email was sent or cc'd as a recipient.

>> **To perform an action on the sender or another recipient:** Display the email, and then tap the sender's name (or email address, if that's what you see) to convert the names (or email addresses or both) of the sender and the other recipients to links. Tap the link for the sender or recipient you want to work with, and Mail displays a list of actions you can perform. These actions include icons for messaging, voice calling, video calling, and emailing the person. You also see the following commands:

- *Add to VIP:* Gives VIP status to the sender or recipient. You might want to assign VIP (very important person) status to key people in your life, such as your significant other, family members, boss, or doctor. A star appears next to any incoming message from a VIP. You can summon mail from all your VIPs by tapping the VIP folder in the list of Mailboxes. To demote a VIP to an NVIP (not very important person), tap the sender at the top of the message, tap the VIP's link, and then tap Remove from VIP.

- *Block this Contact:* Blocks the person, which means you'll no longer receive messages from this person.

- *Search Mail for Contact:* Initiates a Mail search for this person's email address.

- *Send Message:* Creates a new email message addressed to this person.

- *Share Contact:* Enables you to send the person's name or email address or both to someone else via the standard-issue share dialog.

- *Create New Contact:* Adds the person's name and email address as a new card in the Contacts app.

- *Add to Existing Contact:* Adds the person's email address to an existing Contacts card that you specify.

>> **To mark a message as read or unread:** Swipe left on the message in the message list to reveal three buttons: More, Flag, and Trash. Tap More and then tap either Mark as Read or Mark as Unread.

Choose Mark as Unread for messages you may want to revisit at some point. The message is again included in the unread message count on the Mail icon on your Home screen, and its mailbox again has a blue dot next to it in the message list for that mailbox.

>> **To mute a thread:** Tap the version of the reply icon that appears in the bottom-right corner of the message (labeled in Figure 5-5) and then tap Mute. Muting a thread means you won't receive any notifications when new messages in that thread arrive.

>> **To get notified when someone replies to a message:** Tap the reply icon in the bottom-right corner of the message (refer to Figure 5-5) and then tap Notify Me.

>> **To get reminded to deal with a message:** Tap the reply icon in the bottom-right corner of the message (refer to Figure 5-5), tap Remind Me, and then tap when you want to be reminded (such as Remind Me in 1 Hour).

Sending Email

Sending email on your iPad is a breeze. You'll encounter several subspecies of messages: pure text, text with a photo, a partially finished message (a *draft*) you want to save and complete later, or a reply to an incoming message. You can also forward an incoming message to someone else — and in some instances print messages. The following sections examine these message types one at a time.

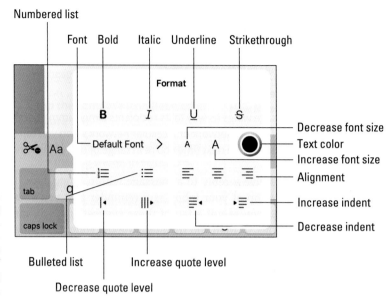

Numbered list

Font   Bold   Italic   Underline   Strikethrough

Format

B   *I*   U̲   S̶

Decrease font size
Default Font >   A   A   ⬤   Text color
Increase font size
Alignment
Increase indent
Decrease indent

Bulleted list   Increase quote level

Decrease quote level

FIGURE 5-9:
The Format
dialog gives
you an
impressive
range of
formatting
options.

Sending a photo or video with an email message

Sometimes a picture is worth a thousand words, and a video can be priceless. When that's the case, follow these steps to send an email message with a photo or video attached:

1. Start a new email message, address it, and type a subject.

2. In the message body, position the insertion point where you want the photo or video to appear.

 3. In the toolbar above the virtual keyboard, tap the insert photo or video icon (shown in the margin).

4. Tap a command from the menu that appears:

- *Photo Library:* Choose an existing photo or video from your iPad's photo library.

- *Take Photo or Video:* Use your iPad camera to take a new photo or shoot a new video.

- *Scan Document:* Scan an entire document.

- *Scan Text:* Scan some text.

5. If you see the Image Size field, tap the image size you want to send: Small, Medium, or Actual Size.

6. Complete and send your message.

TIP

An alternative way to send a photo or video is to open the Photos app, display the photo or video you want to send, tap the share icon at the top of the screen (the square with the upward-pointing arrow), and then tap Mail. A new email message appears with the photo or video embedded in the message. Address the message, type whatever subject and text you like, and then tap the Send button.

Adding an attachment to an email message

If you have a file either on your iPad or in your iCloud Drive that you want to send to someone, follow these steps to attach that document to an email message:

1. **Start a new email message, address it, and type a subject.**

2. **Tap anywhere inside the message body.**

3. **In the toolbar above the virtual keyboard, tap the attach file icon (shown in the margin).**

   Mail opens a Files-based interface for navigating the files on your device, iCloud Drive, or any third-party file-hosting service you may have added to your iPad.

4. **Navigate to and tap the document you want to send.**

   Mail attaches the file to your email.

5. **Complete and send your message.**

Marking up an attachment

If you're attaching a photo or a PDF document, you can take advantage of iPadOS's Markup feature. With a picture attachment or PDF embedded in your outgoing message, long-press the attachment and then tap the markup icon (shown in the margin) from the virtual keyboard's toolbar.

Now that you're in markup mode, you can draw on that image or PDF, tapping the simple annotation tools just below. The tools, which are represented by icons, include several pens (your finger will be that pen unless you use an Apple Pencil or another stylus), a highlighter, and a pencil. You even have a ruler you can use to draw perfectly straight lines.

In markup mode, you have the option to change the color and thickness of the lines and symbols you draw and change the font and size of text.

Tap + in the palette menu to access a menu that enables you to add a sticker, a description, text, a signature, or a shape.

When you're finished with the markup tools, tap Done to exit markup mode and return to the message.

Replying to a message

Some of the messages you receive will be information-only missives that require no further action from you (except perhaps moving them to a folder for safe-keeping). However, many messages require some sort of response, which you can make happen by following these steps:

1. **Display the message that you want to reply to.**

2. **Tap one of the following icons (refer to Figure 5-5).**

   - *Reply:* Opens a response message addressed to the sender

   - *Reply all:* Opens a response message addressed to the sender and to every other recipient of the message (except Bcc recipients, whom you don't know about)

   In both cases, Mail appends *Re:* to the Subject line. Mail also includes the original message as part of the reply.

3. **Write your reply in the space above the original message.**

4. **Tap the send icon (the upward-pointing arrow; refer to Figure 5-8).**

Forwarding a message

Often, you'll receive a message that you think will be of interest to someone who wasn't one of the original recipients. In that case, you can forward a copy of the email to that person, along with a bit of text explaining why you're forwarding the message. To forward a message, follow these steps:

1. **Display the message that you want to forward.**

2. **Tap the forward icon (refer to Figure 5-5).**

   Mail appends *Fwd:* to the Subject line and includes the original message as part of the forward.

3. **In the To field, type the address or the name (if the person is in your Contacts) of the recipient.**

4. **Write your message to the recipient in the space above the original message.**

5. **Tap the send icon (upward-pointing arrow; refer to Figure 5-8).**

Saving a draft

Sometimes you start an email message but don't have time to finish it. When that happens, you can save it as a draft and finish it some other time. Here's how:

1. **Start an email message, as described in one of the previous sections.**

2. **When you're ready to save the message as a draft, tap the Cancel button in the upper-left corner of the screen.**

3. **Tap the Save Draft button to save this message as a draft and complete it another time.**

   If you tap the Delete Draft button, instead, the message disappears immediately without a second chance. Don't tap Delete Draft unless you mean it!

To work on the message again, tap the Drafts mailbox or long-press the compose new message icon. A list of all messages you saved as drafts appears. Tap the draft you want to work on, and it reappears on the screen. When you're finished, you can tap Send to send it or tap Cancel to save it as a draft again.

REMEMBER

The number of drafts appears to the right of the Drafts folder, the same way the number of unread messages appears to the right of other mail folders, such as your inbox.

Scheduling an email to be sent later

Once you complete a message, you might prefer not to ship it right away. Perhaps you want to wait until after some external event has occurred, or perhaps your recipient lives in a different time zone and you don't want your message arriving in the middle of the night.

Whatever the reason, you can schedule the email to be sent later by following these steps:

1. **Complete your message by addressing it, adding a subject line, adding the text, and attaching any required files.**

2. **Long-press the send icon (refer to Figure 5-8).**

   Mail displays a menu of scheduling options. The options you see depend on what time it is, but you always see a couple of suggestions, such as Send 9:00 PM Tonight or Send 8:00 AM Tomorrow. There's also a Send Now command to send the message immediately, and a Send Later command to choose a custom send time.

3. **Tap the send time you want to use.**

   If you tap Send Later, the Send Later dialog appears, which enables you to choose the date and time you want the message sent; tap Done when you've finished.

   Mail sends the message at your selected time.

Unsending an email

It has happened to everyone: you compose an email in haste, tap Send, and immediately realize you've just made a gaffe, which could be anything from a minor typo to sending a love letter to the entire company.

If you'd give your eyeteeth to "unsend" that email, I have good news: You can keep your teeth where they are because Mail has got your back on this one. When you send a message, you actually have up to ten seconds to change your mind! As soon as you hear the iconic "whoosh" sound that Mail makes when it sends a message, you see a link that says Undo Send at the bottom of the folder pane, as shown in Figure 5-10. Tap that button and Mail yanks the message back before the recipient gets a chance to see it. Whew!

FIGURE 5-10:
Tap Undo Send to bring a sent message back from the brink.

TIP

To get more time to unsend a message, choose Settings ➪ Mail ➪ Undo Send Delay, and then tap 20 Seconds or 30 Seconds.

Settings for sending email

You can customize the mail you send and receive in lots of ways. In this section, you explore settings for sending email. Later in this chapter, I show you settings that affect the way you receive and read messages.

You can customize your mail in the following ways:

>> **To hear an alert when you successfully send a message:** Tap Settings ➪ Sounds. Make sure the Sent Mail setting is turned on. You'll know because you'll see a sound type listed (among alert sounds and ringtones), Swoosh by default. Tap Sent Mail to select a different sound or choose None if going silent is your preference.

>> **To add a signature line, phrase, or block of text to every email message you send:** Tap Settings ⇨ Mail ⇨ Signature. The default signature is *Sent from my iPad.* You can add text before or after it or delete it and type something else. Your signature will be affixed to the end of all your outgoing email. You can choose a signature that is the same across all your accounts or select different signatures for each account.

>> **To set the default email account for initiating email from outside the Mail application:** Go to Settings ⇨ Mail ⇨ Default Account. Note that if you have only one email account set up on your iPad, the Default Account setting will not be visible. If you have more than one email account on your iPad, tap the account you want to use as the default. The designated email account is the one that's used when you want to email a picture directly from the Photos app, for example. Also, if you choose one default account, you can dispatch mail from another account when you send your message.

Setting Your Message and Account Settings

I close this chapter with a quick look at a few settings that can make it easier to work with messages and email accounts.

Checking and viewing email settings

Several settings affect the way you can check and view email. You might want to modify one or more, so I describe what they do and where to find them:

>> **To specify how often the iPad checks for new messages:** Tap Settings ⇨ Mail ⇨ Accounts ⇨ Fetch New Data. You're entering the world of *fetching* or *pushing*. If your email account supports push and the Push setting is enabled on your iPad, fresh messages are sent to your iPad automatically as soon as they hit the server. If you turned off push or your email account doesn't support it, the iPad periodically fetches data instead. Choices for fetching are Every 15 Minutes, Every 30 Minutes, Hourly, Manually, and Automatically. Tap the one you prefer. With push email, messages can show up on the lock screen and in Notification Center.

>> **To set the number of lines of each message to be displayed in the message list:** Go to Settings ⇨ Mail ⇨ Preview, and then choose a number. Your choices are 1, 2, 3, 4, and 5 lines of text or None. The more lines of text you display in the list, the fewer messages you can see at a time without scrolling, so think before you choose 4 or 5.

>> **To specify whether the iPad shows the To and Cc labels in message lists:** Tap Settings ⇨ Mail and then turn on or off the Show To/Cc Label setting.

>> **To turn on or off the Ask before Deleting warning:** Go to Settings ⇨ Mail. Next, turn on or off the Ask before Deleting setting. If this setting is turned on, every time you want to delete an email, you must tap the trash (or archive) icon at the top of your email and then tap the red Delete button. When the setting is turned off, tapping the trash icon deletes the message, and you never see a red Delete button.

>> **To change swipe options:** Go to Settings ⇨ Mail ⇨ Swipe Options. Tap Swipe Left to choose an extra option (besides Trash) to appear when you swipe left on a message in the preview pane; the default extra option is Flag. Tap Swipe Right to choose an extra option (besides Remind Me) to appear when you swipe right on a message in the preview pane; the default extra option is Unread.

>> **To flag email addresses that are outside one or more designated domain names:** Tap Settings ⇨ Mail ⇨ Mark Addresses. Type @ followed by the domain name (say, of your company) that you do *not* want marked. If you want to designate multiple domains, separate each with a comma. From then on, when you're composing a message, all email addresses sent to or from the specified domain(s) will appear in blue, while all other mail addresses will be shaded red. Why do this? The idea is that you can more easily identify mail dispatched to or from addresses outside your organization, alerting you to a potential security risk if you're exchanging, say, sensitive information.

>> **To organize your mail by thread:** Tap Settings ⇨ Mail ⇨ Organize by Thread so that the setting is on. Then, as mentioned, you can choose whether to show the most recent message on top and whether to show all messages in a thread, even those since moved to other mailboxes.

Altering account settings

The last group of email settings you explore in this chapter deals with your email accounts. You most likely will never need most of these settings, but I'd be remiss if I didn't at least mention them briefly. So here they are, whether you need 'em or not:

TIP

WARNING

>> **To stop using an email account:** Tap Settings ➪ Mail ➪ Accounts ➪ *account name,* and then flip the switch for Mail off.

This setting doesn't delete the account; it only hides it from view and stops it from sending or checking email until you turn it on again. (You can repeat this step to turn off calendars, contacts, reminders, and notes in a given account.)

>> **To delete an email account:** Tap Settings ➪ Mail ➪ Accounts ➪ *account name* ➪ Delete Account ➪ Delete. Tap Cancel if you change your mind and don't want your account blown away, or tap Delete to proceed.

Deleting an email account also removes calendar entries, contact names, and notes from the given account.

You can find still more advanced Mail settings, reached the same way: Tap Settings ➪ Mail ➪ Accounts ➪ *account name.* From here, your exact path may be different depending on the kind of account you're working with. For example, Gmail requires you to tap Account ➪ Advanced and iCloud requires you to tap Account ➪ iCloud ➪ Mail ➪ Advanced.

REMEMBER

The settings you see under Advanced (sometimes shown as Advanced Settings under a specific email account) will vary by account. This list describes some of the settings you might see:

>> **Specify how long until deleted messages are removed permanently from your iPad:** In iCloud Mail, your choices are Never, After One Day, After One Week, and After One Month. Tap the choice you prefer. Other mail accounts may give you different time frame options or not present this setting.

>> **Choose whether drafts, sent messages, archived messages, and deleted messages are stored on your iPad or on your mail server:** Tap Advanced and then choose the setting under Mailbox Behaviors. You can decide for drafts, sent messages, and trash. If you choose to store any or all of them on the server, you can't see them unless you have an internet connection (Wi-Fi or cellular). If you choose to store them on your iPad, they're always available, even if you don't have internet access. In certain circumstances, you also get to determine whether to delete or archive discarded messages.

WARNING

I strongly recommend that you don't change the next two items unless you know exactly what you're doing and why. If you're having problems with sending or receiving mail, start by contacting your ISP (internet service provider), email provider, or corporate IT person or tech department. Then change these settings only if they tell you to. Again, these settings and exactly where and how they appear vary by account.

>> **Reconfigure mail server settings:** In the Incoming Mail Server or Outgoing Mail Server section of the account settings screen, tap Host Name, User Name, or Password and make your changes.

>> **Adjust SSL, authentication, or IMAP path settings, or the server port:** Tap Advanced and then tap the appropriate item and make the necessary changes.

You're now fully qualified to set up email accounts and send and receive email on your iPad.

Chapter **6**

Text Messaging

ech fads come and go with an inevitability and regularity that would be the envy of the tides themselves. As I write this, artificial intelligence bots — particularly generative AI apps such as ChatGPT — have the tech world mesmerized. A couple of years ago it was Bitcoin and the blockchain (whatever that was). Before that it was virtual reality and the metaverse (whatever that was). It's likely that by the time you read these words, the world's nerds will be oohing and aahing over some other shiny tech trinket. *Sic transit gloria mundi* and all that.

Ah, but while the vulture — oops, I mean *venture* — capitalists and tech bros have been busy ogling the latest and (supposedly) greatest, a quiet revolution has been happening right under their (and our) noses: Text messaging has taken over the world. It wasn't that long ago when texting was dismissed as "that thing teenagers are always doing," as the rest of us fretted about our overburdened email inboxes. Email still holds sway for longer correspondence, but it's taken on an oddly formal, perhaps even fusty, aura. Now, people text each other, end of story.

Happily, the texting thing isn't the sole province of the smartphone because your iPad comes with Messages, an app optimized for communicating with friends, family, and colleagues via text. In this chapter, you get to know Messages by diving deep to explore its many features for making texting easier and more fun, and you learn all the ways that Messages can help you stay in touch with everyone in your life.

iMessage versus SMS/MMS: What's the Difference?

One point of confusion that I need to clear up right off the bat is that the Messages app can deal with two types of messages:

>> **iMessages:** These messages can include not only text but also a wide variety of other media, such as photos, videos, maps, voice recordings, stickers, and animated GIFs. You can also get read receipts, see when the other person is typing a reply, and use Apple Pay. You can send iMessages only to folks who have an iPad, an iPhone, an iPod touch, or a Mac.

>> **SMS/MMS:** SMS (short messaging service) messages are text-only affairs, while MMS (multimedia messaging service) can include photos, videos, and audio. If you're exchanging messages with someone who doesn't have an iPad, an iPhone, an iPod touch, or a Mac, those messages will be SMS or MMS messages.

REMEMBER

To send SMS/MMS messages, your iPad needs to be using the same Apple ID as an iPhone and that iPhone needs to have text message forwarding turned on for the iPad (on the iPhone, choose Settings ⇨ Messages ⇨ Text Message Forwarding, and then tap the switch for your iPad on.)

REMEMBER

You can communicate with people who don't have an Apple device, but messages will be exchanged through SMS text messages or MMS multimedia-type missives. If you're involved in an SMS/MMS schmooze-fest, your message bubbles will be green. If you're exchanging iMessages with others, your bubbles will be blue. The distinction is important because most of the fancy multimedia tricks I tell you about in this chapter won't work unless you're exchanging iMessages.

REMEMBER

In this chapter, I refer to all the missives you send or receive with the Messages app as *text messages*. Unless I specify otherwise, this umbrella term refers to both iMessages and SMS/MMS messages and includes those missives that contain media, not just text.

Sending Text Messages

The next few sections show you various ways to ship out text messages to friends, family, colleagues, and perhaps even a stranger or two. You'll need the Messages app up and running, so this is as good a time as any to tap the Messages icon on the Home screen to launch the app.

Sending a text message to one person

 To start a new text message, tap the little pencil-and-paper (compose) icon in the left pane of the screen (shown in the margin).

At this point, with the To field active and awaiting your input, you can do three things:

>> **If the recipient is in your contacts list, type the first few letters of the name.** A list of matching contacts appears. Scroll through the list if necessary and tap the name of the contact. The more letters you type, the shorter the list becomes.

>> **Tap the blue circled + icon on the right side of the To field to select a name from your contacts list.** If a name in that list is disabled, that contact doesn't have a phone number or an email address that Messages can use to send the message.

>> **If the recipient isn't in your contacts list, type the person's phone number or email address.**

Now tap inside the message box that appears near the bottom of the New Message window. Type your text message. Note that you can start a new line in your text message by tapping the Return key.

 When your text message is ready to go, tap the send icon, shown in the margin.

 If you're sending iMessages, you can make your texts a little more email-like by including a subject line. The Subject field is off by default, but you can turn it on by choosing Settings ⇨ Messages and tapping the Show Subject Field switch on.

TIP

Whoops I: Editing a sent message

Why has texting become our de facto communications tool? I suspect one reason is that texting is super-casual. It generally reflects bad on you if you send a spelling-challenged email, but few people will raise an eyebrow if you ship them a text that contains a few misspelled words. As long as the meaning of your message is clear, most texters have a forgive-and-forget attitude when it comes to spelling and grammatical gaffes.

However, your recipients will definitely be far less forgiving if you make *factual* errors in your texts. Get the date, time, or location wrong for a rendezvous, and you're bound to get a spicy reply. That's why it's always good form to quickly check a text's facts before sending it.

Fortunately, the Messages app has you covered if a too-hasty tap of the send icon means you ship out a message that contains one or more crucial errors. The normal response is to quickly send a follow-up message with the correction, but as long as you sent an iMessage, you can make your changes directly to the message. You can make up to five edits within 15 minutes of sending the message. Your recipient might have already seen the error and, in any case, they can always view the edit history of the message, but you can at least feel good about setting the record straight.

To edit a sent message, follow these steps:

1. **Long-press the sent message you want to edit.**

   Messages displays a pop-up menu of commands you can run, as shown in Figure 6-1.

2. **Tap Edit.**

   Messages opens the message for editing.

   Messages enables you to edit a message only within 15 minutes of sending it, so if you don't see the Edit command, it means you're too late. Sorry about that.

3. **Make your edits to the message.**

4. **Tap Send.**

   Messages sends the edited version of the message.

FIGURE 6-1:
Long-press a message to see this list of commands.

REMEMBER

Whoops II: Unsending a message

If you launch a text at the wrong person, the results can range from minor embarrassment to full-on mortification. Fortunately, as long as you sent an iMessage and you realize your mistake within 2 minutes, the Messages app is happy to enable you to unsend the message, which means the (unintended) recipient is less likely to see it.

To unsend a message, follow these steps:

1. **Long-press the sent message you want to recall.**

   Messages displays a pop-up menu of commands you can run (refer to Figure 6-1).

2. **Tap Undo Send.**

   Messages retracts the message.

REMEMBER

   Messages enables you to unsend a message only within 2 minutes of sending it, so if you don't see the Undo Send command, it means you're out of luck. Bummer.

Sending group text messages

You aren't limited to sending text messages to a single person. Group chats in Messages allow multiple people to carry on a conversation, including sharing images, directions, files, and all the other goodies in Messages (assuming that each person is using an iPad, an iPhone, an iPod touch, or a Mac).

REMEMBER

If even one member of a group chat is not using Messages — for instance, that cousin who insists on using an Android device — all messages in the group chat are sent as SMS or MMS messages. You can tell because your outgoing chat bubbles will be green.

To initiate a group message, tap the compose icon (shown in the margin), and then type in the To field the names or phone numbers of everyone you want to include. When you've finished addressing and composing, tap the send icon to send your message on its merry way.

To name the group, tap the group chat in the list of ongoing chats on the left side of the Messages screen. Then, at the top of the message history for the group chat, tap the bar containing the group chat's members to open a dialog that shows the group chat's details. Tap Change Name and Photo, tap the Enter a Group Name field, and then enter the name you want.

You can see all participants in a group chat by tapping the group chat in your list of chats, and then at the top of the message history for the group chat, tapping the bar containing the group chat's members. If any group members are sharing their location with you, you'll also see a Maps interface with their location in the details dialog. Scroll down to the bottom of the details dialog to see the images and links shared in the group chat and the files sent. To leave a group, tap Leave This Conversation in the details dialog.

To add someone to the group, tap the *X* People button in the details dialog (where *X* is the number of people currently in the group chat), and then tap the Add Contact button.

Dictating a text message

If your hands are busy (perhaps you're in the middle of making pie pastry), you can still compose a text message with your voice by using your iPad's built-in dictation feature. Here's how it works:

1. **Start a new text message or open an existing conversation.**

2. **Tap the microphone icon on the right side of the message field.**

   Note that the microphone icon appears only if you haven't typed text in the message field.

   If you see a dialog asking if you want to enable dictation, tap the Enable Dictation button to make it so.

   Your iPad beeps and you see an icon indicating that dictation is activated, as pointed out in Figure 6-2.

3. **Speak your message.**

   As you speak, your iPad transcribes your words into text, as shown in Figure 6-2.

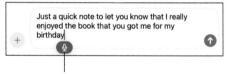

This icon appears while dictation is active

4. **(Optional) Tap the dictation icon to end the dictation.**

5. **Tap Send.**

   Messages sends the text.

FIGURE 6-2:
The dictation icon appears while dictation is active.

Sending an audio message

You can record an audio message and send it to a recipient. Apple calls this feature Tap to Talk, and here's how to take advantage of it.

Start a new text message or open an existing conversation. Tap the + icon to the left of the text-entry field and then tap Audio in the pop-up list that appears, shown in Figure 6-3. (Depending on how your iPad is configured, the menu you see might have more or fewer options than the one shown in Figure 6-3.) Start speaking; your voice appears as a waveform at the bottom of the screen. When you've finished the recording, tap the stop icon that appears to the right of the waveform.

To listen to your recording before you send it, tap the play icon that appears to the left of the waveform. If you're not thrilled with what you've just recorded, tap the X to the left of the recorded message and try again. Once the recording is the way you want it, tap the send icon.

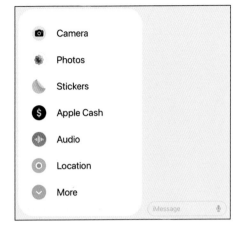

FIGURE 6-3:
Tap + to the left of the message text box to display a menu like this one.

⚠️

WARNING

After you listen to a received audio message, Messages by default deletes the audio message in 2 minutes (unless you tap the Keep button). You can choose Settings ⇨ Messages ⇨ Expire ⇨ Never to have received audio messages never expire.

The recipient of your recorded iMessage will be able to tap a play icon to listen to what you have to say.

Keep in mind that the sound wave icon that lets you record your voice is enabled only if you're sending a Message to a chat partner who's using the iPad, iPhone, iPod touch, or Mac. It won't be available if you're chatting with someone in SMS or MMS mode, which is when your chat bubbles are green.

Sending a doodle

You can use your finger (or a stylus such as an Apple Pencil) to draw a doodle or write message and then send your (literal) handiwork to someone. Here's how:

1. **Start a new conversation or open an existing conversation.**

2. **Tap inside the message text box.**

3. **On the virtual keyboard, tap the handwriting key, shown in the margin.**

   The handwriting pane appears.

4. **In the handwriting pane, use your finger or a stylus to create a doodle or handwrite some text.**

5. **Tap Done.**

6. **(Optional) Add a message to go along with your doodle.**

7. **Tap Send.**

   Messages sends your message.

Sending a photo

If you want to include a photo with a text message, you can send an existing image or use your iPad's camera to take a new photo. Either start a new conversation or tap an existing conversation. Tap + to the left of the message text box to display the pop-up menu shown earlier in Figure 6-3.

From here, you tap one of the following in the menu:

>> **Camera:** Launches the Camera app so that you can take a photo. When you're finished, either tap Done to return to Messages so that you can add some text to go along with the photo or tap the send icon that appears in the Camera app to send your photo right away. (Note that these instructions also apply if you want to use the Camera app to shoot and send a video.)

>> **Photos:** Opens a chooser dialog for your photos. Tap either the Photos tab or the Albums tab, locate and then tap the photo you want to send, and then tap Done to return to Messages. Type some text to go along with the photo (this is optional) and then tap the send icon.

TIP

Another way to text a photo is to open the Photos app, open the photo you want to text, tap the share icon (square with the upward-pointing arrow near the top-left corner of the screen), and then either tap a recent recipient or tap Messages and specify the person to whom you want to text the photo.

REMEMBER

After you add a photo a message but before you send it, you can remove the photo from the message if you change your mind. To remove the photo, tap the X that appears in the upper-right corner of the photo thumbnail.

TIP

If you want to restrict how much bandwidth your texts use (because either you or your recipient have text bandwidth caps), configure Messages to send lower-quality (and therefore smaller) images. Choose Settings ⇨ Messages, and then tap the Low Quality Image Mode switch on.

TIP

Rather than sending a photo, you might prefer to send a prefab animated GIF image. Tap + to the left of the message text box, tap More, tap #images, and then tap the animated GIF you want to send.

Sending your location

If you want to text someone to meet you or pick you up where you are, how do you let that person know where to go? Sure, there's always the old-fashioned method of providing the nearest intersection or address, but Messages offers a more modern way: Send your location in a text message. Here's how it works:

1. **Start a new conversation or open an existing conversation.**

2. **Tap + to the left of the message text box.**

3. **Tap Location.**

   iPadOS asks you to confirm that you want to allow Messages to use your location.

4. **Tap Allow Once.**

   Alternatively, if you think you'll be use the Location feature regularly, you can tap Allow While Using App.

5. **Tap Share and then tap for how long you want to share your location: Indefinitely, Until End of Day, or For One Hour.**

6. **(Optional) Include a message to be sent along with your location.**

7. **Tap the send icon.**

Inviting folks to collaborate on a file

You can use Messages to send an invitation to one or more people to collaborate on a file. For file collaboration to work, you and your recipients must be using Messages with at least iOS 16, iPadOS 16, or macOS 13, and you need to save the file to a location where everyone can access it, such as iCloud Drive.

Follow these steps to use Messages to invite people to collaborate on a file:

1. **Use the Files app to display the file on which you want to set up a collaboration.**

2. **Tap the share icon.**

TIP

   You can combine Steps 1 and 2 by opening the Files and Messages apps in split view (refer to Chapter 2), and then dragging the file to a new message.

3. **At the top of the share sheet, make sure that Collaborate is selected in the pop-up menu, as shown in Figure 6-4.**

4. **To configure the collaboration's settings, tap Only Invited People Can Edit and then follow these substeps:**

   a. *To control who has access to the file, in the Who Can Access section, tap either Only Invited People (only the people you invite via Messages can access the file) or Anyone with the Link (any person who is sent a link to the file can access it).*

   b. *To control what people who have access can do with the file, in the Permissions section, tap either Can Make Changes (people with access can edit the file) or View Only (people with access can't make any changes to the file).*

   c. *To enable invitees to invite other people to collaborate on the file, tap the Allow Others to Invite switch on. (Note that you see this switch only if you tapped Only Invited People in Step a.)*

   d. *Tap Done.*

FIGURE 6-4:
In the share sheet for a document, make sure Collaborate is selected.

5. **In the share sheet, if you see an icon for the person or group you want to invite, tap that icon. Otherwise, tap Messages and use the To field to choose the people you want to invite.**

6. **(Optional) Add a message to the invitees.**

7. **Tap the send icon.**

   Messages sends the invitation to the people or groups you selected.

Sending and receiving money

Did you know you can send and receive money in your Messages app? It's part of Apple Cash, which itself is part of Apple Pay. Although Apple limits the Wallet app to iPhone and Apple Watch, Apple Pay is still part of iPadOS.

Outside Messages, you can use Apple Pay on your iPad on sites that have enabled support for Apple Pay. In Messages, you can both send and receive money that comes from or goes to your Apple Pay balance. You can then use that balance to pay for things or to send money to someone using Apple Cash. If you want to send more money to someone than you have in your Apple Cash balance, Apple Cash will pull from the bank account you've added to Apple Cash. If you're paying for something that costs more than your Apple Cash balance, you can do so using any of the credit cards attached to your Apple Pay account.

Here's how to send or request money via Apple Cash:

1. **Start a new conversation or open an existing conversation.**

2. **Tap + to the left of the message text box.**

3. **Tap Apple Cash.**

   The Apple Cash interface opens.

4. **Tap to choose how much money you want to send (or request).**

5. **Tap Send or Request, depending on what you want to do:**

   - *Tap Send to have the money taken from your Apple Pay balance or your bank account and sent to your iMessage recipient.*

   - *Tap Request to ask that person for money.*

   The amount you're sending or requesting will be added to a new message waiting to be sent.

6. **Tap the send icon to send the money or payment request.**

To view the details of an Apple Pay Cash transaction, tap the black Apple Pay square in your Messages chat. You see who sent the money, when it was sent, the status of the transaction, how much was received, and a transaction ID.

Boosting Your Message with Special Effects

One of the original appeals of text messaging was the inherent simplicity right there in the first word: *text*. Send a recipient some words, they send you a few other words in response, and then it's just words flying back and forth. What could be simpler?

That original plainness was blissful, but it didn't allow for much in the way of nuance or subtlety. And if we've learned anything in the internet age, it's that communicating without subtlety is a recipe for various kinds of disaster. So, that might be why the Messages app — and particularly the iMessages you can exchange with other iDevice and Mac people — have gradually added more and more add-ons and special effects to enhance your outgoing messages. And while these effects can serve the practical use of adding nuance to a message, they can also be a ton of fun when used with a modicum of restraint.

This section takes you through the various add-ons and effects that you can use to give your text messages a boost.

Adding an animation effect to the message bubble

When you send a message, you can make the message stand out for the recipient by adding an animation effect to the message bubble. Follow these steps:

1. **Start a new conversation or open an existing conversation.**

2. **Add your message.**

3. **Long-press the send icon.**

   The Send with Effect screen appears.

4. **At the top of the screen, tap the Bubble tab.**

5. **Tap the effect you want: Slam, Loud, Gentle, or Invisible Ink.**

   Tapping an effect displays a preview of what your recipient will see. Messages also adds a send icon beside the effect name.

   If you decide against adding the effect, tap the X icon that appears below the effects list.

6. **Tap the send icon beside the effect you want to add.**

   Messages sends your message with the bubble effect.

REMEMBER

To "decode" a message received with the invisible ink effect, slide a finger along the message. This will make the text legible for a few seconds.

Adding an animation effect to the message window

If you're looking to up the wow factor for your recipient, send a message with an effect that plays over the entire message window. You can light up the window with fireworks, balloons, confetti, and more. Follow these steps:

1. **Start a new conversation or open an existing conversation.**

2. **Add your message.**

3. **Long-press the send icon.**

   The Send with Effect screen appears.

4. **At the top of the screen, tap the Screen tab.**

   Messages previews the first effect.

5. **Swipe left to preview the next effect, or swipe right to preview the previous effect.**

6. **When you've decided on the effect you want, make sure that it's currently being previewed and then tap the send icon.**

   Messages sends your message with the full-window effect.

Decorating a message with a sticker or two

You can add a bit of fun to a message by plastering it with one or more stickers, which you can create from your photos or from emojis. Here are the steps to follow to add a sticker to a message:

1. **Start a new conversation or open an existing conversation.**

2. **Add your message.**

3. **Tap + to the left of the message text box, and then tap Stickers.**

   Messages displays a dialog for working with stickers.

4. **To create a sticker from a photo, in the toolbar, tap stickers (the second icon from the left), tap New Sticker, choose the photo, and then tap Add Sticker.**

   Messages adds the photo sticker to the Stickers tab. Each photo sticker comes with an Add Effect button (long-press a sticker to see it) which, when tapped, enables you to add a special effect to the photo sticker.

5. **In the toolbar, tab a sticker category.**

6. **Tap the sticker you want to apply.**

7. **Tap outside the dialog to dismiss it.**

8. **Send your message.**

Sending Digital Touch effects

Digital Touch effects first appeared on Apple Watch but are now found also in iPadOS. They allow you to send customized animations designed to convey emotions and other abstract ideas.

When you're composing a message, tap + to the left of the message text box, tap More, and then tap Digital Touch to reveal the Digital Touch interface. Here's how Digital Touch works:

>> **To sketch:** Draw with one finger.

>> **To send a pulsing circle:** Tap with one finger.

>> **To send a fireball:** Tap and hold down with one finger.

>> **To send a kiss:** Tap with two fingers.

>> **To send a heartbeat:** Long-press with two fingers.

>> **To send a broken heart:** Long-press with two fingers, and then drag down.

>> **To switch ink colors:** Tap one of the circles at the top. If you see only one hue option, tap the colored circle to reveal other choices.

>> **To add a picture or video to your Digital Touch effect:** Tap the camera icon in the lower-left corner.

WARNING

Fireball, kiss, heartbeat, and heartbreak Digital Touch messages are sent automatically as soon as you lift your finger. Don't tap or press the screen in Digital Touch mode unless you really mean it.

Next, let's look at the built-in App Store, where you can buy (or download for free) sticker packs, new effects, lyric quoting apps, games you can play with your friends, apps for professional sports, and more. To get free stickers and see what other third-party apps are available, tap + to the left of the message box, and then choose More ⇨ Store.

Inserting memoji

You can use memojis to create a cartoon version of yourself to send in your iMessages as a sticker. Here's how to create your own memoji:

1. **Start a new conversation or open an existing conversation.**

2. **Add your message.**

3. **Tap + to the left of the message text box, tap More, and then tap Memoji.**

   Messages displays a dialog for working with memoji.

4. **Tap New Memoji (+).**

   Messages displays the memoji creator dialog.

5. **Customize your memoji.**

   Tap to choose the skin color, hairstyle, brows, eyes, head, nose, mouth, ears, facial hair, eyewear, and headwear. Each of these categories of features has multiple options to choose from. Spend as much or as little time as you want to create the perfect memoji for you.

6. **Tap Done on the memoji creator dialog.**

That's it! Your new memoji is now available in the list of available memojis and, as noted, will also have stickers based on what you created, premade and ready to go.

If you want to edit, duplicate, or delete a memoji, tap the memoji and then tap the circle with three dots on the left side of the memoji pane. A list of options appears: New Memoji, Edit, Duplicate, and Delete. Then do one of the following:

» Tap Edit to make changes to the memoji you already created.

» Tap Duplicate to use what you already created as the starting-off point for a new memoji. This option is useful if you want to change a hat, glasses, or some other minor feature.

» Tap Delete to permanently delete the memoji you created. You'll be asked to tap Delete again to confirm the deletion. When you do so, the deleted memoji disappears, and the next memoji in your list takes its place.

Tap Done to go back to Messages.

Now that you've created a memoji and have a list of stickers, it's time to insert a memoji sticker in an iMessage. Tap the memoji sticker you want to use to add it to your iMessage input field. Then tap the blue send arrow on the right side of the iMessage input field to send your memoji to your recipient. Or, if you change your mind and want to delete the memoji from your iMessage input field before sending, tap the small gray x-in-a-circle.

Being a Golden Receiver: Receiving iMessages

Text messaging is very much a two-way street. In the last section, you learned the ins and outs of sending text messages. Here, you discover a few useful settings and techniques related to receiving them, as well.

Before getting to all that, note that just the receiving part of texting is pretty close to a no-brainer because you don't need to do anything to retrieve texts that are sent your way. When your iPad receives a text, you see a notification, hear the text sound (choose Settings ⇨ Sounds ⇨ Text Tone to change it), and the Messages app's badge gets updated. Your only job is to open Messages and then tap the conversation to read the new message.

TIP

You can set up a separate text tone for someone in your iPad contacts, which lets you know who's texting based on the sound your iPad plays. In the Contacts app, display the person's card, tap Edit, tap Text Tone, tap the tone you want to use for that person's incoming texts, and then tap Done.

When you are viewing an individual chat or group chat, your messages appear on the right side of the screen in blue bubbles (green bubbles for SMS or MMS messages with someone not using iMessage) and the other person's messages appear in light gray bubbles, whether it's an iMessage, SMS message, or MMS message. When your message has been delivered, that fact will be noted just below the last bubble in your exchange. If there was a problem delivering the message, you'll see Not Delivered instead. If at first you don't succeed, try again.

TIP

One of the annoying quirks of the Messages app is that it shows the time you sent or received a message only for some of the messages in a conversation. If you need to know exactly when you sent a message or received any message, drag the conversation window to the left. The time each message was sent or received appears to the right of each message.

If you receive a picture or video in a message, it appears in a bubble just like text. You can view a still image or live photo inline, or tap the image to have it go full screen. In the case of a live photo, you can tap and hold down on it to play the short recording. (See Chapter 9 for more info on live photos.) If someone sends you a video, you can tap the play icon on the video to play it right in Messages. To have the video take over the full screen, tap the video first and then tap play.

Replying to a message

After you receive a message, there's a good chance you'll want to keep the conversation going by returning some sort of reply. You have three choices:

REMEMBER

>> **Reply to the most recently received message:** Use the message text box at the bottom of the conversation window to ship out your response.

If your sender can accept iMessages, the message text box includes the *iMessage* placeholder text; if the sender can accept only SMS/MMS messages, the message text box includes the *Text Message* placeholder text.

>> **Reply to an earlier message:** Swipe right on the message to which you want to reply. Alternatively, long-press the message and then tap Reply in the pop-up menu that appears. Then use the Reply text box to respond to the message.

>> **Reply with a reaction symbol:** Long-press the message and then tap one of the reaction symbols (Messages calls them tapback symbols) that appear above the message, as shown in Figure 6-5.

WARNING

Tapback works only with other devices running iPadOS, iOS 10 and above, or macOS Sierra and later. If the recipients are using any other operating system, they won't see any cute balloons, just plain old text that reads, "*Your name here* Loved/Liked/Disliked/Laughed At/Emphasized/Questioned *item name here.*"

FIGURE 6-5:
Long-press a message and then tap a reaction symbol.

Changing some receive settings

When determining your settings for receiving iMessages, first things first. Decide whether you want to hear an alert when you receive a message:

>> **If you want to hear an alert sound when you receive a message:** Go to Settings ➪ Sounds ➪ Text Tone, and then tap an available sound. You can audition the sounds by tapping them. You can also create your own tones in GarageBand for iPad.

>> **If you *don't* want to hear an alert when a message arrives:** Instead of tapping one of the listed sounds, tap None, which is the first item in the list of alert tones. You can also turn off alerts for individual chats and group chats. To do so, tap the conversation you want to silence, tap the bar above that chat with the name of the person you're chatting with, and then tap the Hide Alerts button on. Now you won't hear alerts or receive notifications just for that chat!

>> **If you don't want any iMessages:** Turn off iMessage by going to Settings ➪ Messages and tapping the iMessage switch off.

Forwarding a conversation

If you want to forward all or part of a conversation to another iMessage user, follow these steps:

1. **Open the conversation.**

2. **Long-press any text bubble in that chat.**

   A pop-up menu appears.

3. **Tap More.**

   Messages adds check boxes beside each text bubble in the chat and selects the check box the text bubble you long-pressed.

4. **Select the check box beside each message you want to forward.**

5. **Tap Forward (the curved arrow icon at the lower right of the screen).**

   The contents of the selected text bubbles are copied to a new text message.

6. **Specify a recipient.**

7. **Tap the send icon.**

   Messages forwards the selected texts to the recipient.

Deleting texts

If you need to get rid of some messages, you have two choices:

>> **Deleting part of a single conversation thread:** Long-press a text bubble and tap More. Select the check box beside each text bubble you want to delete. Tap the trash can icon at the bottom of the pane, and then tap Delete X Message(s) (where X is the number of messages you selected).

>> **Deleting an entire conversation thread:** Tap the Edit button at the upper left of the Messages list, tap Select Messages, select the check box to the left of each conversation you want to remove, tap the Delete button at the bottom of the pane, and then tap Delete when Messages asks you to confirm. Alternatively, swipe from left on a conversation in the Messages pane, tap Delete, and then tap Delete in the confirmation dialog.

Smart Messaging Tricks

Here are some more things you can do with messages:

>> **Search your messages for a word or phrase.** Type the word or phrase in the search field at the top left of the Messages listing pane. If you don't see the Search field, swipe down on the Messages pane.

TIP

» **Send read receipts to allow others to be notified when you have read their missives.** Tap Settings ➪ Messages and tap the Send Read Receipts switch on.

In iMessages, you can see when your own message has been delivered and read, and when the other person is readying a response. You can also tap the person's name at the top of the conversation pane to reveal the details dialog and then tap Send Read Receipts. Read Receipts is turned on, but only for the person with whom you are chatting.

» **Open a URL included in an iMessage.** Tap the URL to open that web page in Safari.

» **From iMessages, call or FaceTime the person you're texting with.** Tap the circled picture or initials representing the person you're communicating with, and then tap the audio call icon or FaceTime icon to call the person directly. If you tap the person's name at the top of the conversation window to open the details dialog, and then tap the person's Info button, you'll open up the person's full Contacts card.

» **See an address included in an iMessage.** Tap the address to see it on a map in Maps.

» **Choose how you can be reached via iMessage.** Tap Settings ➪ Messages ➪ Send & Receive. Then add another email address or remove existing addresses. You can also select the email address (or phone number) from which to start new conversations.

» **Filter unknown senders.** Tap Settings ➪ Messages and then tap Filter Unknown Senders on to turn off notifications for iMessages from folks who are not among your contacts. You can sort such unknown senders into a separate list. Specifically, after you activate Filter Unknown Senders, the initial Messages screen will display three lists: Known Senders, Unknown Senders, and All Messages (which includes both known and unknown senders).

» **Block a sender.** Block someone who is harassing you or has left your good graces. Tap the person's name at the top of the conversation pane to reveal the details dialog, tap Info, and then tap Block This Caller. You will no longer receive messages or FaceTime calls from this person.

» **Share your location.** Meeting a recipient in an unfamiliar place? In the middle of your conversation, you can share your location on a map. Tap the person's name at the top of the conversation pane to reveal the details dialog and then tap either Send My Current Location or Share My Location. Choosing the latter gives you the option to share your whereabouts indefinitely, until the end of the day, or for one hour. You can monitor how much time is left before your location will no longer be shared.

>> **See all message attachments at once.** Tap the person's name at the top of the conversation pane to reveal the details dialog, where you can browse all the photos, videos, documents, and links from your conversation.

>> **Keep your Messages history.** You can keep your entire Messages history on the iPad permanently, for one year, or for 30 days. Tap Settings ⇨ Messages ⇨ Keep Messages and make your choice.

You are now a certified Messages maven.

3

Banishing Boredom with the Multimedia iPad

IN THIS PART . . .

Explore the world of Apple Music, Books, News, and TV, including Apple's many content subscription services.

Capture good video, watch video, and share video with others.

Shoot photos, store them, edit them, and more.

Chapter **7**

Apple Music, Books, and News

As I discuss at length in Part 4, your iPad is a solid work device that can manage your contacts, keep track of your appointments, and direct you to your next meeting. However, if you believe that all work and no play make Jack and Jill a dull couple, there's no need to put away your tablet. Why not? Because your iPad is loaded with apps that fall on the "play" side of the ledger. These apps enable you to have loads of fun by turning your iPad into a multifaceted multimedia device.

If you're into music, for example, you can get your fill of everyone from Adele to ZZ Top by using the Music app, which gives you access to not only your own music library but also the seemingly infinite supply of tunes offered by the Apple Music subscription service. E-book nerds, too, have a home on the iPad: the Books app, which enables you to read almost any available book from the comfort of your tablet. Finally, if you get your jollies from knowing the latest happenings in the worlds of politics, sports, entertainment, and the like, check out the News app. You explore all these apps and their corresponding services in this chapter.

Music: Listening to Tunes on Your iPad

The Music app is the musical hub inside your iPad. You can not only manage your music library and listen to songs in the Music app but also tap into a library of nearly 100 million songs through the Apple Music subscription service. To get started, tap the Music icon, which in a default Home screen setup is located in the dock, as pointed out in Figure 7-1.

FIGURE 7-1:
Tap the Music icon in the dock to launch the Music app.

The layout of the Music app depends on the orientation of your iPad:

>> **Landscape orientation:** As shown in Figure 7-2, you see the sidebar on the left and the rest of the screen is populated with the currently selected sidebar item.

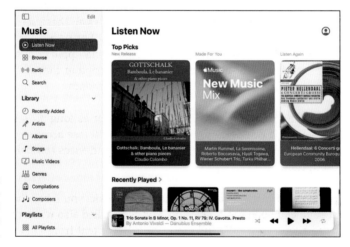

FIGURE 7-2:
The Music app with the iPad in landscape mode.

>> **Portrait orientation:** The entire screen is taken up by the currently selected sidebar item. To get the sidebar onscreen, either swipe right from the left edge of the screen or tap the sidebar icon, shown in the margin. (To hide the sidebar once again, tap anywhere outside of the sidebar.)

The Music app sidebar is home to four icons at the top: Listen Now, Browse, Radio, and Search. You also see a Library section and a Playlists section. In the following sections, you take a closer look at these elements of the Music app.

Listen Now: The Apple Music section of the Music app

You start with the Listen Now section, which is where you find Apple Music, Apple's premium music subscription service. Apple Music gives you access to over 100 million songs. That's right, 100 *million* songs, plus more than 30,000 curated playlists, song recommendations, and Music 1, Apple's streaming music channel with human DJs, sort of like a legacy radio station. You get all this for $10.99 per month or $99 per year, $5.99 per month for college students, or $16.99 per month for a family sharing plan for up to six people. Your first month is free, giving you plenty of time to get hooked on Apple Music before automatic billing kicks in.

TIP

If you just purchased your iPad, there's a good chance it came with an offer of six free months of Apple Music. In the Listen Now tab, look for a button that says Get 6 Months Free. If you see that button, go ahead and tap it to redeem your offer.

TIP

If besides Apple Music you also want access to Apple TV+ (discussed later in this chapter), Apple Arcade (over 200 games), and iCloud+ (extra online storage), consider a subscription to Apple One, which bundles all these services for $19.95 per month (or shared with up to five other folks for $25.95 a month). If you also want Apple News+ (discussed later in this chapter) and Apple Fitness+ (a bunch of different workouts), an Apple One Premier subscription that can be shared with up to five other people will set you back $37.95 a month.

REMEMBER

You'll be married to that subscription price for as long as you want to listen to Apple Music. If you ever stop subscribing, you'll lose access to music you used to stream and any music you downloaded to your devices through your Apple Music subscription.

If you haven't already subscribed to Apple Music, you'll be asked to subscribe the first time you open the Music app. You'll be asked also when you open the Listen Now section because it's full of the curated content from Apple Music.

After you subscribe to Apple Music, you can tap the Listen Now or Browse icons, which are discussed in more detail later, and then tap to hear any artist, genre, playlist, or song. It's that simple! You can tap the iCloud download icon next to a song or album to download that music to your device for offline listening, or stream anything you want when you have a connection to the internet, be it Wi-Fi or cellular. Note that streaming music counts against most cellular data plans; check with your provider if you're unsure.

Finding new music in Browse

The Browse icon in the Music app is all about finding new music, looking at music by genre, and viewing other recommended content from the Apple music team. While Listen Now is centered on what Apple Music thinks you're interested in, Browse offers a more general look at music, especially new releases and other new additions to the Apple Music catalog. Just like with Listen Now, when you have a subscription to Apple Music, you can tap any artist, playlist, genre, song, or other listing and play that music whenever you want.

But unlike Listen Now, Browse also lets you see content whether or not you have a subscription to Apple Music, allowing you to preview songs and see new releases. If you try to play a song, however, you'll be asked to sign in with an Apple ID that has subscribed to Apple Music.

Listening to human DJs in the age of streaming music

Tap the Radio icon to see the Radio section of Apple Music. You'll find several stations algorithmically designed around your music, as shown in Figure 7-3.

But the crown jewel in Apple Music's radio collection, and a feature unique to Apple Music, is Apple Music 1, an internet radio station created by humans and with human DJs. Much of the content is created hands-on by Apple's talented staff, with other content created by big and small artists. You can listen to individual shows with distinct flavors helmed by named DJs. You can tap See Full Schedule to view a schedule of shows; you also see some flagship shows promoted in the large banner at the top of the screen.

FIGURE 7-3:
The Radio section features radio stations built around your music.

To listen to Apple Music 1 or any other radio stations, tap the show or station you want to enjoy. You can view content in the Radio section at any time, but you need an active subscription to Apple Music to listen to those shows.

Managing music in the library

Now let's move on to your music, which you'll find in the Library section of the Music app sidebar. The library is dedicated to songs you've ripped from CDs, downloaded from the iTunes Store or other online music stores, or downloaded from Apple Music for offline listening. You also find songs you've synced to your iPad from your Mac or PC.

If you have multiple Apple devices and want to keep your music library synced between all of them, open Settings ⇨ Music and then tap the Sync Library switch on. With Sync Library, changes to the music library on one device are synced automatically to your other Apple devices.

TIP

For more information on syncing music to your iPad from your Mac or PC, please see Chapter 3.

Figure 7-4 shows an example of the Albums section of the library, where the albums are sorted alphabetically by artist. Each album shows the album cover, the name of the album, and the artist. Tap the sort icon in the upper-right corner of the screen to sort your library by Title, Recently Added, or Artist.

Sort

FIGURE 7-4:
The library shows all the music on your iPad.

Working with playlists

As with individual songs, you can create and listen to playlists on your iPad, or manage playlists synced to your library through the Sync Library feature. Display the Music sidebar and, if you don't see any playlists, tap Playlists to open the section. You see some default playlists, and this is where you'll see any playlists you create. You can tap any playlist to view its contents, and then tap the play icon on the Playlist page to listen to it.

To create a playlist, follow these steps:

1. **Tap All Playlists in the sidebar.**

2. **Tap + (new) in the upper-right corner.**

As an alternative to Steps 1 and 2, open Playlists in the sidebar and then tap the New Playlist button at the bottom.

The New Playlist dialog appears.

3. **(Optional) To add an optional description, tap Description. To add cover art, tap the camera icon on the left side.**

4. **Tap Playlist Title, enter a name for your playlist, then tap Create.**

5. **Tap the Add Music button to add new songs.**

6. **Tap the source you want to use: Listen Now, Browse, or Library.**

Depending on the source, you might need to drill down further into the content. In your library, for example, you might have to tap Albums and then tap the album that has the song or songs you want to add to the playlist.

Music opens the Add to "*Playlist*" dialog (where *Playlist* is the title you entered in Step 3).

7. **Tap each song you want to include, and then tap the Done button in the upper-right corner of the dialog.**

8. **Repeat Steps 5 through 7 as needed to populate your playlist.**

Your new playlist appears in the Playlist section of the sidebar, where you can tap and play it whenever you want.

To edit your playlist, tap it, tap the three dots (. . .) in the upper-right corner of your playlist screen, and then tap Edit. In edit mode, you can change the name of your playlist and add cover art. If it's a playlist you created, you can rearrange the order of the songs by dragging the three lines to the right of each song; you can tap Add Music to add more songs; and you can tap the red delete icon (−) to the left of any song to remove it (then, to confirm, tap the Delete button that appears to the right of the song).

If the playlist is one of Apple's Smart playlists, such as My Top Rated, you can't order, add, or delete the songs.

Searching for music in the Music App

Search may be one of the most important parts of the Music app for many users because that's where you search both your own library and Apple Music for specific artists, songs, albums, and even lyrics. To go to the search screen, tap the

Search icon above the Library heading in the sidebar. To search Apple Music (as I did in Figure 7-5), tap Apple Music if it's not already selected and then type your search term. To search your library, tap Your Library and then enter the search term. When searching either Apple Music or your own library, your iPad will display live results that change the more characters you type.

What about the iTunes Store?

All this talk about Apple Music may have you wondering about Apple's venerable iTunes Store. Never fear, dear reader, because the iTunes Store is still on your iPad, but now it's a separate app from the Music app. If you prefer to own your music, you can use the iTunes Store to buy songs and download them to your iPad whenever you want. (You can also buy movies and TV shows in the iTunes Store app.)

Tap the iTunes Store icon on your Home screen. Figure 7-6 shows the home page of the iTunes Store, which defaults to the Music section. Tap an artist, an album, or a song to view more information, including price. Note that links to Apple Music content in the iTunes Store may take you

FIGURE 7-6:
Buy music from the iTunes Store.

back to the Music app. That may be a little confusing at first — at least I think it is — but it's not surprising considering how hard Apple is pushing its subscription service.

If you buy a song or an album in the iTunes Store, it will be added to your music library. To play your newly purchased music, tap the Music app on your Home screen and then tap the Library icon in the sidebar. If you don't immediately see your new music, open the Playlist section and then tap Recently Added. Your new purchase will be at the top when it has finished downloading.

Songs in the iTunes Store tend to be priced at $0.99 or $1.29, with most albums starting at $7.99. Purchased songs will be charged to your iCloud account, and you'll be asked to sign into your iCloud account if necessary when purchasing from the iTunes Store.

Books: Reading E-books on Your iPad

With its large, sharp screen, the iPad is a natural reading device, so it's no wonder lots of people use their iPad to read e-books. The app of choice here is Books, which offers clear text, useful display and font settings, accurate page numbers, and great page curling and turning effects that (almost) make it feel like you're reading a real book.

Open Books by tapping the Books icon on your Home screen. The layout of the Books app depends on your iPad's orientation:

>> **Landscape orientation:** As shown in Figure 7-7, Books displays the sidebar on the left and the rest of the screen is populated with the currently selected sidebar item.

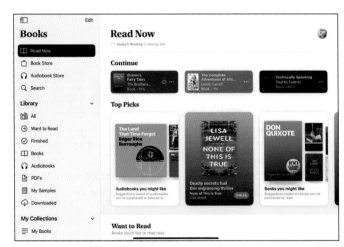

FIGURE 7-7:
The Books app in landscape mode.

>> **Portrait orientation:** The entire screen displays the current sidebar item. To display the sidebar, either swipe right from the left edge of the screen or tap the sidebar icon, shown in the margin. (Tap anywhere outside of the sidebar to hide it.)

The Books app sidebar offers four icons at the top: Read Now, Book Store, Audiobook Store, and Search. You also see a Library section and a My Collections section. In the following sections, you take a closer look at these elements of the Books app.

TECHNICAL STUFF

The default file format for Apple Books is EPUB (.epub), an open format for e-books. You can add EPUB files to Books through file transfers or even by emailing them to yourself and using the Share feature to send them to Books. (In Mail, long-press the EPUB attachment, tap Share, and then tap Books.) I discuss syncing files to your iPad in more depth in Chapter 3. Books also supports Apple's own multitouch format for e-books created with the iBooks Author app on the Mac. Most of the books available through the Book Store are EPUB files, but you'll be happy to know that you don't need to understand or care about the format of these books.

Read Now: Your iPad's bedside table

The Read Now section offers quick access to the books you've most recently opened, as well as books Apple is promoting. The book you're currently reading is at the top of the screen (refer to Figure 7-7), under the Current heading, while books you've opened recently are shown under the Recent heading.

Below the list of current books are books recommended to you based on what you've already read. If you've marked a book as one you'd like to read (I explain how later in the "Buying books in the Book Store" section), it appears in the Want to Read section.

Perusing your personal library

Open the Library section of the sidebar to view all the books you have in your Books iCloud library, whether or not they've been downloaded to your iPad. Books that haven't been downloaded have an iCloud icon below the cover art for the book. Tap that icon to download the book from iCloud to your iPad. Tap a book's cover art to open the book to the last page you had open. If you haven't previously opened a particular book, tapping it will take you to the book's designated starting page.

TIP

To view the table of contents for a book, tap to open the book, tap the reading menu icon (shown in the margin) in the lower-right corner of the screen, and then tap Contents. If you don't see the menu icon, tap anywhere on the page to bring up hidden controls and buttons, including the menu icon. Tap Resume to leave the table of contents and go back to the page you were on.

TIP

If you prefer to have the reading menu icon in the bottom-left corner of the screen, choose Settings ➪ Books and then, in the Reading Menu Position section, tap Left.

As you're reading, you can turn the page using three different gestures:

- ❯❯ **Tap:** Tap the current page's right margin to go to the next page; tap the current page's left margin to go to the previous page.

- ❯❯ **Drag:** Drag the right margin to the left edge of the tablet to go to the next page. As you drag, you slowly turn the page, just as if you were turning a real page on a real book. You'll even see the text of the page you're turning reversed and dimmed, as if you were seeing through a piece of paper. Drag the left margin to the right edge of the iPad to go to the previous page.

- ❯❯ **Flick:** Flick the current page to the left to go to the next page; flick the page to the right to go to the previous page.

TIP

Let's take a second to jump to Settings ➪ Books, where tapping the Both Margins Advance switch on allows you to advance the page by tapping either margin. You can still go back a page by dragging the left margin or flicking right when this setting is active. While you're here, tap Page Turn Animation and then select the animation you prefer: Slide, Curl (the default), or None.

REMEMBER

To close an e-book, tap the screen to display the controls and then tap the X that appears in the upper-right corner of the screen.

Making e-reading easier with a custom font and layout

Reading an e-book on your iPad can be a relaxing, delightful experience, or it can be a stressful, frustrating experience. What makes the difference? Two absolutely vital elements:

- ❯❯ **The font:** The style of the e-book text, including its typeface (some typefaces are easier to read than others) and its size (text that's too small or too large can cause eyestrain).

>> **The layout:** The background color, the screen brightness, and the spacing between lines, words, and characters. Your eyes will protest if you read with dark text on a light screen at night, a too-bright screen, or with text that's all scrunched together.

Many e-books come with poorly designed fonts and layouts, making them a slog to read. Fortunately, the Books app comes with a ton of settings that enable you to configure any e-book to suit your reading style.

 To check out these settings, open an e-book, tap the screen to display the controls (if they aren't displayed already), tap the reading menu icon, and then tap Themes & Settings. Books opens the Themes & Settings dialog, shown in Figure 7-8.

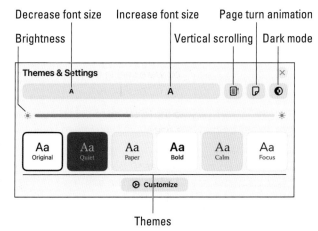

FIGURE 7-8:
Control the
look and
feel of any
e-book with
the Themes &
Settings dialog.

Here are the controls you get to play with:

>> **Decrease Font Size:** Tap to make the font smaller.

>> **Increase Font Size:** Tap to make the font larger.

>> **Vertical Scrolling:** Tap to turn this setting on, which means you now scroll your book vertically instead of horizontally. Tap to turn this setting off to return to horizontal scrolling.

>> **Page Turn Animation:** Tap to choose an animation effect for (horizontal) page scrolling: Slide, Curl, or None.

>> **Dark Mode:** Tap to see a menu of dark mode options: Light (dark text on a light background); Dark (light text on a dark background); Match Device (mirrors whatever dark mode setting you use on your iPad; refer to Chapter 15); and Match Surroundings (the iPad's sensors will switch to dark

mode when you're in a low-light environment and switch to light mode when you're in a brighter environment).

TIP

If you read in the evening or in a dark room, switching to dark mode can make e-book reading much easier and greatly reduce eyestrain.

» **Brightness:** Drag the slider to the right to make the screen brighter; drag the slider to the left to make the screen dimmer.

» **Themes:** Tap a swatch to apply that theme, which includes a typeface, type color, background color, and in some cases bold text. Try out different themes to see if one improves your reading experience.

The Themes & Settings dialog also comes with a Customize button that, when tapped, displays the Customize Theme dialog so that you can tweak the current theme. This dialog has some sample text at the top and the following controls:

» **Font:** Tap to choose a typeface for the theme. Some, but not all, books will list Original as the font, probably at the top of the list. If Original is listed and selected, you're reading your book in the font chosen by the publisher. Below that are several typeface choices, including Athelas, Georgia, Iowan, San Francisco, and Times New Roman, all standard publishing fonts. Fonts are subjective, so feel free to experiment until you find the one you like the best.

» **Bold Text:** Tap this switch on to make the e-book text bold.

» **Customize:** Tap this switch on to reveal the following options:

- *Line Spacing:* Sets the amount of vertical space between each line. For comfortable reading, use a value from 1.2 to 1.5.

- *Character Spacing:* Sets the amount of horizontal space between each character. You shouldn't have to mess with this value for professionally produced e-books. However, some cheaper e-books squish the characters together, so bumping this value up to 10 percent or more can help make such text easier on the eyes.

- *Word Spacing:* Sets the amount of horizontal space between each word. Again, you should only need to increase this value for poorly produced books that have the words set too close together.

- *Justify Text:* When on, aligns the text with both the left and right margins. If you find the word spacing in your e-book is uneven, tapping this switch off can help.

- *Allow Multiple Columns:* When on, displays the text in two columns when your iPad is in landscape mode. If you'd prefer a single column even in landscape mode, tap this switch off.

Searching inside a book

If you're looking for something in a book — it could be all the instances of a particular word, a memorable passage, or some tidbit of information — don't bother swiping to and fro to find what you want. The Books app comes with a Search Book feature that does just what it says on the box: It enables you to search the current book for what you want.

To search the current e-book, tap the screen to display the controls (if they aren't displayed already), tap the reading menu icon, and then tap Search Book. In the dialog that appears, tap inside the text box and then type a word or phrase that represents what you want to find. (You can also type a page number if you want to navigate to a specific page.) The search results appear below the text box. Tap a result and you jump straight to that page, with the word or phrase that matches your search highlighted.

In the top-left corner of the screen, you also see a number with a left-pointing arrow. That number represents the page you were on when you initiated the search; you can tap that number (or the arrow) to return to that page. (When you return to the initial page, Books shows a number and a right-pointing arrow in the top-right corner of the screen. You can tap that number or the arrow to return to the search result.)

Bookmarks that don't fall out

Searching for a favorite passage in an e-book, as I describe in the preceding section, is fine if you have lots of time on your hands. However, for those pages that you return to frequently, you're better off *bookmarking* the page, which adds the page to a special list that enables you to display the page with just a few taps. You can bookmark as many pages as you want.

To bookmark the current page, follow these steps:

1. **In the current e-book, navigate to the page you want to bookmark.**

2. **Tap the screen to display the controls (if they aren't displayed already).**

3. **Tap the reading menu icon.**

   Books displays the reading menu.

4. **Tap the bookmark icon, shown in the margin.**

   Books adds a bookmark for the current page.

To revisit a bookmarked page, tap the screen, tap the reading menu icon, and then tap Bookmarks & Highlights. In the dialog that appears, tap the Bookmarks tab to see the bookmarks you've saved in your current book. Tap a bookmark and the Books app transports you to that page.

To remove a bookmark, you have two choices:

» Display the Bookmarks list, swipe left on the saved bookmark, and then tap the trash icon (delete).

» Navigate to the bookmarked page, tap the bookmark icon that appears in the lower-right corner of the page, and then tap the Bookmark button to turn off the bookmark for that page.

Adding highlights and notes

If you were to open any book I've read, you'd find underlined passages and short notes scribbled in the margin. To me, a book doesn't feel read unless I've engaged with the text in these ways.

If you read physical books like this, you'll be pleased to know that the Books app offers features to engage with e-books in similar ways. Long-press a word in the text, and then drag the selector handles to select the full text you want to work with. In the selection menu that appears, tap one of the following:

» **Highlight:** Tap a color to add that color background to the selected text to make the passage stand out from the rest of the page. (Alternatively, tap the underline icon to underline the selected text.) Adding a highlight is the e-book equivalent of using a pen, pencil, or highlighter to mark up a passage in a physical book.

» **Add Note:** Displays the Note dialog, where you type something related to that text and then tap Done. Books adds a yellow highlight to the selected text and displays a yellow square in the margin to mark that a note has been added to the highlighted text. Adding a note is the e-book equivalent of writing something in the margin of a physical book.

TIP

If you want to make changes to a note, tap the note's highlighted text and then tap Edit Note.

To revisit a highlight or note, tap the screen, tap the reading menu icon, and then tap Bookmarks & Highlights. In the dialog that appears, tap the Highlights tab to see the highlights and notes you've added to your current book. Tap a highlight or note to display that page.

You remove a highlight or note (or both) as follows:

>> **Remove a highlight:** Tap the highlight and then tap Remove Highlight.

>> **Delete a note (but keep its highlight):** Tap the note's highlighted text and then tap Delete Note.

>> **Remove both a note and its highlight:** Tap the note's highlighted text and then tap Remove Highlight & Note.

Buying books in the Book Store

It's time to go shopping in the Book Store. (If you're currently reading an e-book, tap the screen, and then tap the X in the upper-right corner to close the book.) Display the sidebar, and then tap Book Store to open the Book Store screen, shown in Figure 7-9.

The screen is divided in several different categories, with bestsellers and promotional offers at the top. Below the promo section is the For You section, which contains books that Apple recommends for you based on what you've already purchased and read. Other sections include New & Trending books, Top Charts (paid and free bestsellers), Coming Soon, Books We Love (by Apple staff), special offers, and links to browsing by genre. You can also tap Browse Section in the upper-right corner to see a complete list of the Book Store's available sections.

FIGURE 7-9:
Buy e-books in the Book Store.

Tap any book to get a full-screen page of information about that book, as shown in Figure 7-10. Besides the titles, subtitle, and author at the top, you get a description and data such as the book's genre, release date, length, and publisher. The details page also has a Want to Read button that, when tapped, adds the book to the Want to Read section of the sidebar. Most books also include a Sample button that displays a snippet of the book for you to test-read. If you're convinced you want to own the book, tap the book's Buy button to purchase it. (If the book is free, tap the Get button, instead.)

For most e-books, you also see various lists to check out, including More Books Like This, More Books by *Author* (where *Author* is the author of the current book), More Audiobooks by *Author*, Customers Also Bought, and Top Books in *Genre* (where *Genre* is the genre of the current book).

After you purchase a book, you can view it in your library. Tap the book in your library to open it, and then read it as described earlier in the chapter.

Reading books with your ears in the Audiobooks section

The Book Store also has a section for *audiobooks*, recorded books that have been read by a human narrator. Audiobooks can be listened to right in the Books app and are listed in your library along with your e-books. You can view just your audiobooks by displaying the sidebar and choosing Audiobooks in the Library section. Audiobooks in your iCloud library that haven't been downloaded to your iPad will have an iCloud icon below them. Tap the iCloud icon to download the audiobook.

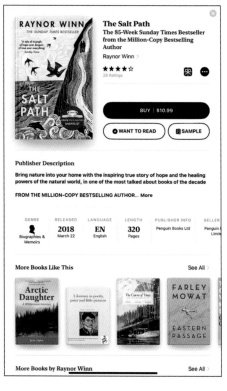

FIGURE 7-10:
Lots of information is available on an e-book's details pane.

TIP

To purchase an audiobook, display the sidebar, and then tap Audiobook Store. You see an audiobook details page that's similar to the e-book details page (refer to Figure 7-10). You can tap Preview to hear a sample, tap Want to Read to save it for later, or tap Buy to purchase the audiobook.

Tap the cover art for the audiobook to open it, as shown in Figure 7-11. Tap the play icon to play the audiobook and tap the pause icon to stop. Tap the 15 icon with an arrow going counterclockwise to back up the recording by 15 seconds, something that's useful if you missed something or were interrupted. You can tap that icon as many times as you want. Tap the 15 icon with an arrow going clockwise to advance the audiobook by 15 seconds.

Tap and drag the timeline below the cover art to advance or rewind the audiobook to a specific point in the recording. Tap and drag the volume button to change the volume.

At the bottom of the screen are four icons: 1x, a quarter moon, the Air-Play icon, and the content icon. The 1x button is a playback speed button. Tap 1x and then tap a playback speed: 0.75x, 1x, 1.25x, 1.5x, 1.75x, or 2x. What speed works for you is subjective, so feel free to try different options to find the speed you like.

The quarter moon icon is a way of playing your audiobook for a certain number of minutes before it automatically stops, a great tool for listening yourself to sleep. Tap the quarter moon icon and choose to end the playing at a time between 5 minutes and 1 hour, when the current chapter ends, or after a custom number of hours or minutes or both.

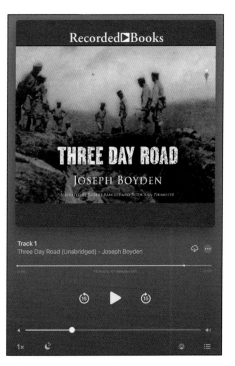

FIGURE 7-11:
Audiobook playback controls are intuitive and easy to use.

The AirPlay icon at the bottom of the screen allows you to choose your audio source. Tap the AirPlay icon to pick between any connected headphones, nearby HomePods, nearby Apple TVs, connected Bluetooth speakers, or any nearby AirPlay-capable speakers.

Tap the contents icon to see a list of tracks for your audiobook. Tap a track to play it or tap X in the upper-right corner of the list to return to your audiobook. Swipe down from the top of the audiobook screen to return to the library view.

News: Staying Informed on Your iPad

Apple got serious about its News app a few years ago, and it got even more serious with the release of iPadOS. The key to Apple's approach to presenting third-party news is human curation, a theme you may have noticed throughout this chapter. Apple uses human curation for many of its news selections, rather than relying solely on computer algorithms to make those decisions. In addition, Apple has focused on layout and presentation to make reading news stories in the News app pleasant and enjoyable. Some of the larger publications use tools that Apple provides to make News app versions of their stories visually appealing.

Tap the News icon on your Home screen to open it. (The first time you open News, you might have to tap through a few introductory screens.) You'll be taken to the today view, as shown in Figure 7-12. The today view includes Top Stories and Trending Stories sections, with stories gaining momentum in the News app. The app includes other curated sections, such as Editor's Picks, For You (recommended stories based on what you tend to read), and articles from the publications and genres you read the most.

Tap the sidebar icon in the upper-left corner of the News app (or rotate the iPad to landscape orientation) to find links to the home pages for specific sections of the app, as shown in Figure 7-13. Near the top of this menu is News+, which is a subscription service offered by Apple, as well as links to Today, Shared with You, Saved Stories, and History, which contains a list of articles you've already read. You'll also see publications you're subscribed to, topics you've chosen to follow, a list of suggested topics, and the Discover Channels button, where you can choose additional publications and topics to follow.

FIGURE 7-12:
Today in Apple News.

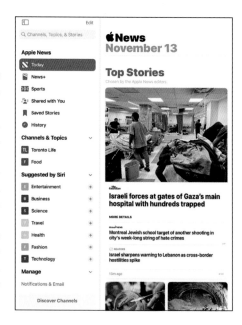

FIGURE 7-13:
The sidebar in the News app.

To edit the publications you follow, tap the Edit button in the upper-right corner of the sidebar. You can remove publications from your follow list by tapping the red circle with a – sign, and then tapping the Unfollow button that is revealed. You can move an item by tapping its icon with three lines and dragging it to the new location.

When reading an article in the News app, you can use the following controls (all pointed out in Figure 7-14) to work with the story: back (returns you to the previous page); save story (adds the article to the Saved Stories section of the sidebar); share story (displays the article's share sheet so you can let other people know about it); suggest more (tells News that you want to see more articles similar to this one); suggest less (tells News that you want to see fewer articles similar to this one); text size (enables you to increase or decrease the size of the article text); and more (displays a menu of commands for working with the story).

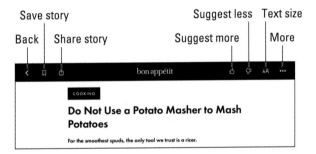

FIGURE 7-14:
The toolbar for a News article.

Chapter **8**

iPad Videography

First came the notion of the *third place:* somewhere other than home or work where a person could go to relax and gather informally with others (think coffee shop, community center, salon). These days we have the idea of the *third screen:* a video screen that a person uses almost as often as their TV and computer screens. You might nominate your smartphone as your third screen (heck, it might even be most people's *first* screen), but what if we restrict the screen to watching video? Ah, that's a different story, and I think it's much more likely that your iPad with its relatively big screen and sharp image is your go-to third screen for watching video.

But your iPad is also equipped with a couple of fancy-schmancy cameras that you can use to shoot your own videos. Even better, you can edit those videos right on your iPad and distribute your filmic masterpieces to friends and family at the tap of an icon.

And with your iPad's front camera, you can take advantage of another useful video feature: face-to-face video chatting with old pals and far-flung family members.

In this chapter, you investigate these iPad video features courtesy of the TV app, the Camera app's video mode, and the FaceTime app. It's a veritable feast for the eyes and ears!

Finding Stuff to Watch

With iPadOS, Apple has brought all its video offerings, even shows you're watching through third-party services, under the umbrella of the TV app. In the TV app, you can find almost all the streaming content available on your iPad, as well as movies and TV shows from the iTunes Store and anything shared from iTunes on your Mac or PC.

You can still go to dedicated apps from third party-services, too. For example, if Netflix is the only subscription service you have, want, or need, get the Netflix app and you're covered.

Watching shows with the TV app

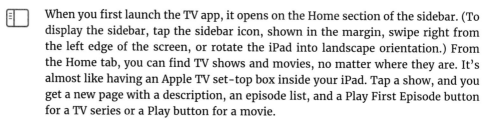 When you first launch the TV app, it opens on the Home section of the sidebar. (To display the sidebar, tap the sidebar icon, shown in the margin, swipe right from the left edge of the screen, or rotate the iPad into landscape orientation.) From the Home tab, you can find TV shows and movies, no matter where they are. It's almost like having an Apple TV set-top box inside your iPad. Tap a show, and you get a new page with a description, an episode list, and a Play First Episode button for a TV series or a Play button for a movie.

You can browse the TV app by genre, hits, trending movies, trending TV shows, and a list of recently watched shows.

If you just want to check out original Apple TV+ programming, that's the job of the sidebar's Apple TV+ tab, shown in Figure 8-1. Apple TV+ is Apple's original content subscription service. Apple TV+ offers subscribers TV shows and movies developed for and available exclusively through Apple TV+. As of this writing, Apple TV+ comes as part of an Apple One subscription or is available on its own for $9.99 per month, with a one-week free trial when you first subscribe. For a limited time — Apple hasn't said when it will end — people who buy a new Apple device get three months of Apple TV+ free. Tap Apple TV+ to see the latest releases and to browse Apple TV+ shows by genre.

Use the sidebar's Library section to find all the shows you've purchased or rented from iTunes as well as other videos. On the left side of the screen are organizational tabs, such as Recent Purchases, TV Shows, Movies, and Genres, as shown in Figure 8-2.

FIGURE 8-1:
The Apple
TV+ tab in
the TV app is
where you find
original Apple
programming.

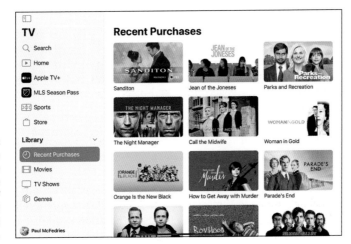

FIGURE 8-2:
The Library tab
in the TV app
is the home
for movies, TV
shows, and
downloaded
videos.

If you can't find what you want by browsing through the Home, Apple TV+, and Library tabs, fear not: Tap the Search tab and run a search. Search also includes tiles for video genres such as Action, Comedy, Documentary, and Sports. Tap one of those tiles and you'll see a screen full of the available titles in that genre.

Renting and buying at the Apple TV Store

The TV app's sidebar includes a Store tab that takes you to the Apple TV Store. The Store features dedicated sections for purchasing or renting episodes of TV shows, for subscribing to channels, and for buying or renting movies, as shown in Figure 8-3.

Pricing varies, but it's not atypical (as of this writing) to fork over $1.99 to pick up an episode of a popular TV show in standard definition or $2.99 for a high-def version. And a few shows are free. You can also purchase a complete season of a favorite show — prices are usually about $24.99 for standard-def and $29.99 to $39.99 for high-def or 4K, when available.

A new-release feature film typically costs $19.99 in high definition or $14.99 in standard def, but you'll also see prices higher and lower.

You can also rent many movies, typically for $2.99, $3.99, or $4.99, though Apple sometimes serves up a juicy 99-cent rental as well, and I've seen rentals as high as $6.99. Not all movies can be rented, and I'm not wild about current rental restrictions — you have 30 days to begin watching a rented flick and 48 hours to finish watching after you've started.

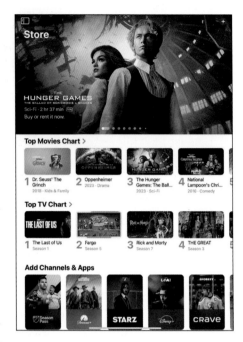

FIGURE 8-3:
Use the Apple TV Store to buy or rent TV shows and movies and to add channels.

Tap a movie listing in the Apple TV Store, and you can generally preview a trailer before buying (or renting) and check out additional tidbits: the plot summary, credits, reviews, and customer ratings, as well as other movies that appealed to people who bought the movie you're looking at. And you can search films by genre or top charts (the ones other people are buying or renting). Apple also groups movies by various themes, such as New & Noteworthy, Standout Discoveries, and What We're Watching.

Watching your own videos

You can find videos you've created in your Photos library, whether they're raw videos you filmed with your iPad or edited videos you created in iMovie. Check out the "Shooting Your Own Videos" section, later in this chapter, for directions on creating movies with the iPad.

Are we compatible?

The iPad works with many popular video standards, such as H.264, MPEG-4, M-JPEG, MP4, M4V, MOV, and HTML5 in Safari. (Note that the iPad does not support Flash.) You may run into a snag if you're trying to watch AVI, DivX, MKV, or other videos formats.

A moment for HEVC

One of iPadOS's big under-the-hood features is High-Efficiency Video Codec (HEVC; also known by the equally unlovely moniker H.265) for storing video. HEVC's claim to fame is smaller video files with the same or higher quality as before.

So far, the file format is used only internally by the Photos app on your Mac and the Camera and Photos apps on your iPhone or iPad running iPadOS. You can't currently export files in the HEVC format, and iPadOS intelligently exports using more common file formats. In other words, you don't need to worry about HEVC; it's just something Apple is using to make videos take up less space. I expect this to change over time because HEVC is an industry standard like its predecessor, H.264.

Playing Video

Now that you know what you want to watch, it's time to find out how to watch it. For these steps, I walk you through watching a movie, but the steps for TV shows and downloaded videos are similar:

1. **On the Home screen, tap the TV icon.**

2. **Display the sidebar and then, in the Library section, tap the subsection that contains what you want to watch: Recent Purchases, Movies, TV Shows, or Genres.**

   You see poster thumbnails for any movies you previously purchased through iTunes — even for those movies you haven't downloaded yet.

3. **Tap the poster that represents the movie or other video you want to watch.**

   You're taken to a movie summary page that reveals a larger movie poster, a description, the genre, the run time, and a Play icon, as shown in Figure 8-4.

FIGURE 8-4:
The movie info
screen.

4. **To start playing a movie (or resume playing from where you left off), tap the Play icon. Or to download the movie to your iPad for later playback, tap the iCloud icon.**

5. **(Optional) Rotate your iPad to landscape mode to maximize the video's view.**

Finding and working the video controls

While a video is playing, tap the screen to display the controls. What you see depends on whether you launched a TV show or movie from the TV app or a video from the Photos app. Figure 8-5 shows the controls that appear when you launch a video from Photos. Here's how to work the controls:

>> **Play or pause the video:** Tap the play/pause icon.

>> **Toggle the volume mute:** Tap the mute icon.

>> **Restart, skip back, or skip forward:** Drag the playhead or tap the scrub bar at the point where you want the video to start playing.

>> **Hide the controls:** Tap the screen again (or just wait for them to go away on their own).

>> **Tell your iPad you've finished watching a video:** For an TV app episode or movie, tap X (close); for one of your own videos, tap < (back) in the top-left corner. You return to the last video screen that was visible before you started watching the movie.

Watching video on a big TV

I love watching movies on the iPad, but I also recognize the limitations of a smaller screen. Friends won't crowd around to watch with you, so Apple offers two ways to display video from your iPad to a TV:

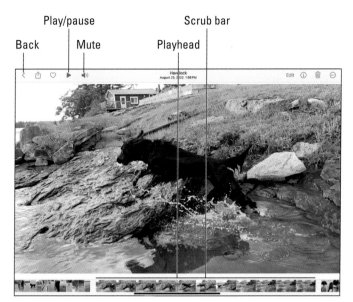

Back · Play/pause · Mute · Scrub bar · Playhead

FIGURE 8-5:
Controlling video.

REMEMBER

» **AirPlay:** Through AirPlay, you can wirelessly stream videos as well as photos and music from the iPad to an Apple TV set-top box connected to a monitor or to an HDTV or a 4K TV. Start watching the movie on the iPad, display Control Center by swiping down from the upper-right corner of the screen, and then tap the screen mirroring icon. Apple TVs on the same Wi-Fi network will be listed as options. Tap the Apple TV you want, and your iPad's screen will be shown on that Apple TV. When you're finished, open Control Center, tap the screen mirroring icon, and then tap iPad.

Although you can stream from an iPad to an Apple TV and switch screens between the two, you can't stream to the iPad a rented movie that you started watching on Apple TV.

» **AV adapter cables:** Apple and others sell a variety of adapters and cables for connecting the iPad to a TV. For instance, Apple sells a Lightning Digital AV Adapter for $49 that lets you connect an HDMI cable (which you'll have to supply) from the tablet to the TV. If you have an iPad Pro with a USB-C port, you can use a similar adapter from Apple called the USB-C Digital AV Multiport Adapter for $69. Both adapters also let you *mirror* the iPad screen on the connected TV or projector. So you can not only watch a movie or video but also view anything else that's on the iPad's screen: your Home screen, web pages, games, other apps, you name it. You can also mirror what's on the screen through AirPlay.

Deleting video from your iPad

REMEMBER

Video takes up space — lots of space. After the closing credits roll and you no longer want to keep a video on your iPad, here's what you need to know about deleting it.

To remove a downloaded video you purchased from Apple in the iTunes Store — the flick remains in iCloud — open up the TV app, display the sidebar, and then tap the Downloaded tab. The Downloaded screen displays the TV shows and movies you've downloaded to your iPad. Tap Edit in the upper-right corner of the screen, and a circle will appear next to each movie or TV show in your list. Select the show you want to delete by tapping its circle, and then tap the Delete button that is now in the upper-right corner of your screen. When your iPad asks if you're sure you want to delete the video, tap Delete Download. (If you change your mind, tap outside the Delete button.)

Shooting Your Own Videos

Your iPad has a great camera on the back, plus the FaceTime camera in the front. Let's take a look at the resolutions you can shoot with the cameras on the current generation of iPads:

>> **Back camera:** 4K video at 24fps (frames per second), 25fps, 30fps, or 60fps; 1080p video at 25fps, 30fps, or 60fps; and 720p HD video at 30fps

>> **Front camera:** 1080p video at 25fps, 30fps, or 60fps

TIP

4K video image quality is astounding but is also a memory hog that claims roughly 170MB for just one minute of video, and that's at 30fps.

You can't choose the video quality of the front camera, but you can follow these steps to choose the video quality for the back camera:

1. **Open the Settings app.**

2. **Tap Camera.**

3. **Tap Record Video.**

4. **Tap the format you want to use for your back-camera video recordings.**

Now that I've dispensed with that little piece of business, here's how to shoot video on the iPad:

1. **On the Home screen, tap the Camera icon.**

2. **Scroll through the list of shooting modes (Photo, Square, Pano, and so on) until Video is selected.**

   When *Video* appears in yellow instead of white, it's selected. You can also choose Time Lapse (which creates a video by stitching together still images shot every few seconds) or Slo-Mo (which captures video in slow-motion).

TIP

   You can't switch from the front to the rear camera (or vice versa) while you're capturing a scene. So before shooting anything, think about which camera you want to use, and then tap the front/rear camera icon, just above the record button, when you've made your choice.

3. **Tap the red record button (labeled in Figure 8-6) to begin shooting a scene.**

4. **When you're done, tap the record button again to stop recording.**

   Your video is automatically saved to the All Photos album, alongside any other saved videos and digital stills that land in the Photos app.

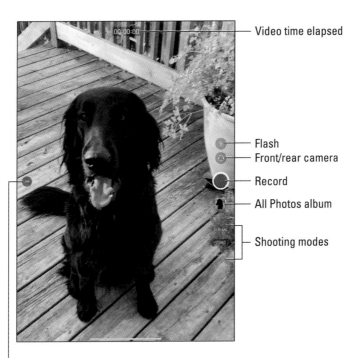

Video time elapsed

Flash
Front/rear camera
Record
All Photos album
Shooting modes

FIGURE 8-6: Lights, camera, action.

Zoom

Going slow

If you have an iPad model that runs iPadOS, you get another shooting benefit: the capability to capture video in slow motion, which I think is truly nifty. Now you can play back in slow motion your kid's amazing catch in the varsity football game.

Depending on your iPad, you'll be able to shoot at 120 frames per second (fps) at 720p or 1080p, or even 240fps at 720p or 1080p. However, the frame rate and resolution you're using to record your slow-motion video won't matter unless you're a professional videographer. And remember that the best camera to use is always the camera you have with you, so set your camera to Slo-Mo and grab the action!

But first things first: To shoot in slow motion, launch the Camera app and select Slo-Mo as your shooting format of choice. Shoot your slow-motion footage the same way you shoot at regular speeds. Note that the white circle surrounding the red shutter icon has teeny-tiny lines around it.

To check out your handiwork, tap the All Photos album (labeled in Figure 8-6), and then tap the slow-motion video you want to watch.

Going fast

The time-lapse camera feature on your iPad has the opposite effect of slo-mo, enabling you to capture a scene and play it back at a warp speed. Even better, every iPad covered in this book sports the time-lapse option. To make a time-lapse video, choose the time-lapse option the same way you select other shooting modes, and then tap the record icon. The app captures photos at dynamically selected intervals. When you're ready to watch the sped-up sequence, tap play as you do with any other video.

Editing what you shot

I assume you captured some really great footage, but you probably shot some stuff that belongs on the cutting room floor as well. No big whoop — you can perform simple edits right on your iPad. Tap the All Photos album just below the shutter button in the Camera app to find your recordings. When you record slo-mo or time-lapse videos, the Photos app creates albums for them so you can find them quickly. (In the Photos app sidebar, look for albums named Slo-Mo and Time-Lapse in the Media Types category.) Select your video, and then:

1. **If the onscreen controls are not visible, tap the video recording.**
2. **Tap the Edit button.**

3. Drag the start and end points along the frame viewer at the bottom of the screen to select only the video you want to keep, as shown in Figure 8-7.

The lines turn yellow.

4. Tap the play icon to check your edit.

5. Tap Done and then tap either Save Video or Save Video as New Clip.

If you choose Save Video, Photos will alter the original file — be careful when choosing this option. Save Video as New Clip creates a newly trimmed video clip; the original video remains intact. The new clip is stored in the All Photos album and in the Videos, Slo-Mo, or Time-Lapse album, depending on its type.

To discard your changes, instead, tap Cancel and then tap Discard Changes.

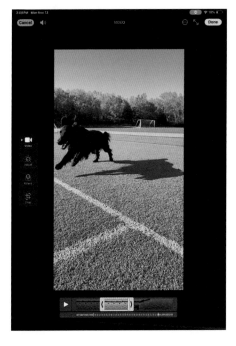

FIGURE 8-7:
Getting a trim.

TIP

For more ambitious editing on the iPad, consider iMovie for iPad, a free app closely related to iMovie for Mac computers. Among its tricks: You can produce Hollywood–style movie trailers, just like on a Mac.

WARNING

Any video edited with the iPadOS version of iMovie must have originated on an iOS or iPadOS device. You can't mix in footage shot with a digital camera or obtained elsewhere.

Sharing video

You can play back in portrait or landscape mode what you've just shot. And if the video is any good, you'll likely want to share it with a wider audience. To do so, open the All Photos album, Videos album, or another album, and tap the thumbnail for the video in question. Tap the share icon, and you can email the video (if the video file isn't too large), send it as a message (see Chapter 6), or keep a copy in Notes.

And you have many other options: If your video is stored in iCloud, you can tap Copy iCloud Link and share the online link to the video with other people. Depending on which apps you have installed, you can share the video in numerous other places, such as X (Twitter), Facebook, Flickr, YouTube, and Vimeo. And if you have an Apple TV box, you can beam the video to a big-screen television via AirPlay.

Seeing Is Believing with FaceTime

I bet you can come up with a lengthy list of people you'd love to be able to eyeball in real time from afar. Maybe the list includes your old college roommate or your grandparents, who've long since retired to a warm climate. That's the beauty of FaceTime, the video chat app. FaceTime exploits the two cameras built into the iPad, each serving a different purpose. The front camera — the FaceTime camera as it's called — lets you talk face to face. The back camera shows what you're seeing to the person you're talking to.

To take advantage of FaceTime, here's what you need:

>> **Access to Wi-Fi or cellular:** The people you're talking to need internet access, too. On an iOS or iPadOS device, you need Wi-Fi or a cellular connection and an internet connection on your iPad. You also need at least a 1Mbps upstream and downstream connection for HD-quality video calls; faster is always going to be better.

WARNING

Using FaceTime over a cellular connection can quickly run through your monthly data allotment and prove hazardous to your budget. However, you can do an audio-only FaceTime call, which can cut down significantly on your data usage.

>> **FaceTime on recipient's device:** You can do FaceTime video only with someone with a device capable of receiving a FaceTime video call. You can also send a link to a Windows user and that person can join your call by pasting the link into a web browser.

Getting started with FaceTime

Now, let's get started with FaceTime by tapping the FaceTime icon on the Home screen to launch the app. If you haven't signed in with your Apple ID, head to Settings ⇨ Apple ID and sign in.

Making a FaceTime call

Now the real fun begins — making a video call. (I say "video call" because you can also make FaceTime audio calls.) Follow these steps:

1. **In the FaceTime app, choose someone to call:**

   - *Your recent calls list:* If you've already made or received a call, tap anyone in your recent calls list to FaceTime that person again. Below the name of each person in the list is the method you used to call the person before (FaceTime or a cellular call). Tapping an entry in this list will duplicate that method of calling.

     Or tap the *i*-in-a-circle to access the full entry in your contacts. At the top of the contacts list you'll see several ways to contact the person: message, call (as in cellular phone call), FaceTime, mail, and Apple Pay.

   - *Your contacts:* Tap the New FaceTime button and the list of recent calls will become the New FaceTime pane. You have two ways to find someone.

     One, start typing a name in the To field, and iPadOS will display all potential matches from your contacts. The more of the person's name you type, the more accurate those suggestions will be. Tap the name you want, and two green buttons appear on the screen. Tap the Audio button to make an audio-only FaceTime call to that person, or tap the Video button to make a video call.

     Two, you can tap the circle with a plus sign to show all your contacts, where you can choose the specific person you want. Tap a name in your contacts list, and you will get the person's entry in your contacts, including multiple ways to contact the person: message, cellular phone call, FaceTime, mail, and Apple Pay.

   - *Create Link:* Tap this button to send a link to someone who doesn't have FaceTime (such as a Windows user). That person can then paste the link into a web browser to join your call.

2. **If you started a new FaceTime call, tap FaceTime to get the call started.**

3. **If necessary, move the picture-in-picture window.**

   When a call is underway, you can see what you look like to the other person through a small picture-in-picture window, which you can drag to any corner of the video call window. The small window lets you know if your mug has dropped out of sight.

4. **(Optional) To toggle between the front and rear cameras, tap the camera icon (labeled in Figure 8-8).**

5. **When you're ready to hang up, tap the End button.**

While you're on a FaceTime call, the following tips will be handy:

Toggle speaker

Toggle camera

Toggle microphone   Switch camera

>> **Rotate the iPad to its side to change the orientation.** In landscape mode, you're more likely to see everybody at once.

FIGURE 8-8:
Tap the screen to see the FaceTime controls.

>> **Silence or mute a call by tapping the microphone icon.** Be aware that you can still be seen even though you're not heard (and you can still see and hear the other person).

>> **Momentarily check out another iPad app by pressing the Home button or swiping up from the bottom of the screen (if your device doesn't have a Home button) and then tapping the icon for the app.** At this juncture, you can still talk over FaceTime, but you can no longer see the person. You also won't be visible to them, which lets them know you're not currently in the FaceTime app. Tap the green bar at the top of the iPad screen to bring the person and the FaceTime app back in front of you.

TIP

Through the split view feature in iPadOS (refer to Chapter 2), you can conduct and view a FaceTime video call while engaged in other activities on the iPad.

Receiving a FaceTime call

Of course, you can get FaceTime calls as well as make them. FaceTime doesn't have to be open for you to receive a video call. Here's how incoming calls work:

>> **Hearing the call:** When a call comes in, the caller's name, phone number, or email address is prominently displayed on the iPad's screen, as shown in Figure 8-9, and the iPad rings.

FIGURE 8-9:
Tap the green button to accept the call.

>> **Accepting or declining the call:** Tap the green accept button to answer the call or the red decline button if you'd rather not. If your iPad is locked when a FaceTime call comes in, answer by sliding the Slide to Answer button to the right, or decline by doing nothing and waiting for the caller to give up. You can also tap Message to send a canned iMessage *(Sorry, I can't talk right now; I'm on my way; Can I call you later?)* or a custom message. Or you can tap Remind Me to be reminded in one hour that you may want to call the person back.

>> **Silencing the ring:** You can press the top button on the iPad to silence the incoming ring. If you know you don't want to be disturbed by FaceTime calls before you even hear a ring, visit Control Center (see Chapter 14) to put your iPad on mute. You can also turn on the do not disturb feature in Control Center to silence incoming FaceTime calls.

>> **Blocking unwanted callers:** If a person who keeps trying to FaceTime you becomes bothersome, you can block that person. In the FaceTime app, you can block a caller who shows up on your caller list by tapping the *i*-in-a-circle next to the caller's name and then tapping Block This Caller. Note that the person isn't notified that you've blocked them. The next time they try to call you, you won't see anything, and the call will just keep ringing on their end until they give up.

>> **Removing people from the call list:** If you don't want to block a caller but don't want the person clogging up your call list, swipe left on the caller and tap Delete.

TIP

You can also receive calls to your iPhone on your iPad, as long as the devices are on the same Wi-Fi network. Go to Settings ⇨ FaceTime and tap the Calls from iPhone switch on.

With that, I hereby silence this chapter. But you can do more with the cameras on your iPad, and I get to that in Chapter 9.

Chapter **9**

iPad Photography

E verywhere you go these days, somebody — or, most likely, a whole bunch of somebodies — has a smartphone a foot or so in front of their face. What are they doing? Why, taking photos, of course. So many photos. This citizen photography (some have called it *smartphoneography,* a term that doesn't exactly trip lightly off the tongue) is a hallmark of the age, but it's almost entirely a smartphone phenomenon. Why? Because the size and weight of even the largest smartphone make it easy to snap a photo at will.

Alas, you can't say that about your iPad. Sure, the iPad mini is reasonably wieldy, but your average iPad or iPad Pro makes an awfully awkward camera. An awkward camera, yes, but not a bad camera. After all, the current generation of the iPad, the iPad Pro (both the 11-inch and 12.9-inch models), and the iPad Air come with a 12-megapixel camera with backside illumination, an impressive *f*/1.8 aperture, and a multi-element lens. The current generation iPad mini has a 12-megapixel camera with an *f*/2.4 aperture.

Even if you use another device (such as an iPhone) as your main camera, you iPad also serves as an excellent photo editor because not only does it come with an impressive set of tools for tweaking images, but that large screen makes it easy to work with those images.

In this chapter, you delve into the details for taking photos with your iPad. However, you spend most of your time working with your iPad's long list of features that enable you to view, share, and edit your photos. I also give you a quick introduction to the barrel-full-of-monkeys-level of fun you can have with the Photo Booth app.

Shooting Photos

Okay, so you're on board (at least temporarily) with the idea that you can use your iPad as a camera. Well then, let's get right to so you can learn what I mean.

Say "Cheese!": Snapping photos

Here are the steps to follow to take a photo with your iPad:

1. **Fire up the Camera app using one of the following techniques:**

   - *On the Home screen, tap the Camera icon.*

   - *On the lock screen, swipe from right to left.*

   - *Drag Control Center down from the top-right corner of the screen and tap the Camera icon.*

   - *Ask Siri (refer to Chapter 14) to open the Camera app for you.*

   However you get here, your iPad has turned into the tablet equivalent of a point-and-shoot camera, although in a much bigger form factor. You're also effectively peering through one of the largest viewfinders imaginable!

2. **Choose the camera you want to use.**

   To toggle between the front and rear cameras, tap the switch camera button (labeled in Figure 9-1).

3. **Use the camera's display to frame your image.**

4. **Select a shooting format:**

   - *Photo:* Think snapshot.

   - *Portrait:* Decreases the depth of field to blur the background, which brings more attention to your subject. This feature is only available on the iPad Pro (all 11-inch models and the third-generation and later 12.9-inch models).

   - *Square:* Gives you a picture formatted to work well as contact photos and to make nice with the popular Instagram photo-sharing app.

   - *Pano:* Short for *panorama,* lets you capture epic vistas.

   - *Video, Slo-Mo,* or *Time Lapse:* I kindly refer you to Chapter 8.

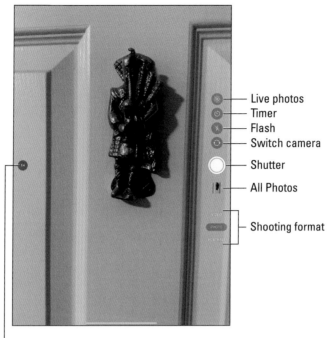

Live photos
Timer
Flash
Switch camera
Shutter
All Photos
Shooting format

FIGURE 9-1:
The features
of the iPad's
Camera app.

Zoom

You move from one format to another by swiping up or down on the shooting format control (pointed out in Figure 9-1) so that the format you've chosen is highlighted and has yellow text.

5. **Snap your photo by tapping the shutter button.**

The Camera app takes the shot and deposits it in the All Photos album, which you can access by tapping its button (labeled in Figure 9-1). I explain what you can do with the images on the iPad later in this chapter.

Going pro: Getting the most out of the Camera app

Here are some tips for working with the Camera app:

>> **Adjust the exposure and focus point.** Tap the portion of the screen that contains the face or object you want as the image's focal point. A small rectangle surrounds your selection, and the iPad adjusts the exposure and focus for that part of the image. (The rectangle is not visible in Figure 9-1.) Your iPad can detect up to ten faces in a picture. Behind the scenes, the camera is balancing the exposure across each face. If you want to lock the focus and exposure settings while taking a picture (for example, if your scene contains moving items that

make the camera change the focus point frequently), long-press the screen at your desired focal point until the rectangle pulses and AE/AF Lock appears at the top of the screen (AE/AF is short for Auto Exposure/Auto Focus). After you take your shot, tap the screen again to make AE/AF Lock disappear.

TIP

Next to the exposure box is the exposure setting, represented by a sun icon. When the exposure box is visible, drag up anywhere on the screen to increase the exposure, or drag down anywhere on the screen to decrease the exposure.

» **Zoom in or out.** Spread two fingers on the screen to zoom in or pinch two fingers to zoom out. Alternatively, long-press the zoom button (refer to Figure 9-1) and then drag the dial counterclockwise to zoom in or clockwise to zoom out. (Note that the zoom button isn't available if you're using the front camera.) On some iPad models, you see a zoom slider that you can drag to set the zoom level.

REMEMBER

The iPad Pro has a 2x *optical zoom*, which means it uses the camera lens to magnify the image. Here, *2x* means the lens doubles the magnification. All the other iPads have up to 5x *digital zoom*, which means the Camera app performs a kind of faux magnification by cropping and resizing the image. (The iPad Pro also has up to 5x digital zoom for magnifications beyond 2x.) This cropping and resizing means that digital zooms are lower quality than optical zooms.

» **Display gridlines to help you compose your picture.** Tap Settings ➪ Camera and tap the Grid switch on. The Camera app now shows two vertical and two horizontal gridlines that divide the screen into nine rectangles.

TIP

Gridlines can help you frame a shot by using the photographic principle known as the rule of thirds, where you place your subject on one of the gridlines instead of in the middle of the screen.

» **Add a level indicator.** Tap Settings ➪ Camera and tap the Level switch on. The Camera app now shows three horizontal bars, where the left and right bars are fixed and the center bar rotates as you rotate the iPad. When your iPad is perfectly level, the three bars line up, become a single line, and turn yellow.

TIP

Photos that aren't straight are probably the most common flaw in iPad photography. You can straighten crooked photos (refer to "In the Digital Darkroom: Editing Photos," later in this chapter), but using the Camera app's level tool can save you that extra work.

» **Interact with camera text.** If the screen you want to shoot has text, tap the text and then tap the live text button that appears. (If you don't see that button, it means your iPad doesn't support this feature.) As shown in Figure 9-2, the Camera app displays the text in a pop-up window. Tap a word (or swipe across a phrase) to select it, and then use the controls in the toolbar to choose the action you want to perform on the selected text (such as copying it or sharing it).

» **Capture a rapid-fire series of photos.** Long-press the shutter button to capture photos in *burst mode*, which takes up to ten photos per second.

» **Capture panoramas.** To shoot a *panorama*, a photo that takes up to 240 horizontal degrees, swipe the shooting format to Pano. Position the tablet so it's where you want your panorama to begin and tap the shutter button when you're ready. Steadily pan in the direction of the arrow. (Tap the arrow if you prefer panning in the opposite direction.) Try to keep the arrow just above the yellow horizontal line. When you've finished shooting your panorama, tap the camera button again to stop.

» **Shoot a photo after a delay.** Tap the timer button (refer to Figure 9-1) and then tap 3s (3 seconds) or 10s (10 seconds) as the time interval between when you press the shutter button and when the picture is captured. The screen displays a countdown leading up to that moment. To turn off the self-timer, tap the Off button.

» **Capture live photos.** Tap the live photos button (refer to Figure 9-1) to turn it on (the button turns yellow and you briefly see Live at the top of the Camera app). When you take a photo, your iPad includes 1.5 seconds of video captured before you press the button and 1.5 seconds after you press the button, which creates a kind of mini-video. When you want to stop taking live photos, just tap that icon again.

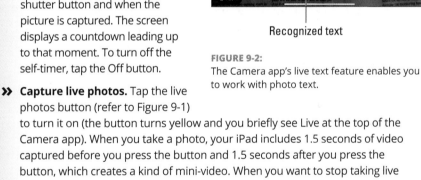

Toolbar   Live text

Recognized text

FIGURE 9-2:
The Camera app's live text feature enables you to work with photo text.

Reducing blurry iPad photos

The iPad camera hardware is topnotch these days, so the iPad generally takes really nice shots. However, one the biggest problems most people have with iPad photos is blurry images, which are caused by not holding the tablet steady while taking the shot.

The latest iPads offer image stabilization, which can reduce blurry images, but it doesn't eliminate them entirely. Fortunately, there are a few other things you can do to minimize blurred shots:

>> Widen your stance to stabilize your body.

>> Lean your shoulder (at least) or your entire side (at best) against any nearby object, such as a wall, doorframe, or car.

>> Hold your breath while taking the shot.

>> In low-light conditions, after you release the shutter button, keep the tablet steady until the photo thumbnail appears. If you move while the iPad is finalizing the photo, you'll blur the shot.

Keep some or all of these pointers in mind while shooting with your iPad, and you'll soon find that blurry iPad photos are a thing of the past.

Now that you know how to shoot photos on your iPad, it's time to learn how to check out your handiwork. In the following sections, I zoom in (pun intended, sadly) on the details.

Browsing and Viewing Your Photos

FIGURE 9-3:
The All Photos tab shows — you guessed it! — all your photos.

Your iPad offers lots of features for working with photos, and you'll find most of those features in an app called Photos. When you launch Photos, the app starts you off in the All Photos tab (check out Figure 9-3), which displays your photos (as well as your videos; see Chapter 8), arranged by the date each was taken, with the newest items at the bottom. You can also organize the photos by date by tapping one of the other tabs: Years, Months, or Days. For example, if you tap Months, you see headings for each month along with a sample image from that month — tap the heading or the image to see that month's photos and then tap the photo you want to view.

The Photos app also comes with a sidebar which you display by tapping the sidebar button in the upper-left corner of the screen (and shown here in the margin), or by swiping right from the left edge of the screen. The sidebar offers the following sections for navigating your photos:

>> **Photos:** This is the main section at the top of the sidebar and it offers the following items:

- *Library:* Displays all your photos and videos.

- *For You:* Displays a few special photos as curated by the Photos app.

- *People & Pets:* Displays headshots for people and pets in your photos. Tap a headshot to see all your photos of that person or furry friend. (If a headshot has no name, tap the headshot, tap Add Name, type the person's name, tap Next, and then tap Done.)

- *Places:* Displays a map and locates your photos on that map. You'll usually need to zoom in on a location to see the individual photos.

- *Favorites:* Displays those photos you've marked as your favorites. Check out the section "Marking a photo as a favorite," later in this chapter.

- *Recents:* Displays the photos you've captured recently, with the most recent at the bottom.

- *Search:* Enables you to search for a photo. In the search box, you can type a person's name, a location name, or any word or phrase that describes what's in the photo you're looking for (such as *dog* or *boat* or *sunset*). If the photo you're looking for contains text, you can also search for that text.

>> **Utilities:** This section offers the following tools:

- *Imports:* Displays photos you've imported to your iPad (for example, via a USB-C card reader or camera adapter connected to your iPad).

- *Duplicates:* Displays photos that appear two or more times in the Photos library. For each duplicate, tap Merge to keep one photo (the one with the higher quality and the more relevant metadata, assuming those differences exist between them) and delete the other (that is, send the photo to the Recently Deleted folder, discussed a couple of paragraphs from now). If the two photos are the same but have different resolutions or formats, Photos will keep the one that is of the highest quality.

- *Hidden:* Displays photos that you've hidden (as I describe in the next bullet point). To unhide a photo, open the Hidden folder (you need to provide your iPad passcode or use FaceID or TouchID to access this folder), display the photo, tap More (the three horizontal dots), and then tap Unhide.

- *Recently Deleted:* Displays photos you've deleted (check out the "Deleting a photo" section) within the last 30 days (any photos you deleted more than 30 days ago are automatically removed from your iPad). Each photo shows how many days it has left to live before it's automatically removed for good. To permanently delete a photo, tap it, tap Delete, and then tap Delete From All Devices. If you deleted a photo by accident, tap it, tap Recover, and then tap Recover Photo.

» **Media Types:** Displays a category for each type of media in your Photos library, such as videos, selfies, live photos, and panoramas. Tap a media type and Photos filters your library to show only the items that use that media type.

» **Shared Albums:** Displays a list of photo albums you've shared with other people.

» **My Albums:** Displays a list of albums that you've created to store your photos (check out "Creating a photo album," later in this chapter).

Navigating and manipulating photos

You can do so much with your photos after they're on your iPad, and it isn't your normal photo–browsing experience. You aren't just a passive viewer because you have some control over what you see and how the pictures are presented:

» **Scroll through your photos.** Once you have an individual photo on-screen, you view more photos by flicking left to view the next photo or flicking right to view the previous image. Alternatively, tap the screen to display a sequence of thumbnails at the bottom of the Photos app window and run your finger along those thumbnails to quickly peruse the photos.

» **Rotate the screen for the best view.** If you have your iPad in portrait orientation and you're viewing a photo that was taken in landscape mode, the Photos app scales down the photo so that it fits the width of the screen and displays white space above and below the photo. Nothing wrong with that, but you can get the best view of the photo by rotating the screen into landscape orientation. The photo rotates, too, but now it satisfyingly fills the whole screen. Rotate the tablet back to portrait orientation when the next photo taken in portrait mode shows up.

» **Flip the iPad.** To show a photo to another person, flip the iPad so that the back is toward you and the bottom is now the top. The Photos app automatically flips the photo right-side up.

» **Zoom in and out of a photo.** If there's a portion of a photo you want to get a closer look at, you can zoom in to magnify the shot. You can zoom in and out in either of the following ways:

- *Double-tap.* To zoom in, double-tap the spot on the photo you want to magnify. Photos dutifully zooms in on the place where you tapped. Double-tap anywhere on the screen to return to the original magnification.

- *Spread and pinch.* To zoom in, spread two fingers apart over the spot you want to magnify. To return to the original magnification, pinch two fingers together anywhere on the screen.

>> **Pan a photo.** After you zoom in on a photo, drag your finger on the screen to move — or *pan* — the photo along with your finger.

>> **Run a slideshow.** To get your iPad to do all the work, start a slideshow that navigates through the photos automatically. Display the first photo you want to appear in the slideshow (or select all the photos you want to include in the slideshow; check out "Selecting photos," next), tap the more icon (three horizontal dots), and then tap Slideshow. To configure the slideshow, tap the screen, and then tap Options. In the pop-up menu that appears, you can change the slideshow Theme, Music, whether the show repeats, and the speed at which the photos change.

>> **Use a photo as wallpaper.** If you have a photo that you'd prefer to use as your iPad wallpaper rather than any of the images supplied by Apple, display the photo, tap the share icon, and then tap Use as Wallpaper. Swipe horizontally to choose a style, choose a color, and then tap Add.

>> **Assign a photo to a contact.** If you have a photo of a person who's in your Contacts list, you can assign that photo to the person so that the picture appears up whenever you receive a FaceTime call or an iMessage from that person. Display the photo, tap the share icon, and then tap Assign to Contact. When your list of contacts appears on the screen, tap the contact who matches the picture. Drag and resize the picture to get it just right. Then tap Choose.

>> **Hide a photo.** If you have some similar photos, you might want to view only one of them when you navigating your photos. If you don't want to delete the other photos, you can hide them instead. Display a photo you want to hide, tap the more icon (three horizontal dots), tap Hide, and then tap Hide Photo. Photos moves the photo to the Hidden album.

TIP

When you're zoomed in on a photo, it's best to reset the magnification before resuming your photo scrolling. Why? Because while you're zoomed in, Photos interprets left and right flicks as panning gestures, not scrolling gestures. You can still get to the next photo, but it takes a lot more work.

Selecting photos

Sometimes you want to perform an action on multiple photos at the same time, whether you're sharing them, adding them to a new album, or deleting them in bulk. Here's how to select multiple photos:

1. **In Photos, tap a specific album or view that contains the photos you want to select.**

2. **Tap Select at the upper right.**

   Photos switches to select mode.

3. **Tap the thumbnail of each photo you want to include in the selection.**

   Alternatively, slide a finger across each photo you want to select.

   Photos adds a check mark to the lower-right corner of each thumbnail you tap (or slide across) and updates the *X* Photos Selected text at the bottom of the screen (where *X* is the number of photos you've selected so far).

   To deselect a photo, tap its thumbnail once again.

Creating a photo album

The Photos app enables you to create your own photo albums right on your device, which is a handy way to organize your shots. Follow these steps to create a photo album:

1. **In the Photos app, display the sidebar.**

2. **At the bottom of the My Albums section, tap New Album.**

   Photos prompts you for an album name.

3. **Type the album name, and then tap Save.**

   Photos displays thumbnails for all your photos.

4. **Tap each image that you want to include in your new album.**

   TIP

   You can filter the displayed photos by using the search box to type a word or phrase that describes the photos you want to include in the album.

   Photos adds a check mark to each selected photo.

5. **Tap Add.**

   Photos creates the new album and adds it to the My Albums section of the sidebar.

REMEMBER

To delete an album you no longer use (but keep the photos on your iPad), display the sidebar, tap Edit, tap the red delete icon to the left of the album, and then tap the Delete button that appears. Photos, still not convinced you mean it, asks you to confirm: Tap Delete Album to finally make it happen.

Marking a photo as a favorite

If you take a lot of photos with your iPad, some of them will be gems, but you'll have to scroll through a ton of not-so-gemlike images to see your favorites. I know you don't have time for that, so what's the solution? Tell your iPad which of your photos are your favorite ones! The Photos app maintains an album named

Favorites that stores these keepers, so you can access your greatest hits with just a few taps.

To mark a photo as a favorite, display it in Photos and then tap the favorite icon (heart).

Streaming photos to Apple TV

If you have an Apple TV that supports AirPlay, you can use AirPlay to stream your photos or a photo slideshow from your tablet to your TV.

Follow these steps to stream photos to Apple TV:

1. **Make sure your Apple TV is turned on.**

2. **In the Photos app, display the album that you want to stream.**

3. **Open the first photo you want to stream.**

4. **Swipe down from the top-right corner of the screen.**

    Control Center appears.

5. **Tap the screen mirroring icon.**

    iPadOS displays a menu of output choices.

6. **Tap the name of your Apple TV device.**

    The Photos app streams the photo to that device and, hence, to your TV.

Syncing photos to other devices via iCloud

This scenario has happened to most of us: You take an amazing photo on your iPad and then later want to show the shot to a friend, but you don't have your iPad with you. Similarly, you might snap a photo on your iPhone, but want to edit the photo on your iPad.

The solution to these and many similar scenarios is to configure your iPad and all your iDevices to sync photos with each other via iCloud. Any photo you take with the iPad can be automatically stored in the cloud and pushed to another iPad or to your PC, Mac, iPhone, iPod touch, or Apple TV (third generation or later). Pictures are synced when your iCloud devices are connected to Wi-Fi.

WARNING

Using the iCloud photo library has a catch: You have to pay for storage. You get 5GB of iCloud storage gratis, but shutterbugs will use that up in a flash. So, you'll likely spring for one of the following monthly plans: 50GB ($0.99 per month), 200GB ($2.99 per month), 2TB ($9.99 per month), 6TB ($29.99 per month), and 12TB ($59.99 per month).

To make this syncing happen, follow these steps:

1. **Choose Settings ⇨ Photos.**

2. **Tap the iCloud Photos switch on.**

3. **(Optional) If you iPad has lots of free space, you can speed up the viewing of photos and videos by tapping Download and Keep Originals, which stores the full-resolution versions of your photos and videos on your iPad.**

   If you stick with the default setting of Optimize iPad Storage, your iPad stores low-res versions of photos and videos and has to download the full-res versions from iCloud when needed.

   Your iPad will now sync photos with other devices on the same Apple account that are also configured to sync photos.

Photos taken on the iPad aren't whisked to iCloud until you leave the Camera app. That way, you get a chance to delete pictures you'd rather not have turn up everywhere. But after you leave the Camera app, all the photos you snapped are synced with your other devices.

Sharing your photos

Apple recognizes that you might want to share your best images with friends and family and have those pictures automatically appear on their devices. iCloud photo sharing enables you to create albums of pictures and videos for sharing and to receive photo streams other people make available to you. Here's how:

1. **On the Home screen, tap Settings ⇨ Photos.**

2. **Tap the iCloud Photos switch on (if it isn't already).**

3. **Tap the Shared Albums switch on.**

4. **Open the Photos app, display the sidebar, and open the Shared Albums list. Then tap All Shared Albums.**

5. **Tap + near the upper-left corner of the screen to open the iCloud dialog, and then type a name for your stream.**

   The name is your call, but I recommend something descriptive, along the lines of *My Trip to Paris* (and you should be so lucky).

6. **Tap Next and choose who will receive your stream.**

   You can type a phone number, a text address, or an email address, or choose one of your contacts by tapping the +-in-a-circle in the To field of the iCloud pop-up window.

7. **Tap Create.**

8. **Add photos as follows:**

    a. *Display the sidebar and tap the shared album you just created.*

    b. *Tap +. When your Photos library appears, tap each photo you want to include.*

    c. *Tap Add.*

9. **(Optional) Enter a comment.**

10. **Tap Post.**

    The recipient will receive an email and can choose to subscribe to your shared album by tapping the button shown.

Setting up an iCloud shared photo library

Rather than sharing one of your albums with family and friends, you might prefer to set up an *iCloud shared photo library,* which is a collection of photos and videos shared between up to six people, where each person can add, edit, and delete photos. The person who sets up the shared library — the *library creator* — provides the iCloud storage for the entire library. Any photos or videos you add to this shared library are moved out of your personal library and into the shared library.

REMEMBER

You and each person who joins your shared library must be using a device that's running at least iPadOS 16.1, iOS 16.1, or macOS Ventura.

Follow these steps to set up an iCloud shared photo library using your iPad:

1. **Choose Settings ⇨ Photos.**

2. **Tap the iCloud Photos switch on, if it's not on already.**

3. **Tap Shared Library and then tap Get Started.**

    At this point you might see a Before You Get Started dialog that displays a list of your devices that need to be upgraded before they can use the shared library. If you see this screen, nod knowingly and tap Continue Anyway.

    The Add Participants dialog appears.

4. **For each person (up to five) who you want to invite to join the shared library, follow these substeps:**

    a. *Tap Add Participants*

    b. *Type the email address (or the name, if the person is in your Contacts) of the person you want to invite. For your contacts, you can also tap + and select the person from the list that appears.*

    c. *Tap Add.*

5. Tap Next.

The Move Photos to the Shared Library dialog appears.

6. Choose how you want to handle moving your existing photos and videos to the shared library:

- *All My Photos and Videos:* Moves everything to the shared library.

- *Choose by People or Date:* Moves only photos that include particular people or that were taken on or after a specified date to the shared library.

- *Choose Manually:* Moves only the photos that you select to the shared library.

- *Move Photos Later:* Skips this step for now.

7. If you want to take a peek at your shared library before sending the invitations, tap Preview Shared Library. When you're done, tap Continue.

If you don't want to bother with the preview, tap Skip instead.

8. Invite the participants:

- *Via text message:* Tap Invite via Messages. In the new text message that appears, type your message, and then tap Send.

- *Via email or other sharing method:* Tap Share Link, and then use the share sheet to choose how you want to share a link to the shared library.

The Share from Camera dialog appears.

9. If you want photos taken with your iPad to be automatically added to the shared library when your iPad detects that other participants are nearby, tap Share Automatically.

If you prefer to add new photos to the shared library manually, tap Share Manually Only instead.

TIP

After your shared library is configured, the Camera app sprouts a new shared library icon (silhouette of two people). You can tap that icon to toggle between sharing new photos directly to your shared library or to your personal library. To hide the shared library icon, choose Settings ➪ Camera ➪ Shared Library, and then tap the Share from Camera switch off.

iPadOS displays a message letting you know the shared library is ready for action.

10. Tap Done.

To access your shared library from the Photos app, display the sidebar, tap Library, tap the more icon (three horizontal dots), and then tap Shared Library, as shown in Figure 9-4. Alternatively, tap Both Libraries to see photos from both the shared library and your personal library. Note that photos in the shared library are marked with the shared library indicator icon, pointed out in Figure 9-4.

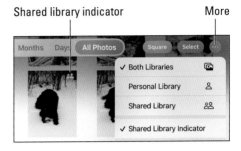

FIGURE 9-4:
Click More to access your shared library.

Deleting a photo

Some of your photos will be admirable works of art that you'll want to view again and again. Others, not so much. If you have a photo that you can't get rid of fast enough, the iPad makes it a cinch to bury the evidence:

1. **Display the objectionable photograph.**

2. **Tap to display the picture controls, if they're not already displayed.**

3. **Tap the trash icon.**

   Photos asks you to confirm the deletion.

4. **Tap Delete Photo (or, if you change your mind, tap anywhere else to cancel).**

   In an instant, the photo is mercifully whisked to the Recently Deleted album, where your iPad will delete it permanently after 30 days.

In the Digital Darkroom: Editing Photos

The iPad isn't the easiest device in the world to use as a camera — it's a bit too big and unwieldy to hold steady. As a result, you might end up with a few less-than-perfect shots. There's not much you can do to fix blurry images (one of the biggest iPad photo faux pas), but other problems can be fixed by enhancing the color or brightness, cropping out extraneous elements, and applying a filter.

Cropping and straightening a photo

Cropping a photo means that you specify a rectangular area of the shot that you want to keep, and everything outside that area is hidden. Why would you do that?

Because cropping enables you to get rid of unwanted elements that appear near the edges of the shot, such as a telephone pole, a piece of garbage, or a glimpse of your finger. Even if your photo contains no such extraneous elements, cropping enables you to give center stage to the subject of a photo.

Straightening a photo means that you rotate the shot either clockwise or counter-clockwise —usually just a few degrees— so that the subject of the photo is level.

Here are the steps to follow to crop and straighten a photo using the Photos app:

1. **Open the photo that you want to edit.**

2. **Tap the photo to display the controls.**

3. **Tap Edit.**

   Photos displays its editing tools.

4. **Tap Crop.**

   Photos displays its tools for cropping and straightening, as shown in Figure 9-5.

5. **To crop the photo, drag a corner or edge of the rectangle that appears around your photo.**

   The idea here is that Photos will retain only that portion of the photo that appears within the rectangle, so drag the corners or edges or both as needed to set the area you want to keep.

6. **To straighten the photo, tap the straighten tool and then drag the slider up or down until the image is level.**

Flip vertically
Rotate
Aspect
Tilt horizontally
Tilt vertically
Straighten

FIGURE 9-5:
The Photos app's cropping and straightening tools.

You're unlikely to need them, but Photos also offers the tilt vertical and tilt horizontal tools that you can use to tilt your photo vertically or horizontally, respectively. If you feel like it, you can also tap the flip vertical tool to flip the photo along its vertical axis.

7. **Tap Done.**

   Photos applies the changes to the photo.

You can get Photos to do some (or even all) of the cropping work for you by tapping the aspect icon (pointed out in Figure 9-5) and then tapping a preset aspect ratio, such as Square, 9:16, or 5:7. You then optionally drag the photo so the portion you want to keep is within the crop.

One annoying photo problem is when the photo appears in landscape mode when your tablet is in portrait orientation (or the photo might appear in portrait mode when your tablet is in landscape orientation). The solution is to tap the rotate icon to rotate the photo 90 degrees to change its orientation.

Applying a filter to a photo

A *filter* is a special effect applied to a photo's colors to give it a different feel. For example, you can enhance a stark image by applying a black-and-white filter such as Mono or Noir.

Follow these steps to apply a filter to an image using the Photos app:

1. **Open the photo that you want to edit.**

2. **Tap the photo to display the controls.**

3. **Tap Edit.**

   Photos displays its editing tools.

4. **Tap Filters.**

   Photos displays thumbnail versions of the photo that demonstrate each filter.

5. **Tap the filter you want to use.**

6. **Drag the slider to adjust the intensity of the filter to your liking.**

7. **Tap Done.**

   Photos applies the filter to the photo.

Making a few adjustments

No matter how good you are at taking photos, you'll most likely need to edit some of your photos to bring out their best features and reduce any deficiencies. The Photos app packs a powerful set of editing tools that you can wield to adjust a photo's exposure, contrast, saturation, and many other for-photography-nerds-only settings.

WARNING

Once you learn how to use the Photos app's image adjustment tools, you'll want to use them for all your photos, or at least those images you want to share with the world. However, you might be tempted to overuse these tools, resulting in photos that look garish, over-processed, and unnatural. Remember that these tools are meant for subtle adjustments only.

Before going through the individual tools, here are the general steps to follow to make adjustments to a photo:

1. **Open the photo that you want to edit.**

2. **Tap the photo to display the controls.**

3. **Tap Edit.**

   Photos displays its editing tools.

4. **Tap Adjust.**

   Photos displays its adjustment tools, as shown in Figure 9-6.

5. **Tap the tool you want to use.**

6. **Drag the tool's slider up or down until the image looks the way you want.**

7. **Repeat Steps 5 and 6 for each type of adjustment you want to make to the photo.**

8. **Tap Done.**

   Photos applies the adjustments to the photo.

FIGURE 9-6:
The Photos app's adjustment tools.

 I should mention right off the top that by far the easiest way to adjust a photo is to tap the auto-enhance tool (shown in the margin), which automatically adjusts the photo's brightness, contrast, color temperature, tint, and saturation. If you like the resulting changes, tap Done and move on with your life. Otherwise, tap Auto again to reverse the adjustments and then make your own adjustments manually.

Besides auto-enhance, Photos offers the following adjustment tools:

 » **Exposure:** Adjust your photo's overall lighting. If your photo is too light (so it looks washed out), try decreasing the exposure (drag the slider up) to darken the photo. If your photo is too dark (so it looks muddy), try increasing the exposure (drag the slider down) to lighten the photo.

- » **Brilliance:** Adjust the brightness of the photo, particularly by adjusting the lighting of the darker parts of the photo. If your photo is well exposed except for the darker parts, increase the brilliance (drag the slider down).

- » **Highlights:** Adjust how intense the brightest parts of the image appear. If your photo has one or more areas that are washed out because they're too bright, reduce the highlights value (drag the slider up) to counter that effect.

- » **Shadows:** Adjust how intense the darkest parts of the image appear. If your photo has one or more areas that show no detail because they're too dark, reduce the shadows value (drag the slider up) to try and bring back some of that detail.

- » **Contrast:** Adjust the distribution of the photo's tones. If the tones in your photo are starkly different, lower the contrast (drag the slider up) to make them more alike. If your photo is bland because the tones are all alike, increase the contrast (drag the slider down) to make the tones stand out.

- » **Brightness:** Adjust all the photo's tones towards white or black. Unlike brilliance, which mostly affects the darker parts of the photo, brightness affects all the photo's tones. If your photo is too dark, increase the brightness (drag the slider down); if your photo is too light, decrease the brightness (drag the slider up).

- » **Black point:** Set the limit for the blackest part of the image. A lower value (drag the slider up) means even the darkest parts of the image will appear gray, while a higher value (drag the slider down) means more of the photo's dark patches will appear black.

- » **Saturation:** Adjust the intensity of the photo's colors. If your photo lacks dynamism, try increasing the saturation (drag the slider down).

- » **Vibrance:** Adjust the (drag the slider).

- » **Warmth:** Adjust the "temperature" of the photo's colors. Drag the slider up to create a cool blue effect; drag the slider down to create a warm red effect.

- » **Tint:** Adjust the amount of green and red tones in the photo. Drag the slider down to add red and reduce green; drag the slider up to reduce red and add green.

- » **Sharpness:** Adjust the contrast of the edges that appear in the photo (for this tool, you can drag the slider only down).

- » **Definition:** Adjust the contrast of areas that appear hazy in the photo (for this tool, you can drag the slider only down).

- » **Noise reduction:** Reduce the graininess of the photo to give the image a smoother look (for this tool, you can drag the slider only down).

- » **Vignette:** Drag the slider down to darken the corners of the photo, which adds a natural frame around the image and draws attention to the interior of the photo.

TIP

If you aren't satisfied with any of the edits you've applied to your pictures, you can always tap Cancel followed by Discard Changes to restore the original. If you tap Done instead and apply the changes, you can still change your mind later. Open the image, tap Edit, tap Revert, and then tap Revert to Original, which will remove all edits made to the pic.

TIP

If you make a ton of little adjustments to a photo, you might be dismayed to think you have to go through the same process for one more of your other photos. Chin up! Once you've completed your adjustments for one photo (but before you tap Done), tap the options icon (three horizontal dots at the top of the screen), and then tap Copy Edits. Now open another photo to which you want to apply the same adjustments, tap the options icon, and then tap Paste Edits. Done!

Editing live photos

With some simple controls that look a lot like the editing tools discussed in Chapter 8, you can trim the length of a live photo, set the *keyframe* (the still that appears when you're not long-pressing a live photo), turn off sound, and more. To edit a live photo, follow these steps:

1. **Open your live photo.**

2. **Tap Edit.**

3. **Tap Live.**

   Photos displays a video timeline that will appear familiar if you read Chapter 8, which covers video features of the iPad.

   If all you want to do is convert your live photo to a boring old regular photo, tap the Live icon at the top of the screen to turn it off and then skip the rest of these steps.

   One of the frames in that timeline will have a white square around it marking the current keyframe.

4. **Drag that square along the timeline until you get a frame you like, and then tap Make Key Photo.**

5. **To mute sound in your live photo, tap the volume icon (speaker near the top-left corner of the screen).**

6. **To trim the length of your live photo, drag the handles at either end of the timeline and move them where you want.**

7. **Tap Done**

   Your live photo will be represented by its new keyframe.

Entering the Photo Booth

Remember the old-fashioned photo booths at the local Five and Dime? Remember the Five and Dime? Okay, if you don't remember such variety stores, your parents probably do, and if they don't, their parents no doubt do. The point is that photo booths (which do still exist) are fun places to ham it up solo or with a friend as the machine captures and spits out wallet-size pictures.

With the Photo Booth app, Apple has cooked up a modern alternative to a real photo booth. Here's how Photo Booth works:

1. **Tap the Photo Booth icon on the Home screen.**

2. **Point the front-facing camera at your face.**

   Your mug appears through a prism of eight rather wacky special effects: Thermal Camera, Mirror, X-Ray, Kaleidoscope, Light Tunnel, Squeeze, Twirl, and Stretch. The center square is the only one in which you come off looking normal.

   You can also use the rear camera in Photo Booth to subject your friends to this form of, um, visual abuse.

3. **Tap one of the special effects (or stick with Normal).**

   If you're not satisfied with the effect you've chosen, tap the icon at the lower-left corner of the app to return to the Photo Booth grid and select another.

TIP

4. **When you have your bizarre look just right, tap the shutter button to snap the picture.**

   Your pic lands in both the All Photos album and the Selfies album.

4

Putting the iPad to Work

IN THIS PART . . .

Shop 'til you drop in the App Store.

Stay on top of your appointments and people with Calendar and Contacts.

Discover time- and effort-saving utilities such as Reminders, Notes, and Clock.

Get from here to there with the Maps app.

Drop in on the handy Control Center.

Get to know Siri, your (mostly) intelligent assistant.

Chapter **10**

Harnessing the Power of Apps

Your iPad comes with an impressive collection of built-in apps, including Safari, Mail, Messages, Calendar, Photos, Music, and Notes. A default installation of iPadOS comes with more than 30 apps. Surely no one needs more than that, amirite?

No, I'm not. For one thing, you might want to use a third-party app instead of one of Apple's default apps. For example, maybe you prefer to use Google Chrome or Mozilla Firefox as your web browser. Maybe you're a diehard Microsoft Outlook fan. Maybe you get your musical kicks from Spotify.

For another, you might have tasks you want to perform on your iPad for which none of the default apps are suitable. Maybe you want to play a game, host a virtual meeting, or just Netflix and chill. That's fine because the App Store is home to nearly 2 million apps, which means that no matter what you want to do with your iPad, there is, as the kids say, an app for that.

In this chapter, you get a bird's-eye view of third-party (that is, non-Apple) apps and your iPad. You don't learn about specific apps. Instead, you find out how to find and download apps on your iPad, and you discover some basics for managing your apps. I also introduce you to your iPad's collection of widgets.

Tapping the Magic of Apps

Apps enable you to use your iPad as a game console, a streaming Netflix player, a recipe finder, a sketchbook, and much, much more. You can run three categories of apps on your iPad:

» **iPad only:** Runs only on an iPad, not on an iPhone, which means you can't even install it on an iPhone. This app is the rarest kind, so you find fewer of these than the other two types.

» **Universal:** Runs on both iPads and iPhones, and the app adjusts to fit the native resolution of whatever device it's running on.

» **iPhone native:** Runs on your iPad but only at iPhone resolution rather than the full resolution of your iPad, as shown in Figure 10-1.

TIP

You can double the size of an iPhone app by tapping the full screen icon in the lower-right corner of the screen (pointed out in Figure 10-1, left). To return the device to native size, tap the normal icon (pointed out in Figure 10-1, right).

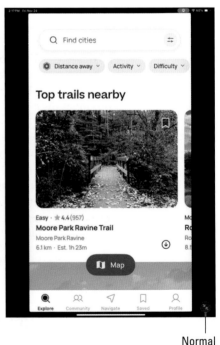

FIGURE 10-1: iPhone apps run at a smaller size (left) but can be increased to double the size (right).

Full screen

Normal

You can obtain and install apps for your iPad in two ways:

» By manually installing apps using the App Store. Check out "Shopping for Apps in the App Store," next, to learn how to install apps.

» By configuring the App Store to automatically download apps you install on your other devices. To enable automatic downloads, choose Settings ⇨ App Store and then, in the Automatic Downloads section, tap the App Downloads switch on. Now all apps you buy on other iPadOS and iOS devices will automagically appear on your iPad.

TIP

After you've obtained an app from the App Store, you can download it to up to ten iOS devices (as long as you log in with the same Apple account or use Family Sharing).

Shopping for Apps in the App Store

The iPad's out-of-the-box collection of apps is impressive, and most of us could happily while away our days playing around with nothing but the default apps. That, of course, would be silly, given that nearly 2 million apps await you in the App Store. That mind-boggling, eye-goggling number means that you're bound to find fistfuls of apps that will make your life easier, cooler, more efficient, and more fun. Best of all, tons of the apps won't cost you a dime, so you can bulk up your iPad without draining your bank account.

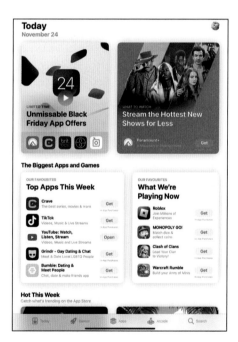

FIGURE 10-2:
The browse icons across the bottom represent different ways to browse the App Store.

Browsing the App Store

To get started, tap the App Store icon on your iPad's Home screen. In the App Store window that appears (see Figure 10-2) are five browse icons at the bottom of the screen, representing five ways to interact with the store.

Here's a summary of what each browse icons does for you:

FIGURE 10-3:
The Apps section displays apps organized by themes, such as iPad Essentials.

>> **Today:** Highlights curated selections from the App Store, including two featured apps at the top, lists of the Biggest Apps and Games, Hot This Week, and themed collections.

>> **Games:** Focuses on iPad games in categories such as What We're Playing, Must-Play Games, and New Games, to name a few. Scroll down and you'll find sections for Top Paid Games, Top Free Games, Popular Games, and more.

>> **Apps:** Displays all the non-game apps available for iPad (see Figure 10-3). It features some apps at the top, and then offers categories such as iPad Essentials, Popular Apps, Made for Kids, and Top Free Apps.

>> **Arcade:** Displays apps related to Arcade, a subscription service offered by Apple. With Arcade, you get on-demand access to more than 200 games, with Apple adding more every week. These are high-quality, top-tier games. Even better, none of them have in-app purchases, which means you can play the entire game without having to spend a penny outside the Arcade subscription itself. You'll find racing games, fighting games, strategy games, simulations, puzzles, mysteries, and so much more. These games are original, with most produced exclusively for Arcade. But here's the best part. Arcade is included with an Apple One subscription or is just $6.99 per month on its own, and that includes everything. (You can get Arcade free for three months if you purchase an iDevice.)

>> **Search:** Enables you to search for the app you want instead of scrolling through the seemingly endless screens of the other browse icons. Type your search word or phrase in the text box at the top of the screen, and then tap Search on the virtual keyboard.

Most pages in the App Store display more apps than can fit on the screen at once. For example, the iPad Essentials section in Figure 10-3 contains more than the four apps initially displayed. Here are a few techniques to help you navigate the Today, Games, Apps, and Arcade sections of the App Store:

» **Swipe from right to left** to display more apps in most categories.

» **Swipe up the screen** to scroll down and display additional categories.

» **Tap the See All link** at the top right of most sections to display all the apps in that section on one screen at the same time.

Doing your research: Getting app details

Browsing and searching for apps in the App Store let you know which apps are available, but how do you know whether an app is worth getting? You can research an app by digging into the details the App Store offers for each app. After tapping an app icon as you browse the store or in a search result, your iPad displays a details screen like the one shown in Figure 10-4.

TIP

Note the blue More link in the app description section, pointed out in Figure 10-4; tap More to read a longer description of the app.

Bear in mind that the app description on this screen was written by the app's developer and may be biased. Never fear, gentle reader: In an upcoming section, I show you how to find app reviews written by people who have used the app (and, unfortunately, sometimes people who haven't).

Age rating

App price

App rating App Store ranking and category

Click to see a longer description

FIGURE 10-4:
The info screen for the buddhify meditation app.

Understanding the age rating

The buddhify app is rated for age 4+ (refer to Figure 10-4). The rating means that the app may contain content unsuitable for children under 4. Other age ratings are 9+, 12+, and 17+, each designed to help parents manage what games and apps their kids are using.

Checking requirements and device support for the app

Remember the three categories of apps mentioned at the beginning of the chapter, in the "Tapping the Magic of Apps" section? Scroll down the page to the Information section (not shown in Figure 10-4), tap Compatibility, and you'll find that this app requires iPadOS 10.0 or later.

Reading reviews

The Ratings & Reviews section of the details screen offers reviews written by users of the app. Each review includes a star rating, from zero to five. If an app is rated four stars or higher, you can safely assume that most users are happy with the app.

Figure 10-4 shows that this app has a rating of 4.7 stars based on 980 user ratings. That means most of the people who reviewed it think it's a great app. Tap See All to read more user reviews.

REMEMBER

Don't believe everything you read in reviews. People find some amazingly bad reasons to give apps bad — and sometimes good — ratings. Take App Store ratings and reviews with a grain of salt and try to find the reviews that resonate with you. I also like to look for a preponderance of opinions to help weigh the ones to take seriously. Lastly, make sure the review you're reading is for the current version — reviews of older versions may not apply to the new version.

Downloading a free app

Amazingly, quite a few of the App Store apps cost precisely nothing. Nada. Zip. You may think these freebies would be amateurish or too simple to be useful. It's true that some of them are second-rate, but a surprising number are full-fledged apps that are as polished and feature-rich as the commercial apps.

REMEMBER

In the App Store's browse screens, the free apps say Get on the right side of the app info. If you're seeking a good place to get your collection of free apps off the ground, tap Apps and then peruse the Top Free Apps list.

REMEMBER

A huge number of apps support a pricing model called *in-app purchases.* This model works by letting you download the app either for free or for a low price; the free or cheap version includes basic app features. However, if you want more features, longer play, more lives, more levels, or any other kind of app extension, you need to pay for it. Note that in-app purchases can amount to quite a bit of money if you're not careful. Check out Chapter 17 to learn how to impose restrictions on a child's iPad, such as disabling in-app purchases.

TIP

You can determine whether an app supports in-app purchases by opening the app's info screen and looking at the app's Get button (if the app is free) or the app's price button. If the app supports purchased add-ons, you see the phrase "In-App Purchases" in fine-print-sized text to the right of the button.

Follow these steps to download and install a free app:

1. **In the App Store, locate and tap the app you want to download.**

    The app's details screen appears.

2. **Tap the Get button.**

    App Store displays a confirmation dialog.

3. **Tap Install.**

    The App Store asks for your Apple ID account password.

    Alternatively, if you've set up Touch ID or Face ID (refer to Chapter 17), the App Store asks you to use those methods to confirm your download, so you can skip Step 4.

4. **Type your password, and tap Sign In.**

    The App Store downloads the app. An icon for the app appears on the Home screen, along with a progress bar that tracks the download and install process. (The icon title changes from Loading to Installing and finally to the name of the app itself.)

Purchasing an app

Many iPad apps are extremely sophisticated, so it's not surprising that some of them will set you back a few bucks. To make sure you don't waste your money, read the description of the app, and be sure to read any reviews that other folks have submitted.

If a commercial app seems worthwhile, follow these steps to purchase and install it:

1. **In the App Store, locate and tap the app you want to buy.**

   The app's details screen appears.

2. **Tap the price button.**

   App Store displays a confirmation dialog.

3. **Tap Purchase.**

   The App Store asks for your Apple ID account password.

   Alternatively, if you've set up Touch ID or Face ID (refer to Chapter 17), the App Store asks you to use those methods to confirm your download, so you can skip Step 4.

4. **Type your password, and tap Sign In.**

   The App Store charges your Apple ID credit card and then downloads the app, which appears on your Home screen after a few seconds or minutes.

Messing with Your Apps

Once you've installed a few apps to go along with the default apps that shipped with your iPad, the overwhelmingly majority of the time you'll perform just two tasks with those apps: starting them and navigating between them (I describe app multitasking in sumptuous detail in Chapter 2). However, you ought to know a few other app-related techniques, including how to use App Library, change an app's settings, remove an app from the Home screen, and delete an app. The next few sections take you through the not-even-close-to-gory details.

Check out App Library

If your iPad Home screen consists of just three or four pages, it's never much of a chore to find the app you need. However, once you have a half dozen pages or more, you might find that you're spending far too much time frantically swiping left and right to find the app you want to use.

One solution is to search for the app you want: Swipe down on the center of the screen to display the Search sheet. Tap a recent app if it appears in the Siri Suggestions section (you can tap Show More to — you guessed it — show more apps); otherwise, start typing the app name in the Search box and then tap the app when it shows up in the results.

Another solution is to take advantage of App Library, which you can open either by tapping the App Library icon, which appears on the far-right end of the dock, or by swiping left on the last Home screen page.

If there's no App Library icon on your iPad's dock, tap Settings ⇨ Home Screen & App Library and then tap the Show App Library in Dock switch on.

As shown in Figure 10-5, the resulting screen has four main features:

>> A Search box at the top that gives you another way to search for an installed app

>> A Suggestions category that list the apps you use most often

>> A Recently Added category that lists three apps you've installed most recently and a four-app icon that, when tapped, displays all the apps in this category

>> A collection of categories for all your other apps: Utilities, Games, Social, and so on

FIGURE 10-5:
A typical iPad App Library.

By default, iPadOS doesn't show app icon badges in App Library. (An app icon badge is a red circle with a white number that tells you how many new items the app has for you.) If you use App Library frequently, you might want to display those badges so you know if an app has new content you should check out. Tap Settings ⇨ Home Screen & App Library and then, in the Notification Badges section, tap the Show in App Library switch on.

Tweaking an app's settings

Most apps work just fine right out of the box, but sometimes an app's default configuration rankles. In that case, it's time to cross your fingers and hope that the app offers some way to reconfigure itself to fix whatever's bothering you. That reconfiguration, if it exists, will come via the app's settings, which enable you to customize the app in the same way the options in the Settings app enable you to customize your iPad. However, if you're used to desktop apps, which usually offer an extensive list of customization options, note that iPad apps almost always have just a few settings, and some apps don't offer any settings.

Depending on the app, you can configure the app's settings in one or both of the following ways:

>> **Via the app:** Some apps have a settings feature that you can access in the app itself. How you access the settings feature varies by app, but look for a settings icon (usually a gear) or a more icon (usually three dots; see Figure 10-6).

More

>> **Via the Settings app:** Tap Settings on the Home screen, and then scroll down the list of categories on the left until you get to an alphabetical list of apps that have settings. Tap an app in the list to display its settings.

FIGURE 10-6:
Some apps (such as Google Chrome, shown here) offer in-app settings.

Taking an app off the Home screen

If you have an app you use only occasionally, you can tidy up your Home screen a bit by taking that app's icon off the Home screen. The app will remain installed on your iPad, but now you'd have to launch the app either by running a search to locate it or by displaying it in the App Library.

Here's how to remove an app from the Home screen:

1. **Long-press the app icon.**

2. **Tap Remove App.**

   iPadOS asks you to confirm.

3. **Tap Remove from Home Screen.**

   iPadOS plucks the app's icon from the Home screen. However, the app remains in the App Library, so you can still open the app from there.

Offloading unused apps

Rather than manually taking low-use apps off your Home screen, as I describe in the preceding section, you can instead get your iPad to do all the work for you. That is, you can configure your iPad to automatically *offload* apps you haven't used in a while, which removes the app (thus saving some storage space on your iPad) but leaves the app's icon available in the Home screen and leaves the app's data intact. When you need to use an offloaded app, tap it; iPadOS immediately reinstalls the app (assuming it's still available in the App Store) and you're good to go.

Follow these steps to offload your apps automatically:

1. **Choose Settings ⇨ App Store.**

2. **Tap the Offload Unused Apps switch on.**

    iPadOS now automatically offloads any app you haven't used in a while. iPadOS indicates an offloaded app by adding a cloud icon to the right of the app's name.

Deleting an app

If you have an app you no longer use, you can delete it to reduce Home screen clutter and recover some storage space on your iPad. Here's how to delete an app on your iPad:

1. **Long-press the app icon.**

2. **Tap Remove App.**

    iPadOS asks you to confirm.

3. **Tap Delete App.**

    A dialog appears, informing you that deleting this app also deletes all its data.

4. **Tap Delete.**

    iPadOS removes the app and its data from your iPad.

Working with Widgets

As long as you're running iPadOS 15 or later on your iPad, your Home screen is populated not only by apps but also by a collection of widgets. A *widget* is a scaled-down version of an app that shows you current info from that app. Here are some examples:

» The Calendar widget shows you today's appointments and what's coming up in the next day or two.

» The Weather widget shows the current conditions in your neck of the woods.

>> The News widget shows the current top stories.

>> The Photos widget shows a random photo from one of your albums.

Viewing your widgets

You have two ways to view and interact with your widgets:

>> Display the first Home screen page, where a subset of your widgets appears at the top.

>> From the first Home screen page or from the lock screen, swipe right from the left edge of the screen to open today view, where your widgets appear in a vertical column on the left side of the screen, as shown in Figure 10-7. Swipe down and up on this column to scroll through the available widgets.

FIGURE 10-7:
Your widgets appear in today view.

Most widgets are there for information purposes only. If you want to open the widget's underlying app, just tap the widget. If the app is part of a *stack* (two or more widgets), swipe up or down within the stack to navigate the widgets.

Adding a widget

Tons of widgets are available, so if one of your installed apps has a widget that's not available either on the first Home screen page or in today view, you can follow these steps to add the widget:

1. **Open the widgets for editing:**

    ● *If today view is onscreen:* Scroll down to the bottom of the today view column and tap Edit.

    ● *If the first Home screen page is onscreen:* Long-press any widget and then tap Edit Home Screen. The widgets and app icons start wiggling.

2. **Tap + in the upper-left corner of the screen.**

   iPadOS displays a widgets sheet with the installed apps that have widgets listed on the left.

3. **Tap the app with the widget you want to add.**

   Note that the first form of the widget appears at this point. For many widgets, you can swipe left to browse other forms of the widget before adding it.

4. **Tap Add Widget.**

   iPadOS adds the widget.

5. **Tap and drag the new widget to the position you prefer.**

6. **To create a stack, tap and drag the widget and drop it on top of another widget that you want to be in the same stack.**

7. **Tap Done.**

Removing a widget

If you have a widget you no longer use, you can remove it to clean up your first Home screen page and your today view. Here's how to remove a widget:

1. **Long-press the widget icon.**

   You can long-press the widget either on the first Home screen page or in today view.

2. **Tap Remove Widget.**

   A dialog appears, reassuring you that removing the widget doesn't delete the app or any of its data.

3. **Tap Remove.**

   iPadOS removes the widget.

Chapter **11**

Staying in Touch: Managing Events and Contacts

One of the paradoxes of modern life is that as your dealings with other people become more important, you store less and less of that information in the easiest database system of them all — your memory. That is, instead of memorizing where and when you're meeting for coffee tomorrow or the phone number of the person you're meeting, you now store all that info electronically. In the end, getting all the info out of your head and storing it somewhere safe is a good thing because it means you can use your brain for more important things (such as figuring out how to get the other person to pay for that coffee).

When it comes to your iPad, storing these kinds of facts electronically means adding the details of your upcoming events to the Calendar app and adding the contacts details of your colleagues, customers, friends, and family to the Contacts app. Even better, if you sync this data via iCloud, as I describe in Chapter 3, you need only enter an event or a contact once on your iPad and the info will propagate to your other devices automatically. Sweet!

In this chapter, you explore the social side of your iPad via the Calendar and Contacts apps. You learn how to navigate the Calendar app, add events, and manage different calendars. You also learn how to add folks to the Contacts app and manage and edit all that contact info.

Working with the Calendar App

Your iPad comes with an app called Calendar that you can use to track upcoming happenings, such as appointments, birthdays, meetings, and dinner dates. Calendar calls these items *events* and offers lots of useful tools for tracking, managing, and remembering the events of your life.

You need the Calendar app up and running for this chapter, so head for the Home screen and tap the Calendar icon. Figure 11-1 shows the Calendar app in portrait mode.

REMEMBER

You don't have to see only your iCloud account calendars in the Calendar app. If you add a third-party account such as Google, Microsoft Exchange, or Outlook.com to your iPad (refer to Chapter 5), you can view that account's calendars, as well. Choose Settings ⇨ Mail ⇨ Accounts, tap the third-party account, and then tap the Calendars switch on.

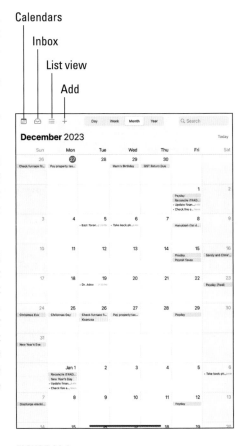

Calendars
Inbox
List view
Add

FIGURE 11-1:
Your tablet's administrative assistant: the beautiful and talented Calendar app.

Navigating the calendar

The key to getting around in the Calendar app efficiently is to take advantage of its various views, represented by the following four options at the top of the screen:

>> **Day:** Shows the events of a single day. To navigate this view, tap a date near the top of the screen. To see more dates, scroll the displayed dates left or right.

>> **Week:** Shows all your events for the selected week. To navigate this view, scroll the screen left or right.

TIP

In many countries (including the United States), week view defaults to showing Sunday as the first day of the week. If that doesn't work for you, you can designate any day you prefer as the start of the week. Choose Settings ➪ Calendar, tap Start Week On, and then tap the day you want to use as the start of your week.

>> **Month:** Shows the titles of all your events for a given month. You navigate this view by scrolling up or down.

>> **Year:** Shows a full calendar year. The dates on which you have scheduled events appear with a colored background. You navigate this view by scrolling up or down.

REMEMBER

Month view shows just the title of each event, along with a color-coded bullet that tells you in which calendar the event resides. To see more details for an event, tap it. Calendar displays info such as the event's time, location, notes, and attendees.

You never know when someone will invite you to lunch or to a get-together. Happily, if you have your trusty iPad at your side, you can check your schedule and add and edit events directly in the Calendar app. The next few sections provide the details.

Adding an event to your calendar

Follow these steps to add a basic event (I cover more advanced features, such as repeating events and alerts, a bit later in this chapter):

1. **Display the date on which the event occurs.**

2. **Long-press the time when the event occurs.**

   In month view, long-press the date. You can also tap + (add; refer to Figure 11-1). The New Event dialog appears, as shown in Figure 11-2.

3. **In the Title box, enter a title for the event.**

4. **(Optional) In the Location or Video Call box, select a location for the event.**

FIGURE 11-2:
Fill in the New Event dialog to add an event to your calendar.

5. **Tap Starts, and then set the time and date when your event begins.**

   If you're creating your event after long-pressing a date in month view, you need to tap the All-Day switch off before you can set a start time for the event. I show you how to create all-day events later in this chapter.

6. **Tap Ends, and then set the time and date when your event finishes.**

7. **If you have two or more calendars, tap Calendar, and then tap the calendar to which you want to assign this event.**

8. **(Optional) In the Notes box (you need to scroll to the bottom of the New Event dialog to see it), enter your notes for the event.**

9. **Tap Add.**

   Calendar adds the new event to your calendar.

TIP

The default events created by Calendar have a duration of an hour, but you can change that duration if the default doesn't work for you. Choose Settings ⇨ Calendar ⇨ Duration for New Events, and then tap the default duration you want Calendar to use.

Editing an event

According to Murphy's Law of Calendars, after you add an event to your schedule, something about the event will inevitably change: the start time, the end time, the location, or perhaps all three. That's fine with you because Calendar makes it easy to edit the event and keep your schedule accurate.

TIP

If you just want to change the start or end time (or both), switch to either day or week view. Then long-press the event until Calendar adds selection handles to it. Drag the top selection handle to change the start time; drag the bottom selection handle to change the end time; drag any other part of the event up or down to move it to a new time. If you're in week view, you can also drag the event left or right to move it to a new date.

Follow these steps to edit an event:

1. **Display the date that contains the event you want to edit. In day view, navigate to the date.**

   In week or month view, open the week or month that contains the date.

2. **Tap the event.**

3. **Tap Edit.**

   Calendar displays the event data in the Edit Event dialog (which looks alarmingly like the New Event dialog shown previously in Figure 11-2).

4. **Make your changes.**

5. **Tap Done.**

   Calendar saves your work and returns you to the event details.

Repeating an event

Lots of events are one-offs: They come, they go, and you move on with your life. However, you probably also schedule many different types of events that recur on a regular schedule: annual birthdays and anniversaries; a monthly departmental meeting at work; a weekly running club or book club. You might think these would be a hassle because they require you to put in regular work scheduling them, but that's not the case. Why not? Because Calendar comes with a repeat feature where, given an event that recurs multiple times, you add only the next event and then ask Calendar to automatically repeat the event at the required recurrence interval (monthly, weekly, every 10 days, or whatever). You can configure the event to either repeat indefinitely or stop on a particular date.

Here are the steps to follow to repeat an existing event:

1. **Display the date that contains the event you want to edit.**

   In day view, navigate to the date. In week or month view, open the week or month that contains the date.

2. **Tap the event.**

   Calendar opens the event info.

3. **Tap Edit.**

   Calendar displays the event data in the Edit Event dialog.

4. **Tap Repeat. In the list that appears, tap the repeat interval you want to use.**

5. **Tap End Repeat, and then tap one of the following choices:**
   - *Never:* The event repeats indefinitely.
   - *On Date:* The event repeats only up to the date you specify.

6. **Tap Done.**

   Calendar repeats the event.

Converting an event to an all-day event

Consider the following list of event types:

>> Birthday

>> Anniversary

>> Trade show

>> Sales meeting

>> Conference

>> Vacation

What do all these types have in common? Their duration is effectively all day. A birthday or an anniversary is literally an all-day event; a vacation is (usually) a multi-day event; and a work-related event such as a trade show or sales meeting usually lasts the whole workday.

Why is this important? Well, suppose you schedule a trade show as a regular event that lasts from 9 a.m. to 5 p.m. When you examine that day in the Calendar app day or week view, you see a big fat block that covers the entire day. If you also want to schedule meetings that occur at the trade show, Calendar lets you do that, but it shows these new events on top of the existing trade show event. This makes the schedule hard to read, so you might miss an event.

To solve this problem, configure the trade show (or whatever) as an all-day event. Calendar removes the event from the regular schedule and displays it separately, near the top of the day view or on the top part of the week view. That leaves the regular schedule free for other events.

Follow these steps to configure an event as an all-day event:

1. **Display the date that contains the event you want to edit.**

   In day view, navigate to the date. In week or month view, open the week or month that contains the date.

2. **Tap the event.**

   Calendar opens the event info.

3. **Tap Edit.**

   Calendar switches to the Edit Event dialog.

4. **Tap the All-Day switch on.**

5. **Tap Done.**

   The Calendar app saves the event, returns you to the calendar, and now shows the event as an all-day event, as shown in Figure 11-3.

Adding an alert to an event

FIGURE 11-3:
All-day events appear in the All-Day section, near the top of the day and week views.

In exchange for a hefty slice of your savings, dozens of productivity gurus out there will tell you their secrets to being a productive and stress-free member of society. Let me save you a ton of money by letting you in on the most important of these secrets: Get stuff out of your head and into some kind of form where it can't be forgotten.

The gurus offer elaborate systems for doing this, but when it comes to handling events, Calendar's alert feature is all you need. If you have an important event coming up, don't fret that you might miss it. Instead, add it to your schedule and then configure Calendar with an alert to let you know when the event is about to happen (which could be a minute, an hour, or a day before — whatever works for you). Alerts appear also in your iPad's Notification Center, so even if you miss the actual alert, you can still see the notification.

Follow these steps to set an alert for an event:

1. **Display the date that contains the event you want to edit.**

   In day view, navigate to the date. In week or month view, open the week or month that contains the date.

2. **Tap the event.**

   Calendar opens the event info.

3. **Tap Edit.**

   Calendar displays the event data in the Edit Event dialog.

4. **Tap Alert and then tap the number of minutes, hours, or days before the event you want to see the alert.**

   If you're editing an all-day event, you can set the alert for 9 a.m. on the day of the event, 9 a.m. the day before the event, 9 a.m. two days before the event, or a week before the event.

5. **To set up a backup alert, tap the Second Alert option and then tap the number of minutes, hours, or days before the event you want to see the second alert.**

6. **Tap Done.**

   The Calendar app saves your alert choices and returns you to the calendar.

TIP

You can set a default alert time for different event types. Choose Settings ⇨ Calendar ⇨ Default Alert Times. Tap the event type you want to configure (Birthdays, Events, or All-Day Events), and then tap the default alert time you want Calendar to use.

REMEMBER

Calendar plays a chime each time it displays an alert. If you find these sounds annoying, you can turn them off. Choose Settings ⇨ Sounds, tap Calendar Alerts, and then tap None.

Getting more out of the Calendar app

The basic features of the Calendar app — multiple views, color-coded calendars, repeating events, all-day events, and event alerts — make it an indispensable time-management tool. But it has a few more tricks up its sleeve that you ought to know about, and these are covered in this section.

Setting the default calendar

If you have multiple calendars on the go, each time you create an event the Calendar automatically chooses one of your calendars by default. It's no big whoop if every now and then you have to tap the Calendar setting and choose a different calendar. However, if you have to do this most of the time, it gets old in a hurry, particularly when I tell you there's something you can do about it. Follow these steps to configure the Calendar app to use a different default calendar:

1. **Open the Settings app.**

2. **Tap Calendar.**

   The Calendar settings appear.

3. **Tap Default Calendar.**

   The Default Calendar screen appears.

4. **Tap the calendar you prefer to use as the default.**

   The Calendar app now uses that calendar as the default for each new event.

Responding to meeting invitations

The iPad has one more important icon in the Calendar app. It's the inbox icon in the top-left corner (refer to Figure 11-1). If you partake in iCloud, have a Microsoft Exchange account, or have a calendar that adheres to the CalDAV (Calendaring Extensions to WebDAV [Web Distributed Authoring and Versioning]) internet standard, you can send and receive meeting invitations.

If you have any pending invitations, you'll see them when you tap the inbox, which is separated into new invitations and invitations to which you've already replied. You can tap any of the items in the list to see more details about the event to which you've been invited. (Note that the Calendar's inbox is not the same as your email inbox.)

Suppose a meeting invitation arrives from your boss. You can see who else is attending, check scheduling conflicts, and more. Tap Accept to let the meeting organizer know you're attending, tap Decline if you have something better to do (and aren't worried about upsetting the person who signs your paycheck), or tap Maybe if you're waiting for a better offer.

TIP

You can choose to receive an alert every time someone sends you an invitation. Choose Settings ⇨ Notifications ⇨ Calendar ⇨ Customize Notifications and make sure the Invitations switch is on.

Subscribing to calendars

You can subscribe to calendars that adhere to the CalDAV and iCalendar (.ics) standards, which are supported by the popular Google and Yahoo! calendars and by the Mac's Calendar app. Although you can read entries on the iPad from the calendars you subscribe to, you can't create entries from the iPad or edit the entries that are already present.

To subscribe to one of these calendars, tap Settings ⇨ Mail ⇨ Accounts ⇨ Add Account. Tap Other and then tap Add CalDAV Account or Add Subscribed Calendar. Next, enter the server where the iPad can find the calendar you have in mind and, if need be, enter a username, a password, and an optional description.

Sifting through Contacts

You need Contacts up and running for the rest of this chapter, so head for the Home screen and tap the Contacts icon. Contacts is best used in landscape mode, which shows the Contacts pane on the left and the currently selected contact on the right, as shown in Figure 11-4. If you prefer to work in portrait mode, you can display the Contacts pane by tapping the sidebar icon in the top-left corner (and shown in the margin).

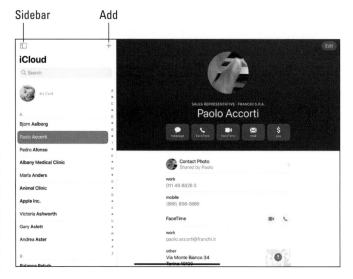

Sidebar Add

FIGURE 11-4:
In landscape mode, you see the Contacts pane on the left and the current contact's details on the right.

Navigating your contacts

If you have a healthy number of contacts, you need to know how to navigate the Contacts list. Here are the basic techniques:

>> Flick up and down to scroll through the list.

>> Tap a letter on the right side of the Contacts pane to leap directly to the contacts whose last names begin with that letter.

>> Use the Search box at the top of the Contacts list to type a few letters of the name of the contact you want to view, and then tap the contact in the search results.

Creating a contact

The next time you realize someone's missing from your contacts, you can fire up your trusty tablet and follow these steps to tap that person's vital statistics right into the Contacts app:

1. **Open the Contacts app.**

2. **In the top-right corner of the Contacts pane, tap + (add).**

    Contacts displays the New Contact dialog.

3. **(Optional) To change the contact picture, tap Add Photo, tap the type of picture — Camera (that is, take a new photo), Photos (use an existing photo), Memoji, Monogram, or Emoji — and then follow the screens that appear to create/select the picture you want to use.**

4. **In the First Name and Last Name fields, type the contact's name.**

   If you're entering the contact data for a company or other organization, skip this step and proceed directly to Step 5.

5. **In the Company field, type either the contact's place of business or the name of the business you're adding as a contact.**

6. **For each type of data you want to add (such as a phone number, an email address, or a pronoun), follow these substeps:**

   a. *Tap Add* Type, *where* Type *is the type of data (Phone, Email, and so on).*

   b. *On the left side of the new field that appears, tap the existing value, and then tap the label that best describes the data you're adding (such as Mobile, Home, or Work for a phone number).*

   c. *On the left side of the new field, add the data.*

7. **Tap Done.**

   Contacts saves your work and adds the new contact.

Editing a contact

People move, change jobs, enter into witness-protection programs, and generally refuse to stand still for even a moment. It's frustrating, but you still need to keep each person's contact data up to date if you want to stay in touch. Here are the general steps to follow to edit an existing contact:

1. **Tap the contact you want to edit.**

2. **Tap Edit.**

   Contacts opens the contact's data for editing.

3. **Make your changes to the contact's existing data.**

4. **Tap Done.**

   Contacts saves your edits and takes the contact out of editing mode.

Deleting a contact

It feels good to add contacts, but you don't get a lifetime guarantee with these things: Friends fall out or fade away, colleagues decide to make a new start at another firm, clients take their business elsewhere, and some of your acquaintances simply wear out their welcome after a while. You move on and so does your Contacts list. The best way to proceed is to delete the contact to keep the list trim and tidy.

Follow these steps to delete a contact:

1. **Tap the contact you want to delete.**

2. **Tap Edit.**

   The contact's data screen appears.

3. **Tap the Delete Contact button at the bottom of the screen.**

   Contacts asks you to confirm the deletion.

4. **Tap Delete Contact.**

   Contacts removes the contact.

Getting more from the Contacts app

Adding and editing data using Contacts is blissfully linear: Tap a field label to change it and then tap inside a field to add the data. If you remember to take advantage of the onscreen keyboard's context-sensitive keys (such as the .com key that materializes when you type a web address), contact data entry becomes a snap.

Contacts is straightforward on the surface, but if you dig a bit deeper, you find some useful tools and features that can make your contact management duties even easier.

Creating a custom field label

When you add information to a contact, you add not only the data itself but also a label that describes the data. Common labels are Home, Work, School, and Mobile. These labels are most useful when you have multiple instances of contact data, such as phone numbers and email addresses, because the labels make it easier to differentiate between them.

If the preset labels don't fit a particular tidbit of contact data, one solution would be to select the Other label. However, that's not very descriptive (to say the least!), so you're almost always better off taking a few extra seconds to create a custom label, like so:

1. **Tap the contact you want to work with.**

2. **Tap Edit.**

   The contact's data opens for editing.

3. **Tap the label beside the field for which you want to create the custom label.**

   The Label dialog appears.

4. **Tap Add Custom Label.**

   Contacts adds a blank line to the Label dialog.

5. **Type your custom label.**

6. **Tap Done.**

   Contacts saves your custom label and applies it to the contact field.

REMEMBER

Contacts remembers your custom label, which means you're free to apply it to any type of contact data. For example, you can create a label named University and apply it to a phone number, an email address, a web address, or a physical address.

Adding fields to a contact

The New Contact dialog (which appears when you add a contact) and the editing screen (which appears when you edit an existing contact) display not only the fields you need for basic contact info (such as First Name, Last Name, and Company) but also lots of extra fields for adding phone numbers, email addresses, the person's birthday, important dates (such as an anniversary), and a related name.

REMEMBER

A related name is another contact who is related to the contact you're editing. For example, if you also have the contact's brother in your Contacts list, tap Add Related Name, tap the *i* icon (more info), tap the brother's name in the list of contacts, tap the field label (the default is mother), and then tap the relationship type.

Despite these additional fields, the contact data screen still lacks quite a few common fields. For example, you might need to specify a contact's prefix (such as Dr. or Professor), suffix (such as Jr., Sr., or III), or job title.

Thankfully, Contacts is merely hiding these and other useful fields where you can't see them. You can add about a dozen hidden fields to any contact. Follow these steps to do so:

1. **With the contact's data open for editing, tap Add Field.**

   The Add Field dialog appears.

2. **Tap the field that you want to add.**

   Contacts adds the field to the contact.

3. **If the field has a label, tap the label box to choose a new one if needed.**

4. **Type the field data.**

5. **Repeat Steps 1 to 4 to add more fields as needed.**

6. **Tap Done.**

   Contacts closes the editing screen.

Deleting fields from a contact

People change, and so does their contact info. Most of the time these changes require you to edit an existing field, but sometimes people actually shed information. For example, they might get rid of a landline or they might shutter a website. Whatever the reason, you should delete that data from the contact to keep the data screen tidy and easier to navigate.

To delete a contact field, follow these steps:

1. **In the Contacts list, tap the contact with which you want to work.**

2. **Tap Edit.**

   The editing screen appears.

3. **Tap the red delete icon to the left of the field you want to trash.**

   Contacts displays a Delete button to the right of the field.

4. **Tap Delete.**

   Contacts removes the field.

5. **Tap Done.**

   Contacts closes the editing screen.

Creating a new contact from a vCard

Typing a person's contact data is a tedious bit of business at the best of times, so it helps if you can find a faster way to do it. If you can cajole a contact into sending his or her contact data electronically, you can add that data with just a couple of taps.

What do I mean when I talk about sending contact data electronically? The world's contact management gurus long ago came up with a standard file format for contact data: the vCard. It's a kind of digital business card that exists as a separate file. People can pass this data along by attaching their (or someone else's) card to an email message.

If you get a message with contact data, you see an icon for the VCF file, as shown later in Figure 11-5. To get this data into your Contacts list, follow these steps:

1. **On the Home screen, tap Mail to open the Mail app.**

2. **Tap the message that contains the vCard attachment.**

3. **Tap the icon for the vCard file.**

   Mail opens the vCard, as shown in Figure 11-5.

FIGURE 11-5:
If your iPad receives an email message with an attached vCard, an icon for the file appears in the message body.

4. **Do one of the following:**

   - *If the person is already in your Contacts list but the vCard contains new data, tap Add to Existing Contact, and then tap the contact.*

   - *Otherwise, tap Create New Contact.*

Sorting contacts

By default, Contacts displays your contacts sorted by last name (or company name, for businesses) and then by first name (to resolve cases where people have the same last name). That makes sense in most cases, but you might prefer a friendlier approach that sorts contacts by first name and then by last name. Follow these steps to make it so:

1. **Open the Settings app.**

2. **Tap Contacts.**

   The Contacts settings appear.

3. **Tap Sort Order.**

   The Sort Order settings appear.

4. **Tap First, Last.**

   Contacts now sorts your contacts by first name.

TIP

While you have the Contacts settings onscreen, you can also tap Display Order to change how Contacts displays the first name and last name of each contact: First, Last (the default display) or Last, First.

Linking contacts

The people you know most likely have contact entries in more than one account, meaning you might end up with redundant entries for the same person. The iPad solution is to *link* contacts. Find the contact in question, tap Edit, scroll to the bottom of the Edit screen, and tap Link Contacts. Choose the related contact entry and then tap Link. It's worth noting that the linked contacts in each account remain separate and aren't merged.

IN THIS CHAPTER

» **Writing things with Notes**

» **Remembering things with Reminders**

» **Timing things with Clock**

» **Eyeballing things on the lock screen**

» **Figuring out these notification things**

» **Learning some things about Personal Hotspot and AirDrop**

Chapter **12**

Indispensable Apps and Utilities

Most new iPad users shuttle between a few popular apps that come with iPadOS: Safari, Mail, Photos, Music, Calendar, and Contacts. These apps are great and useful, for sure, but your iPad comes with a fistful of other built-in apps. Are they all awesome? Nope, not even close. However, a few are good enough and useful enough to merit the adjective *indispensable.*

That might seem like hyperbole, but in this chapter, I try to change your mind. Here you explore three often-overlooked apps that I think you'll find truly useful: Notes, Reminders, and Clock. You also examine the lock screen, notifications, Personal Hotspot, and AirDrop — four utilities that can make your day-to-day life easier and more productive.

Jotting Stuff Down with Notes

Notes enables you to create short documents called — no surprises here — *notes*, which you can use when you want to write something but bringing out the heavy artillery of a word processor seems like overkill. Each note could be a shopping list, a to-do list, a quick observation, a few brainstorming ideas, or just about anything you want to get out of your head and onto (digital) paper. Over the years, Notes has gained many useful features, including "sketch with your finger" mode, checklists, and support for various media types. In addition, many apps now allow you to save data directly to the Notes app (after tapping the share icon). Finally, all your notes can be synced across all your enabled Apple devices via iCloud.

To create a note, follow these steps:

1. **On the Home screen, tap the Notes icon.**

2. **Tap the new note icon in the upper-right corner (and shown in the margin) to start a fresh note.**

   The virtual keyboard appears.

3. **Type your note, such as the one shown in Figure 12-1.**

Figure 12-1 points out a few Notes features and shows a sample note with the following: a title, a list formatted as a checklist, a table with two columns and two rows, and then some handwriting.

TIP

If you're in a hurry or you want to quickly jot something down without having to switch out of your current app, you can also create a Quick Note. From the bottom-right corner of your iPad, swipe towards the center of the screen to display the Quick Note window on top of your current app. (If that doesn't work for you, choose Settings ➪ Multitasking & Gestures, make sure the Swipe Finger from Corner switch is on, and then use the Bottom Right Corner pop-up list to select Quick Note.) Tap out your note and then tap Done. Now that's quick!

Other things you can do with the Notes app include the following:

>> If your iPad is in portrait orientation, tap the sidebar icon in the upper-left corner of the screen to display either a list of all your notes or — if you sync Notes with more than one account, such as iCloud, Google, or Yahoo! — the notes for the currently selected folder from one of the services you sync with. The sidebar appears automatically when your iPad is in landscape orientation.

>> When the sidebar is onscreen, tap a note to open and view, edit, or modify it.

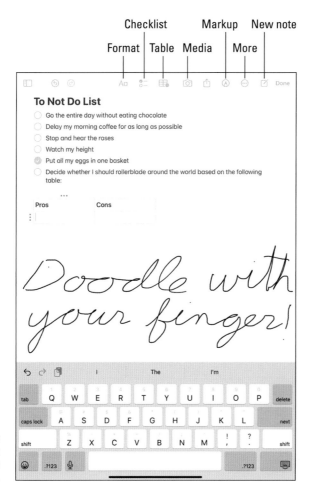

Format | Table | Media | More | New note

Checklist | Markup

FIGURE 12-1:
A note on
the go in the
Notes app.

➤ If your iPad is in portrait orientation, tap Folders in the upper-left corner when the sidebar is onscreen; if your iPad is in landscape orientation, tap the sidebar icon. Either way, in the Folders pane that appears, tap a folder to display its contents.

➤ Tap the checklist icon (shown in the margin) to start a checklist. Then, for each item, type the item text and tap Return to start a new item. After your last item, tap Return twice to end the checklist. You can also convert existing text into a checklist by selecting the text and then tapping the checklist icon.

➤ Tap the media icon (shown in the margin) to take a picture with the camera, select a picture from your Photos library, or scan a document to add to the note you're writing. The document scanner automatically senses and scans a document into the Notes app, crops it, and removes any skewing or glare. If you have a recent generation iPad and Apple Pencil, you can then use Apple Pencil to fill in the blanks or sign the document.

>> Tap the markup icon (shown in the margin) to display the markup tools you can use to create a new finger sketch.

>> Tap the more icon (shown in the margin) to scan a document into the note; pin the note to the top of its folder; lock the note with a password so that the note can't be changed; send a copy of the note or otherwise share the note via the Share sheet; move the note to another folder; display horizontal or vertical lines (or both) for easier handwriting; or delete the note.

Tap the more icon and then tap Customize Toolbar to rearrange or remove items from the Notes toolbar.

When the keyboard is displayed, you can

>> Tap the table icon (shown in the margin) to create a table with two columns and two rows. To add a new row below the current row, tap inside a current row, tap the three vertical dots that appear just to the left of the row, and then tap Add Row. To add a new column to the right of the current column, tap inside a current column, tap the three horizontal dots that appear just above the column, and then tap Add Column.

>> Tap the format icon (shown in the margin) to format text. Select the text before you tap it to change its format. Use the Format dialog to apply a style such as Title, Heading, or Body; apply formatting such as bold or italic; create a bulleted list, dashed list, or numbered list; and change the indent. Depending on the cursor's location in the note, you may get other options.

Finally, one of my favorite iPadOS features for those with an Apple Pencil and a compatible iPad: You can tap the lock screen with your Apple Pencil to launch Notes to a blank page so you can begin taking notes instantly. If this doesn't work for you, tap Settings ⇨ Notes ⇨ Access Notes from Lock Screen, and then tap Always Create New Note. If you prefer to continue working on your most recent note, instead, tap Resume Last Note.

Nudging Yourself with Reminders

The Calendar app (check out Chapter 11) is an excellent tool for tracking appointments, meetings, and other events. By adding an alert to an event you get a digital tap on the shoulder to remind you when and where your presence is required.

However, our days are sprinkled with tasks that don't quite qualify as Calendar-level events, such as making a phone call, starting the laundry, or turning on the oven. These tasks need to be done — and need to be done at a certain time — but it seems like too much effort to add them as Calendar events.

For such mini events, you're better off using the Reminders app, which displays a notification to remind you when it's time to perform the task. Tap the Reminders icon on your Home screen, and your iPad displays a screen that will look at least a little like the one shown in Figure 12-2, which is divided into two panes:

>> **Sidebar:** The left side of the screen displays various lists for your reminders. The top part contains the default lists maintained by the app, including Today (reminders due on this date); Scheduled (reminders that run at a specified date and time); All (every reminder you've set); Flagged (reminders you've marked with a flag icon); and Completed (reminders you've finished). The My Lists section of the sidebar starts with Reminders, which is the default list. When you create your own lists (as I describe in the next section), they appear here.

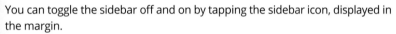

You can toggle the sidebar off and on by tapping the sidebar icon, displayed in the margin.

>> **Reminders:** The right side of the screen displays the reminders in whatever list you select in the sidebar.

Creating a time reminder

Most of your reminders will be *time reminders*, which alert you to do something on a specific day at a specific time. Follow these steps to set up a time reminder:

1. **In the sidebar, tap the list you want to use to store the reminder.**

If you're just starting out, the default list is Reminders. Check out the section "Creating a list and setting the default list" to learn how to set up new lists for your reminders.

2. **On the right side of the screen, at the bottom, tap New Reminder.**

Reminders creates a new reminder.

3. **Type the reminder text.**

4. **Tap the more info icon (displayed in the margin).**

The Details dialog appears, as shown in Figure 12-3.

Time reminder   Location reminder

More   Flag   More

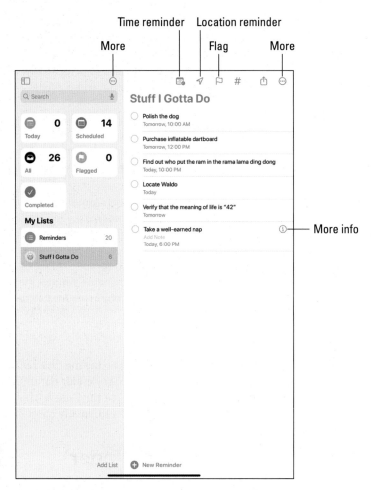

Stuff I Gotta Do

○ Polish the dog
  Tomorrow, 10:00 AM

○ Purchase inflatable dartboard
  Tomorrow, 12:00 PM

○ Find out who put the ram in the rama lama ding dong
  Today, 10:00 PM

○ Locate Waldo
  Today

○ Verify that the meaning of life is "42"
  Tomorrow

○ Take a well-earned nap   ⓘ —— More info
  Add Note
  Today, 6:00 PM

FIGURE 12-2:
The
Reminders app.

5. **(Optional) Tap the Date switch on and then use the calendar that appears to set the date of the reminder.**

Skip this step if you're setting your time reminder for later today.

6. **Tap the Time switch on and then use the controls that appear to set the time of the reminder.**

REMEMBER

You can leave the Time switch off to create an all-day reminder that appears at 9 a.m. on the date you choose. To choose a different time for your all-day reminders, choose Settings ➪ Reminders, tap Time in the All-Day Reminders section, and then set the time you prefer.

7. **If you want Reminders to poke you before the time you set in Step 6, tap Early Reminder and then tap how long before the event you want to be nagged.**

8. **If you want to set up a repeat interval for the reminder, tap the Repeat setting and make a selection.**

9. **If you want to assign a priority to the reminder, tap the Priority setting and choose None, Low, Medium, or High.**

10. **Fill in the rest of the reminder fields as needed.**

    For example, you can use the Notes text box to add background text or other information about the reminder. If the reminder is associated with a web page, you can paste the address in the URL text box. You can also tag a reminder by tapping Tags and then tapping an existing tag or typing a new one.

11. **Tap Done.**

    Reminders saves the reminder.

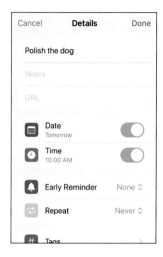

FIGURE 12-3:
The Details dialog is where you set your reminder date and time.

TIP

As an alternative to the preceding steps, you can tap the time reminder icon (shown in the margin), and then either tap one of the default dates (such as Tomorrow or This Weekend) or tap Custom and then use the Date & Time dialog to specify a date and time. Type your reminder text and fill in any other details you need.

Creating a location reminder

Another way to set a reminder is to use a location. The Reminders app then creates a kind of border — called a *geofence* — around that location. When your iPad crosses that geofence, the reminder notification appears. You get to choose if the reminder appears when you're arriving at the location or leaving it. Here are the steps to follow to set up a location reminder:

1. **In the sidebar, tap the list you want to use to store the reminder.**

2. **On the right side of the screen, at the bottom, tap New Reminder.**

    Reminders creates a new reminder.

3. **Type the reminder text.**

4. **Tap the more info icon (displayed in the margin).**

    The Details dialog appears.

5. **Tap the Location switch on.**

6. **Tap Custom.**

   You might need to drag the location circles to the left to bring the Custom circle onscreen.

7. **Use the Search box to specify the address of the location you want to use, and then tap the location when it appears in the search results.**

   Alternatively, you can tap Current Location to use your present whereabouts.

8. **To have the reminder appear when your iPad first comes within range of the location, tap Arriving. If you prefer to see the reminder when your iPad goes out of range of the location, tap Leaving instead.**

9. **Tap < Details.**

10. **Follow Steps 9 through 11 from the "Creating a time reminder" section to fill in the reminder details.**

Setting a reminder for when you message someone

Have you ever said to yourself, "I must remember to mention Y the next time I text so-and-so"? Then, when you finally do text that person, you completely forget to include any mention of Y? I suspected as much.

Well, I'm happy to report that those incidents are now in your past because you can create a reminder that pops up the next time you send a text to someone using the Messages app. Here's how to set it up:

1. **In the sidebar, tap the list you want to use to store the reminder.**

2. **On the right side of the screen, at the bottom, tap New Reminder.**

   Reminders creates a new reminder.

3. **Type the reminder text.**

4. **Tap the more info icon (displayed in the margin).**

   The Details dialog appears.

5. **Tap the When Messaging switch on, and then tap Choose Person.**

   A list of your contacts appears.

6. **Tap the recipient.**

7. **Follow Steps 9 through 11 from the "Creating a time reminder" section to fill in the reminder details.**

Creating a list and setting the default list

The Reminders app comes with a preset list named Reminders. That list might be all you need, but you can also create your own lists. For example, you might want to keep your personal and business reminders separate.

Feel free to create your own list whenever you like by following these steps:

1. **In the bottom-right corner of the sidebar, tap Add List.**

   Reminders displays the New List dialog.

2. **Type the name of your list.**

3. **Tap List Type and then select one of the following:**

   - *Standard:* Creates a list without any special features.

   - *Groceries:* Creates a list that automatically organizes grocery items added to the list by category (such as Meat, Produce, and Breads & Cereals).

   - *Smart List:* Creates a list that automatically stores reminders from other lists that meet the criteria you specify, such as a specified tag or a specified priority.

4. **Tap a color swatch.**

   Reminders uses this color for the list title and other text.

5. **Tap an icon.**

   Reminders displays this icon to the left of the list in the sidebar.

6. **Tap Done.**

   The Reminders app adds the list to the My Lists section of the sidebar.

The default list is the one that Reminders uses when you don't specify a particular list when you create a reminder. Follow these steps to set a particular list as the default:

1. **Choose Settings ⇨ Reminders.**

   The Reminders settings appear.

2. **Tap Default List.**

   The Default List screen appears.

3. **Tap the list you want to use as the default.**

Completing a reminder

When a reminder is complete, you don't want it lingering in its list, cluttering the screen and making it hard to look through your remaining reminders. To avoid that, once the reminder is done, tap the radio button to the left of it. This tells Reminders that the reminder is complete, and the next time you display the list, you won't see the reminder (although you can always tap the sidebar's Completed list to see your completed reminders).

Deleting a reminder

If you no longer need a reminder, it's a good idea to delete it to keep your reminder lists neat and tidy. To delete a reminder, follow these steps:

1. **In the sidebar, tap the list that contains the reminder you want to delete.**

   Reminders displays the list's reminders.

2. **Swipe left on the reminder you want to delete.**

   Reminders displays a Delete button.

3. **Tap Delete.**

   Reminders deletes the reminder.

Taming Time with the Clock App

You might think that the Clock app just tells you the time. Yep, sure, it does that, but the Clock app also does so much more. For example, it can tell you the current time in just about any city in the world. The app also enables you to set alarms, time events with a stopwatch, start a countdown timer, and more.

 To get started, tap the Clock icon on your Home screen. Alternatively, swipe down from the top-right corner of the screen to open Control Center and then tap the timer icon (shown in the margin) to open the Clock app with its timer feature displayed.

The Clock app has four icons across the bottom of the screen: World Clock, Alarms, Stopwatch, and Timers. I talk about each of these features in the next four sections.

Seeing the time anywhere in the world

Want to know the time in Beijing or Bogota? Tap the Clock app's World Clock icon to display the time in numerous cities around the globe. When the clock face is dark, it's nighttime in the city you chose; if the face is white, it's daytime.

To add a city to the world clock, tap + in the upper-right corner and then use the virtual keyboard to start typing a city name.

As you type, the iPad displays a list of places where the city or country name includes what you've typed. For example, typing *ve* brings up Andorra la Vella, Andorra; Caracas, Venezuela; and Las Vegas, U.S.A., among others. Keep typing until the city you want appears in the results, and then tap the city to add a clock for that location. You can create clocks for as many cities as you like, though only six cities fit onscreen at a time (in landscape orientation). Note, too, that you can drag the clocks around the screen to set your preferred arrangement.

To remove a city from the list, tap Edit and then tap the red circle with the white horizontal line that appears to the left of the city.

Setting an alarm

Ever try to set the alarm in a hotel room? It's remarkable how complicated setting an alarm can be, on even the most inexpensive clock radio. Like almost everything else, the procedure is way more straightforward on the iPad:

1. **At the bottom of the Clock app, tap the Alarms icon.**

2. **Tap + in the upper-right corner of the screen.**

   The Add Alarm dialog appears.

3. **Choose the time of the alarm by rotating the hour, minute, and AM/PM wheels.**

4. **Tap Save.**

That's what you can do with a regular alarm clock. What's the big deal, you say? Well, you can do even more with your iPad alarm. In the Add Alarm dialog, you can also do the following:

>> **Set the alarm to go off on other days.** Tap Repeat and then tell the iPad the days you want the alarm to be repeated, as in Every Monday, Every Tuesday, Every Wednesday, and so on.

>> **Name your alarm.** If you want to call the alarm something other than, um, Alarm, tap the Label field and use the virtual keyboard to type another descriptor.

>> **Choose your own sound.** Tap Sound to choose the tone that will wake you up. You can even use songs from your Music library and any custom tones stored on your iPad.

>> **Set the snooze to sleep in.** Tap Snooze on (showing green) to display a Snooze button along with the alarm. When your alarm goes off, you can tap the Snooze button to shut down the alarm for nine minutes.

You know that an alarm has been set and activated because of the tiny status icon (surprise, surprise — it looks like an alarm clock) that appears on the status bar in the upper-right corner of the screen.

An alarm takes precedence over any tracks you're listening to on your iPad. Songs or videos with sound pause when an alarm goes off and resume when you turn off the alarm (or tap the Snooze button).

WARNING

When your ring/silent switch is set to Silent, your iPad still plays alarms from the Clock app. It stays silent for FaceTime calls, alert sounds, or audio from apps, but it *will* play alarms from the Clock app.

Although it seems obvious, if you want to actually *hear* an alarm, you have to make sure that the iPad volume is turned up loud enough for you to hear.

Timing events with the stopwatch

Are you helping a friend or family member train for an upcoming track meet? Do you want to know how long it takes to peel a half-dozen carrots (hey, whatever floats your boat)? Whenever you need to time something, the Stopwatch function can provide an assist. Open it by tapping Stopwatch at the bottom of the Clock app.

Your first concern is whether to use the default digital stopwatch or to swipe left on the stopwatch to switch to the old-school (in a good way) analog stopwatch.

When you're ready, tap Start to begin the timing. When your trainee arrives at the finish line or you're finished with those carrots, tap Stop to shut off the timing. Note, too, that along the way you can also tap the Lap button as often as needed to monitor the times of individual laps (or carrots).

Starting a countdown timer

Cooking a hard-boiled egg or Thanksgiving turkey? Again, the Clock app comes to the rescue. Tap Timers at the bottom of the Clock app, and then rotate the hours, minutes, and seconds wheels to set the length of time you want to count down. Tap When Timer Ends, choose the ringtone that will signify time's up, and then tap Set.

TIP

To configure your iPad to stop the current audio or video playback when the timer finishes (if, say, you plan on falling asleep and don't want the media to play indefinitely), tap When Timer Ends and then tap Stop Playing. When the timer is done, your iPad stops the playback and displays the lock screen.

Tap Start when you're ready to begin. You can watch the minutes and seconds wind down on the screen. Or tap Pause to pause the countdown temporarily. If you need to end the timer prematurely, tap Done.

If you're doing anything else on the iPad — admiring photos, say — you hear the ringtone and a *Timer Done* message appears on the screen at the appropriate moment. Tap OK to silence the ringtone.

Lurking on the Lock Screen

The lock screen is what appears when you first turn on or wake up your iPad. You can quickly access the features and information you need most from the lock screen, even while the iPad is locked.

From the lock screen, you can do the following without unlocking your iPad first:

» Swipe left to open the camera (swipe up from the bottom to return to the lock screen).

» Swipe right to display today view.

» Swipe down from the top-center of the screen to search.

» Swipe down from the upper-right corner of the screen to open Control Center.

» Swipe up from the center of the screen to display Notification Center.

» Tap the screen with an Apple Pencil to start a new note.

» Long-press the top button to invoke Siri.

TIP

To fine-tune what appears on the lock screen, tap Settings ⇨ Touch ID & Passcode (or Settings ⇨ Face ID & Passcode, if your iPad supports Face ID). In the Allow Access When Locked section (refer to Figure 12-4), use the switches to toggle which features are available in the lock screen.

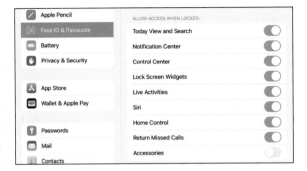

FIGURE 12-4: The switches in the Allow Access When Locked section enable you to control what's available from the lock screen.

Navigating Notifications

When your iPad is locked, notifications appear on the lock screen; when it's unlocked, they appear at the top of the screen.

To summon older notifications to the forefront of your iPad screen when it's unlocked, all you need is the magical incantation — that is, a swipe from the top of the screen downward. Go ahead and give it a try. I'll wait.

Here's the rest of what you need to know about navigating notifications:

REMEMBER

» **Open a notification on the lock screen.** Tap the notification, and then authenticate with Touch ID, Face ID, or your passcode.

Multiple notifications for the same app appear as a stack in Notification Center. To open or clear a notification in a stack, first tap the stack to display the available notifications as a list, and then tap or swipe the notification you want to mess with. (If you want multiple notifications for an app to always appear in list form, choose Settings ⇨ Notifications and then tap List in the Display As section.)

» **Open a notification on an unlocked iPad.** Tap the notification.

» **Mute an app's notifications.** Swipe any of the app's notification from right to left, tap Options, and then tap Mute for 1 Hour or Mute for Today.

- >> **Clear a single notification.** Swipe the notification from right to left and then tap the Clear button.

- >> **Clear all of an app's notifications:** Swipe the app's notification stack from right to left, and then tap Clear All.

- >> **Clear all notifications.** Display Notification Center and then tap the little x-in-a-circle in the top-right corner. The *x* turns into a Clear button; tap the Clear button and all notifications are cleared. If you have notifications from previous days, repeat this procedure for each one.

That's how to summon and use notifications. There's still a bit more to know — including how to change the notification settings for individual apps — but you have to wait until the chapter on the Settings app (that would be Chapter 15).

Sharing Your Internet Connection with Personal Hotspot

Personal Hotspot is a feature that lets your iPad with Wi-Fi + Cellular share its cellular high-speed data connection with other devices, including computers and other iPads. Here's how it works:

1. **Choose Settings ⇨ Cellular Data ⇨ Set Up Personal Hotspot.**

2. **Tap the Allow Others to Join switch to on.**

3. **Tap Wi-Fi Password and create or change the password for the Wi-Fi network you create.**

Now Wi-Fi or Bluetooth devices, or a single USB-enabled device, can join your Personal Hotspot network and share your iPad's cellular data connection.

REMEMBER

Your Personal Hotspot network adopts your iPad's name.

Most carriers offer support for Personal Hotspots in some or all of their data plans in the United States. Some don't, so check with your carrier if a Personal Hotspot option doesn't appear in the Settings app (and, of course, if your iPad has cellular capabilities).

Some carriers don't charge extra for this feature, but the data used by connected devices counts against your monthly data plan allotment. To find out how much cellular data you're using, tap Settings ⇨ Cellular Data and scroll down until you get to Cellular Data, which displays your cellular usage for the current period as well as data used while roaming.

Dropping In on AirDrop

The most straightforward way to share a file with someone is to send that person a copy of the file via, say, an email message. But if the other person is using an iPad, an iPhone, or a Mac, the easiest way to get that file from here to there is via AirDrop, which sends the file over the air using a temporary network connection set up between the two devices. For AirDrop to work, both devices must

>> Be on the same Wi-Fi network

>> Have Bluetooth turned on

>> Be within about 30 feet (around 9 meters) of each other

>> Have AirDrop enabled

In that last item, *enabled* means you've configured AirDrop to allow connections from other users. I show you how to configure AirDrop in a moment, but you should know that you have three options:

>> **Receiving Off:** You don't allow any AirDrop connections (that is, AirDrop is disabled).

>> **Contacts Only:** You allow AirDrop connections only from people who have an Apple ID and that Apple ID's email address (or phone number) is in your Contacts app. For this to work, both you and the other person must also be signed in to iCloud.

>> **Everyone for 10 Minutes:** You allow AirDrop connections from anyone who meets the requirements I just listed. For security, iPadOS allows this level of access for only 10 minutes.

To configure AirDrop, iPadOS gives you two methods:

» **Settings:** Choose Settings ➪ General ➪ AirDrop, and then tap the option you prefer.

» **Control Center:** Swipe down from the top-right corner to display Control Center. Long-press anywhere in the antennas section (the group in the top-left corner of Control Center), long-press the AirDrop icon, and then tap your preferred option.

When you want to send someone nearby some content via AirDrop, follow these steps:

1. **Using the appropriate app on your iPad, display the content you want to send.**

   For example, if you want to send someone a link to a web page, you'd first display that page in Safari.

2. **Tap the share icon (shown in the margin).**

3. **Either tap someone who has the AirDrop icon added to their avatar, or tap AirDrop and then tap the person.**

   If the recipient accepts the connection, AirDrop sends the content.

IN THIS CHAPTER

» Taking a guided tour of the
   Maps app

» Searching for coffee shops,
   bakeries, and other nearby
   essentials

» Putting yourself on the map

» Answering the age-old question:
   "Can I get there from here?"

Chapter **13**

Navigating the World

The science fiction writer Arthur C. Clarke once said that "any sufficiently advanced technology is indistinguishable from magic." Your iPad is bursting at the seams with advanced technology, but the one trick your iPad does that really does seem like magic is mapping. Not only does your iPad somehow know your exact location, but it also knows the exact location of pretty much everything else in the world *and* it can show you how to get from here to there. Magic? Not really, but it *is* impressive. I'm sure you'll find endless uses for the Maps app.

In this chapter, you explore Maps and discover all that it can do, from mapping addresses, to showing your current location, to getting directions on how to get from A to B (and back).

Mapping Locations

The Maps app is the Grand Central Station of mapping on your iPad. To get this trip started, tap the Maps icon on your iPad's Home screen. The first time you open Maps, you'll likely be pestered with a dialog similar to the one shown in

Figure 13-1. Here, Maps is asking for permission to use your location. Your location is kind of important for using a mapping app, so you need to do two things here:

>> **Make sure the Precise setting is on.** (If it's off, tap it.) When Precise is on, Maps can determine your location to within about 10 meters, or about 30 feet. Refer to Chapter 15 for more on this setting.

>> **Tap Allow While Using App:** This gives Maps permission to use your location, but only when you're using Maps. When you switch to a different app, Maps can no longer access to your location.

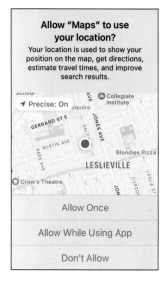

You now come face-to-face with a screen that's essentially just a big map. You use Maps in two main ways:

>> To view locations on the map

>> To get specific directions for getting from one location to another

FIGURE 13-1:
If Maps begs you to use your location, have mercy on the app and allow it.

The next few sections show you numerous ways to map a location. I get to the directions part of the tour a bit later in this chapter.

Mapping a location by searching for it

Maps knows — or seems to know — the location of just about anything. If it's situated somewhere on planet Earth and has an address or a name, chances are you can map it by running a search in the Maps app. Here's how:

1. **Tap inside the Search Maps box near the upper-left corner of the Maps screen.**

2. **Start typing some text that specifies the location.**

   You can type any of the following:

   • The name of the location

   • The address of the location

   • A word or phrase that describes the location

   As you type, Maps displays a list of locations that match what you've entered so far.

3. **In the search results, tap the location you want to map.**

Maps inserts a pin for the destination on the map and displays an information card with data about the location, as shown in Figure 13-2.

The location's info card often displays a ton of data about the location (the more public the location, the more data you see). The data shown on the card can include the location's phone number, street address, hours of operation, website address, and perhaps a photo or two. The card might also display reviews of the location from TripAdvisor (a service that offers user-generated ratings and reviews of millions of locations around the world).

FIGURE 13-2:
Tap your location in the search results and Maps shows you where it is and displays some info about it.

Dropping a pin

In the preceding section, I went through the steps involved in searching for a specific location. That technique works like a treat provided you have a specific location in mind (and know the address or name of that location). However, sometimes you just want to investigate a block or a neighborhood, not a specific location.

No problem. Maps enables you to create a *dropped pin,* which is a pushpin icon that Maps inserts on any spot that you long-press. Handily, Maps also displays the Dropped Pin information card, which tells you the address of the dropped pin, its latitude and longitude, and the name of any nearby businesses (such as a shop or restaurant).

You also get the location's Look Around icon (if that feature is available for the location) in the lower-right corner so you can peek at what's located where you dropped the pin. (The Look Around feature is discussed next.)

Looking around your destination

The Maps app gives you a kind of bird's-eye view of a location and its surrounding area. That overview is usually enough to allow you to get your bearings, but it's often helpful to come down from the clouds and get right onto the street to see exactly what's there. You could literally get right onto the street by traveling to the destination, but what if you want to look around before you go?

You can definitely do that by taking advantage of a Maps feature called Look Around, which shows you still images (taken from a vehicle or on foot) of whatever location you're interested in. (Look Around is Apple's equivalent or the Street View feature in Google Maps.) As I write this, Look Around is available in most major cities in the US and Canada, as well as in more than 60 locations around the world, including London, Edinburgh, Dublin, Tokyo, Sydney, Brussels, and Prague.

 To use Look Around, map your location and then tap the Look Around icon at the bottom of the screen (and shown in the margin). With Look Around enabled, use the following techniques to, well, look around:

>> **Pan the scene.** Drag a finger left or right, up or down.

>> **Move forward in the scene.** Tap the screen.

>> **Zoom in or out on the scene.** Pinch or spread two fingers on the screen.

>> **Switch to full-screen mode.** Tap the enter full screen mode icon (two arrows facing away from each other).

>> **Exit full-screen mode:** Tap the exit full screen mode icon (two arrows facing toward each other).

>> **Exit Look Around:** Tap Done.

You are here: Mapping your current location

Go to your local mall and chances are that somewhere near the entrance you'll see a kiosk that contains a map that you can use to locate the store you want. To help you orient yourself, these maps almost always have a "You Are Here" marker that specifies the location on the map and, therefore, the location of *you*.

 When you're in an unfamiliar part of town or in a city you've never visited before, wouldn't it be great to come across a kiosk that has a "You Are Here" marker? Well, if you have your iPad with you, the Maps app can do that! Tap the tracking icon (shown in the margin). Maps navigates to your overall area and then displays a blue beacon that marks your exact location. Tap the tracking icon a second time and Maps orients the map to face in the same direction as your iPad and also rotates the map along with your iPad.

TECHNICAL STUFF

How does your iPad know your current location? It's hideously complex, but it boils down to your iPad having three (or four) internal hardware doodads that can pick up location information from devices. The internal doohickeys are the Bluetooth and Wi-Fi antennas for all iPads, plus the GPS (Global Positioning System) and cellular antennas, if your iPad comes with cellular network hardware. The Bluetooth, Wi-Fi, and cellular antennas pick up location data from nearby Bluetooth beacons, Wi-Fi hotspots, and cellular network towers, respectively. The GPS receiver gets its location data from in-orbit GPS satellites.

Putting a contact on the map

When you add a contact to your iPad's Contacts app (see Chapter 11), you can include a street address for that person or business. That's cool, but it's even cooler to know that you can map that address by following three measly steps:

1. **From your iPad's Home screen, tap the Contacts icon.**

2. **Tap the contact you want to work with.**

   The Contacts app displays the contact data for the person or business.

3. **Tap the street address that you want to map.**

   Your iPad switches to Maps and drops a pin on the contact's address.

Mapping an address from an email message

If you receive an email message that includes a street address (say, as part of the sender's signature), you might want to know where that address is located. You could copy the address from the message and then paste it into the Search Maps text box in the Maps app, but there's no need to go to that much trouble. Instead, you can follow these much easier steps:

1. **In the Mail app, display the message that includes the address.**

2. **If the address is displayed as a link (that is, it's underlined), tap the address and skip the next step. Otherwise, long-press the address.**

   When you long-press the address, Mail shows a map preview of the location and displays a list of actions.

3. **Tap Open in Maps.**

   Maps opens and drops a pin on the address.

TIP

If you want Maps to provide directions to the location, long-press the address in the message and then tap Get Directions.

Saving a location as a favorite

If you know the address of the location you want to map, you can add a pushpin for that location by opening Maps and running a search on the address. That is, tap the Search Maps box, type the address, and then tap the location in the search results.

That's no big deal for one-time-only searches, but what about a location you map frequently? Typing that address over and over would get old in a hurry, I assure you. You can save time and tapping by telling Maps to save the location in its favorites list, which means you can access it with just a few taps.

Use either of the following techniques to add a location to the favorites list:

» Map the location you want to save and then tap Add to Favorites at the bottom of the location's information card.

» In the Favorites section that appears under the Search Maps text box, tap Add, search for the location you want to add, and tap it in the search results. Use the Details pane to name the favorite, and then tap Done.

To map a favorite location, follow these steps:

1. **If you have a location's information card displayed, tap X (close) in the upper-right corner to close the card.**

2. **If you don't see the favorite you want in the Favorites section (just below the Search Maps text box), tap More.**

   Maps displays the Favorites pane.

3. **Tap the location you want to map.**

   Maps displays the appropriate map and adds a pin for the location.

Sharing a map

To send someone a map via email, text message, AirDrop, or some other sharing method, follow these steps:

1. **Map the location you want to send.**

2. **In the location's information card, tap Share.**

   Maps displays a list of ways to share the map.

3. **Tap the method you want to use to share the map.**

   If the method you choose is not text-based (if you choose AirDrop, for example), you're done.

4. **If the method is text-based (such as an email or text), fill in the rest of your message and send it.**

Mapping locations with Siri voice commands

The Siri voice-activated assistant (see Chapter 14) can be used to control Maps with straightforward voice commands. You can display a location, get directions, and even display traffic information. Long-press the top button until Siri appears.

Here are some commands you can use for mapping locations:

» **To display a location in Maps:** Say "Show *location*" (or "Map *location*" or "Find *location*" or "Where is *location*"), where *location* is an address, a name, or a Maps favorite.

» **To get directions:** Say "Directions to *location*," where *location* is an address, a name, or a Maps favorite.

» **To see the current traffic conditions:** Say "Traffic *location*," where *location* can be a specific place or somewhere local, such as "around here" or "nearby."

» **To get your current location:** Say "Where am I?" or "Show my current location."

Getting There from Here: Navigating with Maps

You'll often map locations just to see where they are. However, most of the time, you'll bring up a location on the map because you want to go there, by car, transit, walking, or whatever.

When you map a destination — using an address search, a name search, a dropped pin, or a tap on a contact or email address — and you know your way around town, just knowing where the destination is located might be enough to enable you to navigate there on your own.

But if the destination is far away or in an unfamiliar town, you'll likely need some help with navigation duties. Maps can ride shotgun with you not only by showing you a route to the destination but also by providing the distance and time it should take and by giving you street-by-street, turn-by-turn instructions, whether you're driving or walking. It's one of the sweetest Maps features, and the next few sections provide the details.

Getting directions to a location

Here are the basic steps to follow to get directions to a location:

1. **Use Maps to add a pushpin for your destination.**

   Use whatever method works best for you: search for an address or a name, drop a pin, tap a contact or email address, or tap a favorite.

2. **On the location's information card, tap Directions.**

   Maps displays several possible routes, as shown in Figure 13-3.

3. **To use a different starting point:**

   a. *Tap the From location (which defaults to My Location, meaning your current location).* Maps opens the Change Stop pane.

   b. *In the Search box, start typing the name or address of the new location.*

   c. *Tap the location when it appears in the search results.* Maps returns to the routes and updates them to account for your new starting point.

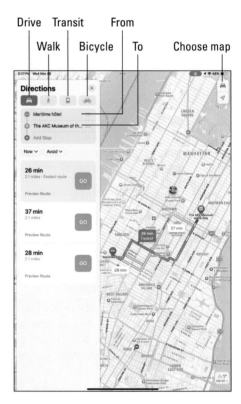

FIGURE 13-3:
Maps offers a few driving routes originating from your current location.

4. **Tap the icon for the type of directions you want: drive, walk, transit, or bicycle.**

   These icons are labeled in Figure 13-3.

5. **To add a stop to your journey:**

   a. *Tap Add Stop.* Maps opens the Add Stop pane.

   b. *In the Search box, start typing the name or address of the stop.*

   c. *Tap the stop location when it appears in the search results.* Maps returns to the routes and updates them to include your new stop.

6. **To change the order of a route stop, use the stop's drag button (the three horizontal lines on the right side of the stop) to drag the stop to the location you prefer.**

7. **Tap the Go button for the route you want to take.**

   Maps displays the first leg of the journey.

Maps features turn-by-turn directions. This means that as you approach each turn, Siri tells you what to do next, such as "In 400 feet, turn right onto Main Street." Maps also follows along the route, so you can see where you're going and which turn is coming up. By tapping the screen, you can see your estimated time of arrival, remaining travel time, and distance remaining.

Getting live traffic information

Okay, it's pretty amazing that your iPad can tell you precisely where you are and how to get somewhere else. However, in most cities, it's the getting somewhere else part that's the problem. Why? One word: traffic. Maps may tell you the trip should take 10 minutes, but that could easily turn into a half-hour or more if you run into a traffic jam.

That's life in the big city, right? Maybe not. If you're in a major North American city, Maps can most likely supply you with — wait for it — real-time traffic conditions. This amazing tool can help you avoid traffic messes and find alternative routes to your destination. The Maps app can also display traffic construction spots, and it gathers real-time information from Maps users to generate even more accurate traffic data. If you're in the middle of turn-by-turn directions, Maps will even recognize an upcoming traffic delay and offer an alternative route around it!

To see the traffic data, tap the choose map icon that appears above the tracking icon in the upper-right corner of the screen (refer to Figure 13-3). The icon changes depending on the currently selected map (drive, walk, transit, or bicycle).

In the Choose Map dialog that appears, tap Driving (if it's not selected already) and then tap X (close).

Maps now displays the following:

>> An orange line to indicate traffic slowdowns.

>> A red line to indicate very heavy traffic.

>> Roadwork icons (black exclamation points inside yellow circles) to indicate construction sites. Tap a roadwork icon to see more information about the work, as shown in Figure 13-4.

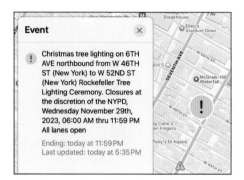

FIGURE 13-4:
Tap a roadwork icon to see info about the construction.

Getting directions with Siri voice commands

You can also use Siri to get directions and display traffic information. Long-press the top button until Siri appears.

Here are the commands you can use:

>> **To get directions:** Say "Directions to *location*," where *location* is an address, a name, or a Maps favorite.

>> **To see the current traffic conditions:** Say "Traffic *location*," where *location* can be a specific place or somewhere local, such as "around here" or "nearby."

Chapter **14**

Taking Control

When you want your iPad to do your bidding, you usually put the magic of multitouch to work: You tap this, double-tap that, swipe something else, and so on. These and other touchscreen gestures such as pinching and spreading aren't difficult, but doesn't it sometimes feel like you have to perform a seemingly endless sequence of gestures to accomplish some tasks? We're all going to end up with calluses on our fingers if we keep this up!

Or you can try a smarter approach and take advantage of some iPad features that drastically reduce or even eliminate the number of gestures you perform to make some tasks happen.

The first of these features is Control Center, which you can open with a quick swipe. Control Center offers one- or two-tap access to many common iPad settings, including Wi-Fi, Bluetooth, Focus, brightness, and volume.

The second feature is Siri, the intelligent, voice-activated virtual personal assistant living like a kind of digital genie inside your iPad. Siri responds to your voice commands for tasks such as opening an app, setting an alarm, scheduling an appointment, and retrieving information. It sounds like the stuff of science fiction and, well, I suppose it is.

Finally, you can also dictate text instead of typing it using the virtual keyboard.

In this chapter, you investigate all these ways of controlling your iPad.

Controlling Your iPad from Control Center

Your iPad is jammed to the hilt with useful tools and features. That's a good thing, but most of the time those tools require several swipes and a few taps to access. Those actions aren't a big deal for tools you use only every now and then, but they can become tedious if you have tools that you use constantly.

That tedium is likely why the iPadOS programmers decided to fix the problem by creating Control Center. This special screen offers quick and easy access to no less than 15 of the most useful iPad tools. And when I say "quick and easy," what I really mean is a swipe. That is, you swipe down from the top-right corner of any screen (even the lock screen or an app screen) to open Control Center.

TIP

To deny access to Control Center from the lock screen, choose Settings ⟹ Touch ID & Passcode (or Face ID & Passcode). Then, in the Allow Access When Locked section, tap the Control Center switch off.

REMEMBER

If Control Center doesn't work for you from an app screen, choose Settings ⟹ Control Center and then tap the Access within Apps switch on. Frustratingly, some apps disallow access to Control Center. When that happens, you'll have to swipe up from the bottom of the screen to go back to the Home screen, and then swipe down from the upper-right corner to display Control Center.

Figure 14-1 shows Control Center, but note that your version might display more or fewer icons depending on your iPad model and iPadOS version. To close Control Center, tap outside it.

The top-left portion of Control Center displays a group of icons representing your iPad's radios:

FIGURE 14-1:
Control Center is a mere swipe away.

>> **Airplane mode:** Toggles airplane mode on and off (refer to Chapter 15).

>> **AirDrop:** Displays a menu of AirDrop settings (refer to Chapter 12). You see this icon if your iPad is not a Wi-Fi + Cellular model.

>> **Cellular data:** Toggles the use of cellular data on and off (refer to Chapter 15). You see this icon instead of the AirDrop icon when your iPad is a Wi-Fi + Cellular model.

TIP

Long-press anywhere in the antennas group to expand the group. If your iPad is a Wi-Fi + Cellular model, the expanded group includes icons for AirDrop and Personal Hotspot (refer to Chapter 12).

>> **Wi-Fi:** Disconnects from the current Wi-Fi network (refer to Chapter 15). Tap this icon again to reconnect to the network.

>> **Bluetooth:** Disconnects from all Bluetooth devices (refer to Chapter 15). Tap this icon again to turn the Bluetooth antenna back on. Note that you'll need to reconnect to any devices that went into sleep mode while your iPad's Bluetooth was turned off.

The top-right portion of Control Center displays another group that contains the music controls: previous, play, and next. You also get an AirPlay icon (shown in the margin) that you can tap to display a list of AirPlay speakers or Apple TVs on your network.

Long-press the music control group to display an expanded version that shows more detail about what's currently playing and includes two sliders: one for controlling where you are in the song and one for controlling the volume.

The rest of Control Center consists of individual icons arranged below the previous two groups. Here's a quick summary of what's available:

>> **Rotation Lock:** Toggles your iPad's rotation lock on and off (refer to Chapter 18).

>> **Screen Mirroring:** Displays a menu of nearby Apple TVs or other compatible devices to which you can mirror your iPad's screen (refer to Chapters 8 and 9).

>> **Brightness:** Controls the screen brightness (refer to Chapter 15). Long-press the Brightness slider to get a larger slider and buttons that toggle the following features: Dark Mode, Night Shift, and True Tone (all covered in Chapter 15).

>> **Volume:** Controls the volume of whatever's playing on your iPad. Long-press the Volume slider to get a bigger version of the slider that gives you a tad more precision.

>> **Focus:** Displays buttons for each focus you've set up. Tap a focus to toggle it on and off. Each focus also has a more icon (three horizontal dots) that you can tap to display options for controlling the length of the focus. There's also the New Focus button, which you can tap to create a focus. (Refer to Chapter 15 to learn about Focus.)

>> **Silent Mode:** Toggles silent mode on and off. When your iPad is in silent mode, most sound output is disabled, but you still hear alarms and the audio portion of any media you play.

>> **Timer:** Opens the Clock app with the Timers tab displayed (refer to Chapter 12). Long-press the timer icon to create a timer without switching to the Clock app: Use the slider to set the timer duration, and then tap Start.

>> **Notes:** Opens the Notes app and starts a new note (refer to Chapter 12). Long-press the Notes icon to display a list of note types you can create: New Note, New Checklist, New Photo, and Scan Document.

>> **Camera:** Opens the Camera app. Long-press the Camera icon to display a list of shooting modes: Selfie, Video, Photo, Portrait Selfie (iPad Pro only) or Slo-mo (all other iPads).

TIP

The preceding icons are what you get in a default configuration of Control Center. iPadOS enables you to remove some of these icons, and it also offers quite a few other icons that aren't displayed by default. To customize Control Center to suit your working (or playing) style, follow these steps:

1. **Choose Settings ⇨ Control Center.**

2. **If you use the Home app, tap the Show Home Controls switch on to add the Home app's controls to Control Center.**

3. **To remove an icon from Control Center, tap the red remove icon (–) to the left of the icon name in the Included Controls section and then tap the Remove button that appears.**

4. **To add an icon to Control Center, tap the green add icon (+) to the left of the icon name in the More Controls section.**

5. **In the Included Controls section, you can change the position of any icon by dragging up or down the three horizontal lines that appear to the right of the icon name.**

Controlling Your iPad with Voice Commands? Siri-ously!

You can make things happen on your iPad via voice commands by using the Siri app, which not only lets you launch apps but also gives you voice control over web searching, appointments, contacts, reminders, map navigation, text messages, notes, and much more.

Getting started with Siri

First, make sure that Siri is enabled by choosing Settings ⇨ Siri & Search and then tapping the Press Top Button for Siri switch on. When iPadOS asks you to confirm that you want to use Siri, tap Enable Siri.

While you're here, you might want to tap Listen For and then tap one of the following:

>> **"Hey Siri":** Tap this option to start Siri by saying the phrase "Hey Siri."

>> **"Siri" or "Hey Siri":** Tap this option to start Siri by saying the word "Siri" or the phrase "Hey Siri."

Either way, your iPad then takes you through a brief setup procedure to ensure that Siri recognizes your voice.

Also, you should tell Siri who you are so that when you say references such as "home" and "work," Siri knows what you're talking about. In the Siri & Search screen, tap My Information, and then tap your card in the Contacts list.

Summoning Siri

You activate Siri by using any of the following techniques:

>> Long-pressing the top button

>> Saying "Hey Siri" or "Siri" (assuming you enabled this feature in the Siri settings, as I describe in the preceding section)

>> Tapping twice on the outside of an Apple AirPod

>> Long-pressing the microphone button on a Bluetooth headset

WARNING

You can invoke Siri from the lock screen, but you might consider this feature a mixed blessing. Not having to type a passcode to get Siri to do its thing is convenient. On the other hand, if your iPad ends up with the wrong person, that person would be able to use Siri to send an email or a message in your name, post to Facebook, or tweet, bypassing whatever passcode security you thought was in place. If you find this potential scenario scary, choose Settings ⇨ Siri & Search and tap the Allow Siri When Locked switch off. For more on Settings, read Chapter 15.

TIP

Siri is often easier to use if you define relationships within it. So, for example, instead of saying "Call Sandy Evans," you can more naturally say "Call mom." You can define relationships in two ways:

>> **Via the Contacts app:** Open the Contacts app, tap your contact card, tap Edit, tap Add Related Name, and then tap the relationship you want to use. Tap the blue more icon to open the contacts list and then tap the person you want to add to the field.

>> **Via Siri:** Activate Siri, say *"Name is my relationship,"* where *Name* is the person's name as given in your Contacts list, and *relationship* is the connection, such as *wife, husband, spouse, partner, brother, sister, mother,* or *father.* When Siri asks you to confirm, say "Yes."

What happens next is up to you. You can ask a wide range of questions or issue voice commands. Note that after you ask your first question, the Siri orb stays onscreen in the lower-right corner, although Siri stops listening after it answers your query. Tap the orb to put Siri back in listening mode.

Siri on the iPad can also launch apps — Apple's own as well as third-party apps. You might say, "Show me how to get home," and Siri will fire up Maps to help you on your way. Or you can say, "Find a good Italian restaurant near Barbara's house," and Siri will serve up a list, sorted by Yelp rating. Using Open Table, Siri can even make a restaurant reservation.

Apple has also opened up Siri to third-party app developers. For example, you can have Siri arrange a ride through Uber or Lyft, or pay a debt on your behalf through Apple or apps such as Venmo or Square Cash.

If you ask about a favorite sports team, Siri will retrieve the score of the team's last game or the game in progress. And if you're rummaging through a longish email that you can't quite get through at the moment, you can have Siri set a reminder for you to follow up later in the evening.

Figuring out what to ask

The beauty of Siri is that there's no designated protocol you must follow when talking to it. Asking, "Will I need an umbrella tomorrow?" produces the same result as, "What is the weather forecast around here?" Siri makes its share of mistakes, of course, but Apple's long-view approach is making Siri better at understanding the meaning of your words.

Another cool feature is that Siri can identify the name and artist of the musical track that's playing. Just ask Siri what song is playing and it'll name that tune. When the song is properly identified, you even get a chance to buy it.

If you're not sure what to ask, invoke Siri and then say "Help." Siri displays the Siri's Here to Help dialog, which you can tap to display a web page that has some sample questions or commands. You can tap any of the links on the page to see even more samples.

Here are some ways Siri can lend a hand . . . um, I mean a voice:

- » **FaceTime:** "FaceTime *phone number*" or "FaceTime my spouse."
- » **Music:** "Play Frank Sinatra" or "Play Apple Music." "What song is this?" "Rate this song three stars."
- » **Messages:** "Send a message to Nancy to reschedule lunch."
- » **Apple Pay:** "Apple Pay $10 to Johnny Appleseed."
- » **Translation:** "Translate 'I miss you so' in French."
- » **Sports:** "Did the Warriors win?"
- » **Calendar:** "Set up a meeting for 9 a.m. to discuss funding."
- » **Reminders:** "Remind me to take my medicine at 8 a.m. tomorrow."
- » **Maps:** "Find an ATM near here."
- » **Mail:** "Mail the tenant about the recent rent check."
- » **Photos:** "Show me the photos I took at Samuel's birthday party."
- » **Stocks:** "What's Apple's stock price?"
- » **Web search:** "Who was the 19th president of the United States?"
- » **Knowledge:** "How many calories are in a blueberry muffin?"
- » **Clock:** "Wake me up at 8:30 in the morning."
- » **Trivia:** "Who won the Academy Award for Best Actor in 2003?"
- » **X:** "Send tweet, 'Going on vacation,' smiley-face emoticon" or "What is trending on X?"

TIP

If you have trouble getting Siri to understand your voice (or if you're unable to speak), you can still use Siri by typing your requests. To activate this feature, choose Settings ⇨ Accessibility ⇨ Siri, and then tap the Type to Siri switch on.

Siri also seeks your permission before sending a dictated message. That's a safe-guard you might come to appreciate. However, if you dislike the extra step, you can turn off this safeguard by choosing Settings ⇨ Siri & Search ⇨ Automatically Send Messages, and then tapping the Automatically Send Messages switch on.

Making Siri smarter

From Settings ⇨ Siri & Search ⇨ Language, you can tell Siri which language you want to converse in. Siri is available in English (with many country variations), as well as versions of Chinese, Danish, Dutch, Finnish, French, German, Hebrew, Italian, Japanese, Korean, Malay, Norwegian, Portuguese, Russian, Spanish, Swedish, Thai, and Turkish.

You can tap Siri Responses to request voice feedback from Siri all the time (tap Prefer Spoken Responses), just when you're using a hands-free headset (tap Prefer Silent Responses), or automatically, that is, let Siri figure it out (tap Automatic).

You can tap Siri Voice to choose whether Siri has a male or female voice. If you're using English, you can even choose Siri's accent: American, Australian, British, Indian, Irish, or South African.

Touchless Text: Dictating Your Writing

All iPads that run iPadOS offer a dictation function, so you can speak to your iPad and have the words you say translated into text. It's easy and works pretty well. Even if you're comfortable with the virtual keyboard or use an accessory keyboard, dictation is often the fastest way to get your words into your iPad.

When you want to use your voice to enter text, tap the microphone key (shown in the margin) on the virtual keyboard that appears in the app you're using. Begin speaking right away.

The first time you tap the microphone key, you might see a dialog asking if you want to enable dictation. You can always enable or disable dictation later. Go to Settings ⇨ General ⇨ Keyboard and tap the Enable Dictation switch on or off. If you set the switch off, you won't see the microphone key on the keyboard.

When you've finished dictating your text, tap the microphone key to end the dictation. (Dictation also turns itself off if it receives no voice input from you for 30 seconds.)

TIP

Here are a few of ways you can improve your dictation experience:

>> For punctuation, you can say the name of the mark you need, such as "comma" (,), "semicolon" (;), "colon" (:), "period" or "full stop" (.), "question mark" (?), "exclamation point" (!), "hyphen" (-), or "at sign" (@).

>> You can enclose text in parentheses by saying "open parenthesis," then the text, and then "close parenthesis."

- » To surround text with quotation marks, say "open quote", then the text, and then "close quote."

- » To render a word in all uppercase letters, say "all caps" and then say the word.

- » To start a new paragraph, say "new line."

- » You can have some fun by saying "smiley face" for :-), "winky face" for ;-), and "frowny face" for :-(.

- » The better your iPad hears you, the better your results will be:

  - A wired headset with a microphone is great when you have a lot of ambient noise nearby.

  - A Bluetooth headset or Apple's AirPods or AirPods Pro may be better than the built-in microphone.

  - If you use the iPad's built-in mic, make sure the iPad case or your fingers aren't covering it.

WARNING

When dictation is enabled, information is shared with Apple's servers if your iPad can't process speech locally. This hasn't stopped me from taking advantage of dictation, but if you have particular privacy concerns, it's helpful to keep this in mind.

5
The Secret Life of an iPad

IN THIS PART . . .

Explore the most useful iPad settings that aren't discussed in depth elsewhere in the book.

Peruse my comprehensive guide to troubleshooting the iPad.

IN THIS CHAPTER

» **Modifying your Apple ID settings**

» **Configuring settings for Wi-Fi, Bluetooth, and cellular connections**

» **Customizing your iPad's display settings**

» **Messing around with the settings for notifications, location, and Control Center**

» **Make sense of your iPad's most useful settings**

Chapter **15**

Tweaking Settings

hen you liberate a new iPad from its box and turn it on for the first time, you run through a short series of screens to configure a few settings, and then you're ready to go. One of the perks of getting an iPad is that you can be up-and-surfing (or whatever) in just a few minutes.

However, the cost of that short on-ramp is an iPad configured by Apple to suit the most common users. Yes, that mercifully brief setup procedure enabled you to customize your iPad a bit, but those options are just a few of the hundreds of settings offered by iPadOS via the Settings app. Yep: *hundreds*.

Sure, tons of those settings redefine the word *esoteric* and should come with a "For geeks only" label. However, just as many settings redefine the word *useful* and should have an "Everyone is welcome" label. You can take advantage of these more useful settings to make your iPad more efficient, less bothersome, and more suited to your personal style.

In this chapter, you break open the Settings app and explore what it has to offer to make your iPad life better. Because I cover some settings elsewhere in this book, I don't dwell on every setting here. Nor do I describe every setting in the order in which Apple lists them. But you still have plenty to digest to help you make the iPad your own.

Checking Out the Settings App

To get the party started, tap the Settings icon on your iPad's Home screen. When you first open Settings, you see a display something like Figure 15-1, with a scrollable list of categories and apps on the left and a pane on the right that corresponds to whichever category or app is selected (which, in Figure 15-1, is the General category). I say "something like" because Settings on your iPad may differ slightly from what's shown here.

TIP

In Figure 15-1, note the Search box near the top-left corner, just under the Settings heading. You use this box to search for settings, which is incredibly useful given that it's often impossible to remember where the Settings app hides some of its preferences. However, the Search box isn't displayed by default, for some bizarre reason. To reveal the Search box, drag the category list down a bit.

You must scroll down to see the entire list of categories and apps. Also, if you see a greater-than symbol (>) to the right of a setting, the setting has a bunch of options. Throughout this chapter, you tap such a setting to check out those options.

As you scroll to the bottom of the list on the left, you come to all the settings pertaining to some of the specific third-party apps you've added to the iPad. (See Chapter 10.) These settings aren't visible in Figure 15-1.

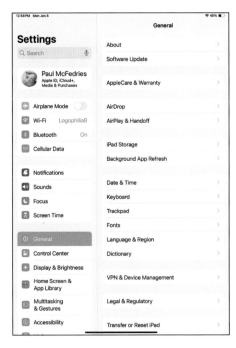

FIGURE 15-1:
The Settings app offers a list of categories and apps on the left and the settings for the selected category or app on the right.

We all have different collections of apps on our iPads, so settings related to those programs will also be different.

Apple ID Settings

The first thing to note in the Settings app is the section at the top with your Apple ID info. You'll see your name, your profile photo, and a partial description of the settings available in this category. Tap your name, and you'll find a variety of settings for both your Apple ID and Apple services, as shown in Figure 15-2.

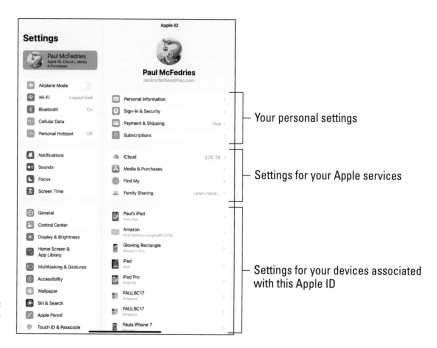

FIGURE 15-2:
Apple ID
Settings.

Here's a summary of the settings:

>> **Profile photo:** At the top of the Apple ID page, tap your profile photo (which, if you don't have a photo yet, will just be your initials) and then use the controls that appear to take a photo, choose an existing photo, create an image using emoji or text, or select one of the predefined images.

>> **Personal Information:** Edit the name, date of birth, and communication preferences associated with your Apple ID.

>> **Sign-In & Security:** Edit your Apple ID email addresses and phone numbers, change your password, and manage other security-related settings. In particular, if you're not using two-factor authentication, I highly recommend that you turn it on. Two-factor authentication means that Apple uses your specified trusted devices or phone numbers to verify your identity whenever you sign in to your Apple ID.

- » **Payment & Shipping:** Manage which credit cards you have attached to your iCloud account. Included is a place to enter your shipping address for Apple Store purchases.

- » **Subscriptions:** Manage your app subscriptions. In particular, you can cancel any subscription by tapping it and then tapping Cancel Subscription.

- » **iCloud:** Manage your iCloud settings (refer to Chapter 3). At the top you see your total iCloud storage and how much of it you've used. Tap Manage Account Storage to, well, manage your iCloud storage, taking note of all your iOS and iPadOS backups. If need be, you can buy more storage; tap Change Storage Plan to get started.

- » **Media & Purchases:** Tap this setting, tap View Account, and then enter your Apple ID password (or confirm your identity with Face ID or Touch ID, if you have either one set up) to see settings associated with media and purchases via the App Store, iTunes Store, and Apple Books.

- » **Find My:** Manage the Find My feature specific to the device you're using at the moment. At the very least, ensure that Find My iPad is turned on by selecting Find My ⇨ Find My iPad and then tapping the Find My iPad switch on. (It's also a good idea to tap the Send Last Location switch on, which saves a lost iPad's last location before its battery dies.) You can also set which of your Apple devices is used to determine where you are when it comes to sharing your location. You can also see everyone you might have shared your location with.

- » **Family Sharing:** Manage or set up your iCloud Family Sharing plan.

- » **Device list:** Every device associated with your Apple ID. Tap through to any of them and you'll see the device's Find My settings, model name, operating system version, and serial number. You can also remove any device from your account (except the iPad you're using) by tapping Remove from Account.

- » **Sign Out:** Sign out of your Apple ID. This usually means removing local copies of data such as calendars and contacts, but Settings give you the chance to retain any of this data (which is a good idea if you're just signing out temporarily).

Controlling Your iPad's Antennas

Your iPad's innards are stuffed with sensors and other electronic gewgaws, including some antennas that your iPad uses to exchange data. There's an antenna for Wi-Fi signals, another for Bluetooth connections, and a cellular antenna on iPad models that support cellular networks. The next few sections take you through a few settings for controlling your iPad's antennas.

Flying with airplane mode

Your iPad offers settings to keep you on the good side of air-traffic communications systems. No matter which iPad you have — Wi-Fi only or a model with cellular — you have airplane mode.

Using a cellular radio or Wi-Fi on an airplane is restricted to when the pilot says it's okay. But nothing is wrong with using an iPad on a plane to read, listen to music, watch videos, peruse pictures, or play games. None of these activities require Wi-Fi, Bluetooth, or cellular data, so go ahead and enable airplane mode by tapping the Airplane Mode switch on.

Enabling airplane mode initially disables each of the iPad's radios: Wi-Fi, Bluetooth, and cellular (depending on the model). While your iPad is in airplane mode, you can't surf the web, get a map location, send or receive emails, sync through iCloud, use the iTunes or App Store, or do anything else that requires an internet connection. If a silver lining exists here, it's that the iPad's long-lasting battery will last even longer — good news if the flight you're on is a lengthy one.

REMEMBER

One quirk of airplane mode is that if you turn it on and then enable Wi-Fi, Bluetooth, or both, iPadOS leaves those features enabled the next time you turn on airplane mode.

How do you know when airplane mode is on? The appearance of a tiny airplane icon on the status bar at the upper-right corner of the screen (and shown in the margin) is your reminder that airplane mode is turned on. Just remember to turn it off when you're back on the ground.

TIP

If in-flight Wi-Fi is available on your flight, which is increasingly the case, you can turn on Wi-Fi independently, as I describe in the next section, leaving the rest of your iPad's wireless radio safely disabled. Bluetooth, which I get to shortly, can also be enabled independently.

Working with Wi-Fi connections

Wi-Fi is typically the fastest wireless network you can use to surf the web, send email, and perform other internet tricks on the iPad. You use the Wi-Fi setting to determine which Wi-Fi networks are available to you and which one to join. To see your iPad's Wi-Fi settings, tap the Wi-Fi category in the Settings app.

At the top of the Wi-Fi settings page, you can tap the Wi-Fi switch to toggle the Wi-Fi antenna on and off. When the Wi-Fi switch is on, all Wi-Fi networks in range are displayed, as shown in Figure 15-3.

To the right of each network, you see three (or sometimes just two) icons:

>> **Lock:** Tells you the network is protected by a password. If you don't see this icon, it means you can join the network without entering a password. When you're in a hotel, at an airport, or at another location, you might still have to enter a password after joining even if the lock icon is not present.

>> **Signal strength:** Indicates the robustness of the network's signal (the more black bars in the icon, the greater the strength). A weak network signal usually means your connection will be slow and unreliable.

>> **Info:** Displays settings related to the network.

FIGURE 15-3:
When the Wi-Fi switch is on, you see a list of the nearby Wi-Fi networks.

WARNING

Be careful when joining open networks (such as those in coffee shops or other public places) as well as networks you don't know. Malicious actors might try to snoop on any unencrypted data on a network you don't control.

You can also turn on and off the Ask to Join Networks setting. However, networks your iPad is already familiar with are joined automatically (as long as the Auto-Join switch is on in the network's settings), whether the Ask to Join Networks feature is toggled on or off. If the Ask feature is off and no known networks are available, you have to select a new network manually. If the Ask feature is on, your iPad will ask if you want to join new networks as they become available. Either way, you see a list with the same Wi-Fi networks in range.

If you used a particular network automatically in the past but no longer want your iPad to join it, tap the info icon next to the network in question (in Wi-Fi settings) and then tap Forget This Network. The iPad develops a quick case of selective amnesia.

Sometimes you may want to connect to a network that's not shown on the Wi-Fi list. If that's the case, tap Other at the bottom of the network list and use the keyboard to enter the network name. Tap to choose the type of security setting the network is using (if any). If you're not sure what to choose, the default WPA2/WPA3 will usually do the job. Finally, type the network password and then tap Join.

WARNING

Connecting to unfamiliar open networks carries risks. Malicious hackers may be able to get to your personal or business data. Be careful when joining unknown networks, especially open ones.

Making Bluetooth connections

Of all the peculiar terms you may encounter in techdom, *Bluetooth* is one of my favorites. The name is derived from Harald Blåtand, a tenth-century Danish monarch, who, the story goes, helped unite warring factions. And, I'm told, *Blåtand* translates to *Bluetooth* in English. (Bluetooth is all about collaboration between different types of devices — get it?)

On the iPad, you can use Bluetooth to communicate wirelessly with a compatible Bluetooth headset, such as Apple's AirPods and AirPods Pro, or to use an optional wireless keyboard, such as Apple's Smart Keyboard. Such accessories are made by Apple and others.

To ensure that your iPad works with a Bluetooth device, it typically has to be wirelessly *paired,* or coupled, with the chosen device. If you're using a third-party accessory, follow the instructions that came with that device so it becomes *discoverable,* or ready to be paired with your iPad. Then, in the Settings app, tap the Bluetooth category and make sure the Bluetooth switch is on so

FIGURE 15-4:
Paired and nearby Bluetooth devices appear in the Bluetooth setting screen.

that the iPad can find such nearby devices and the devices can find the iPad. The nearby Bluetooth devices that your iPad finds are displayed in the Other Devices section of the Bluetooth settings screen, as shown in Figure 15-4. Once you pair with a device, it appears in the My Devices section.

Tap a Bluetooth device to initiate the pairing. (Unless the device already appears in the My Devices section, which means your iPad and the device are already paired so you're good to go.) In some cases, the Bluetooth device requires you to enter a passkey. (This is usually the case with Bluetooth keyboards, for example.) You won't need a passkey to pair every kind of device, though. You won't need a passkey when pairing the iPad with a wireless speaker, for example. Most Bluetooth devices work up to a range of about 30 feet and don't require line of sight.

 Unless you turn Bluetooth off, it's on by default. To see if it's on, pull down from the top-right corner of the screen to access Control Center. The Bluetooth icon (shown in the margin) shows white on a blue background in Control Center when Bluetooth is on. To disconnect any Bluetooth devices currently connected to your iPad, tap the Bluetooth icon in Control Center so that it turns black with a white background. Note, however, that this does not turn off Bluetooth on your iPad — it only disconnects from connected devices. To turn off Bluetooth, which saves battery life, go to Settings ⇨ Bluetooth and tap the Bluetooth switch off. If you want to disconnect a single Bluetooth device, choose Settings ⇨ Bluetooth, tap the device's info icon and then tap Disconnect.

One common Bluetooth conundrum is that once your iPad has paired with a Bluetooth device, your iPad will connect to that device automatically in the future. That sounds great, but what if you'd prefer to pair the Bluetooth device with something else — say, your iPhone or Mac? One solution would be to keep your iPad far away from the Bluetooth device, so that the connection doesn't happen automatically. Alternatively, you can tell your iPad to forget the device. In Settings ⇨ Bluetooth, tap the device's info icon and then tap Forget This Device.

Roaming among cellular data options

If you have a cellular model iPad, you'll see another group of settings. The options appear on the right pane of the Settings screen when you tap the Cellular Data category:

>> **Cellular Data:** If you know you don't need the cellular network when you're out and about or are in an area where you don't have access to the network, turn it off. Your battery will thank you later. But even if you have access to a speedy cellular network, be prudent; in a 4G environment where you can easily consume gobs of data, your data allowance may run out all too quickly. And if you haven't set up your cellular data plan yet, you can get started by tapping the carrier of your choice directly in Settings ⇨ Cellular Data. Data rates apply.

>> **Cellular Data Options:** You may unwittingly rack up lofty roaming fees when exchanging email, surfing with Safari, or engaging in other data-heavy activities while traveling abroad. Turn off Data Roaming to avoid such potential charges.

>> **Personal Hotspot:** Share your iPad's data connection with any other devices you carry. Just know that extra charges may apply — and even if they don't, you'll rack up that much extra data. You or the owner of the device piggybacking on your internet connection must enter the designated password generated by the iPad for the Hotspot connection to make nice. You can use the hotspot feature via Wi-Fi or Bluetooth, or by connecting a USB-C-to-USB or Lightning-to-USB cable. See Chapter 12 to find out how to use Personal Hotspot.

>> **SIM PIN:** The tiny *SIM,* or *Subscriber Identity Module,* card inside your iPad with cellular holds important data about your cellular account. To add a PIN or a

passcode to lock your SIM card, tap SIM PIN. That way, if someone gets hold of your SIM, the person can't use it in another iPad without the passcode.

REMEMBER

If you assign a PIN to your SIM, you have to enter it to turn the iPad on or off, which some might consider a minor hassle. And be aware that the SIM PIN is different from and may be in addition to any passcode you set for the iPad, as described later in this chapter.

>> **Current Period:** Tells you how much cellular data you've used in the current billing period. There's also a separate Current Period Roaming value.

>> **Apps:** Toggle cellular data for individual apps. When an app's switch is on, it means the app is authorized to use your iPad's cellular connection to transfer data; turn off an app's switch to force the app to wait until your iPad is connected to Wi-Fi to get its data.

>> **Wi-Fi Assist:** When on, this setting enables your iPad to automatically employ cellular data to enhance a weak Wi-Fi connection.

>> **iCloud Drive:** When on, this setting authorizes your iPad to use the cellular network to exchange documents and data with iCloud Drive.

>> **iCloud Backup:** When on, this setting authorizes your iPad to use the cellular network to back up to iCloud.

Managing Notifications

One of the hallmarks of our age is that everyone wants to get your attention. On your iPad, those requests for attention usually come in the form of *notifications,* which are "Hey, look over here!" signals that come in one, two, or sometimes all three of the following forms:

>> **Banner:** A text alert that appears at the top of the iPad screen.

>> **Sound:** A brief chime, chirp, or other sound effect.

>> **Badge:** A small, red circle with a white number inside it that appears in the upper-right corner of an app icon and sometimes in the app itself. The badge number tells you how many new app items you haven't yet seen (such as unread email messages in the Mail app).

At first, these notifications (I talk about how to manage them in Chapter 12) seem like a wonderful innovation because they help ensure that you don't miss anything important. Unfortunately, notifications also help ensure that you don't miss anything *un*important, either, which means they can quickly become a distracting nuisance. The secret to staying sane when working with your iPad is to manage your notifications before they start managing *you*.

Customizing all notifications

In the Settings app, tap the Notifications category to display a screen similar to the one shown in Figure 15-5.

The top of the Notifications screen offers the following settings that apply to your iPad's notifications as a whole:

FIGURE 15-5:
Use the Notifications settings to take control of your iPad's notifications.

>> **Display As:** Determines how notifications appear in the lock screen. Tap Count to see the total number of notifications at the bottom of the lock screen (tap the count to see the notifications); tap Stack to see the notifications piled on top of each other at the bottom of the lock screen (with the most recent notification on the top of the stack); or tap List to see the notifications as a list, with the most recent at the top of the list.

>> **Scheduled Summary:** Tap this setting and then tap the switch on to activate a notification summary, which displays your non-urgent notifications at the time you specify.

>> **Show Previews:** Tap this setting and then tap when you want your iPad to show previews in your notifications. A *preview* is a bit of the notification's underlying item, such as the beginning of an email or text or some of the particulars of an appointment.

>> **Screen Sharing:** This setting is off by default, which means you don't receive notifications while you're sharing your screen (such as when you mirror your iPad screen to a TV, as I describe in Chapter 8). That's probably for the best, but you can turn on this setting if you're expecting something important.

>> **Siri Suggestions:** Tap this setting and then tap the Allow Notifications switch off to disable Siri's suggestions for tasks you might want to do next. If you leave this switch on, you can use the app-specific switches to turn off Siri suggestions for particular apps.

Customizing app notifications

Other than the general notification settings I ran through in the preceding section, you manage notifications on an app-by-app basis. In the Notifications settings, tap an app to adjust its settings. In Figure 15-6, you see notification settings for the Calendar app, as indicated by the word Calendar at the top of the screen. Some apps may offer more options than you see here, while other apps may offer fewer options.

Here's a rundown of the settings shown in Figure 15-6, starting at the top:

FIGURE 15-6:
The notification settings for Calendar.

>> **Allow Notifications:** Tap this switch on or off to enable or disable notifications for the app.

>> **Always Deliver Immediately:** When this switch is on, iPadOS delivers time-based notifications right away and leaves them onscreen for an hour so you'll be much less likely to miss them.

>> **Alerts:** This section enables you to customize the notification alert options:

- Lock Screen: Deselect this check box if you don't want this app's notifications to appear on the lock screen.

- Notification Center: Deselect this check box if you don't want this app's notifications to appear in Notification Center.

- Banners: Deselect this check box if you don't want this app's notifications to appear onscreen as a banner.

- Banner Style: Choose between temporary banners, which stay at the top of your screen for a few seconds before automatically disappearing, and persistent banners, which stay at the top of your screen until you perform an action, such as flicking them away or tapping them to go to the app. Note that you see the Banner Style setting only if you leave the Banners check box selected.

- Sounds: Choose from a variety of sounds for many Apple notifications. Apps such as Instagram, however, give you control over only whether or not you hear the sound they chose.

- Badges: Display the number of pending alerts on the app's icon on your Home screen.

» **Show Previews:** See a preview of whatever you're being notified about. In the case of Instagram, the preview would be a thumbnail image of the post you're being alerted about.

» **Notification Grouping:** Allow your iPad to group notifications as it sees fit or to group them by app, or simply turn Notification Grouping off for the selected app.

» **Customize Notifications:** Choose which features of the app can generate notifications.

Apps that don't take advantage of the settings in Settings ⇨ Notifications can still offer notifications, but you'll have to scroll down to the apps section on the left side of Settings and tap the app you want to alter.

Minimizing distractions with Focus

Apple understands that sometimes you don't want to be bothered by notifications or other distractions, no matter how unobtrusive they might be. The result is a feature aptly named Focus, which you activate to silence your iPad's alerts and notifications, leaving you free to, yep, *focus* on your work.

You activate a focus via Control Center (refer to Chapter 14) by tapping Focus and then tapping the focus you want to turn on: Do Not Disturb, Personal, Driving, Work, or a custom focus you've created.

You configure a focus by tapping Settings ⇨ Focus, and then tapping the focus you want to customize:

» **Do Not Disturb:** Turns off all notifications, alerts, and calls until you deactivate the focus. In the settings, you can allow notifications from selected people and apps; customize the look of the lock screen and Home screen; schedule when Do Not Disturb kicks in and when it turns off; and add filters, which enable you to customize how certain apps or system settings work when Do Not Disturb is activated.

» **Driving:** Turns off all notifications, alerts, and calls while you're driving. In the settings, you can allow notifications from selected people.

» **Personal:** Turns off all notifications, alerts, and calls during your personal time. In the settings, you can allow notifications from selected people and apps; customize the look of the lock screen and Home screen; schedule when this focus turns on and off; and add filters.

>> **Work:** Turns off all notifications, alerts, and calls during your work time. In the settings, you can allow notifications from selected people and apps; customize the look of the lock screen and Home screen; schedule when this focus turns on and off; and add filters.

>> **Custom:** Tap + in the upper-right corner and then choose an area of focus such as Mindfulness or Reading. You can also choose Custom to create your own focus. Follow the screens to set up your new focus.

Location, Location, Location Services

By using the onboard Maps, Camera, or Reminders app (or any number of third-party apps), the iPad makes good use of knowing where you are. With Location Services turned on, your iPad has the capability to deliver traffic information and suggest popular destinations in your vicinity. And at your discretion, you can share your location with others.

The Wi-Fi–only iPad can find your general whereabouts by triangulating signals from Wi-Fi base stations and Bluetooth beacons. iPads with cellular capabilities use Wi-Fi, Bluetooth, plus built-in GPS to help determine your location.

If such statements creep you out a little, don't fret. To protect your right to privacy, when you launch an app that would like to use location data, you see a dialog similar to the one displayed in Figure 15-7. Here, the Calendar app is requesting permission to use the iPad's location tools to determine your location. Most of the time you see the following four options:

>> **Precise:** Determines whether the app can use your exact location (to within about 10 meters, or about 30 feet) or just an approximate location (to within about 2 kilometers — about a mile and a quarter — in urban locations and to within about 10 kilometers — about 6 miles — in rural locations). Tap Precise to toggle this setting between on and off.

>> **Allow Once:** Allows the app to use your location just this time. The app will ask again the next time you run it.

>> **Allow While Using App:** Allows the app to use your location, but only when you're using the app. When you switch to a different app, the previous app no longer has access to your location.

>> **Don't Allow:** Prevents the app from using your location.

The iPadOS service that manages location data is called Location Services, and you can customize this service by tapping Settings ⇨ Privacy & Security ⇨ Location Services. You have two ways to make your location more private:

>> **Shut off all app access to your location:** Tap the Location Services switch off.

>> **Shut off access to your location for a specific app only:** Tap the app, and then tap Never. Alternatively, you can choose Ask Next Time Or When I Share (to force the app to ask you permission) or While Using the App (to allow the app to use your location only when you have the app onscreen). You can also toggle access to your specific location by toggling the Precise Location switch off or on.

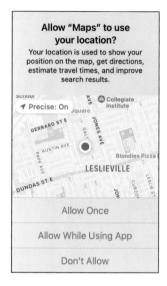

FIGURE 15-7:
Maps asks permission to know where you are.

Customizing Your iPad's Look and Feel

New iPad users often report that, once they get a handle on working with the touchscreen and its various gestures, using an iPad feels natural. It feels like this is the way we're *supposed* to operate a computer. However, that inherent naturalness doesn't mean that how the iPad looks, what it sounds like, and how you interact with it are necessarily just right for you. As the next few sections show, the Settings app offers quite a few preferences that just might make your iPad even easier to work with.

Setting sound settings

In the Settings app, the Sounds category enables you to customize your iPad's sonic output. Here's a quick look at the options available in the Sounds settings:

>> **Silent Mode:** Tap this switch on to prevent your iPad from playing sounds such as notifications, ringtones, and system alerts. This setting is a bit of a misnomer, however, because your iPad will still play sounds associated with timers, alarms, music, and videos.

>> **Ringtone and Alerts:** Drag this slider to set the volume of the ringtone that plays when a call comes in (left is quieter, right is louder).

>> **Change with Buttons:** Leave this switch off to lock the ringer volume, which means that pressing the volume buttons on the side of the iPad will have no effect on the ringer volume. Tap this switch on to use the volume buttons to adjust the ringer volume.

>> **Ringtone, Text Tone, and so on:** For each of the events in this list, tap the event and then tap the sound you want to hear when that event occurs. You can purchase sounds by tapping Tone Store, which take you to the Tones section of iTunes Store. To turn off the event sound, instead, tap None (not available for the Ringtone event).

TIP

To set a custom ringtone or text tone or both for one of your contacts, open the Contacts app, tap that person, and then tap Edit. For a custom ringtone, tap Ringtone, tap the sound effect you want to use, and then tap Done. For a custom text tone, tap Text Tone, tap a sound effect, and then tap Done. Tap Done to exit edit mode.

>> **Keyboard Clicks:** Tap this switch off to silence the (truly annoying) sound your iPad makes when you tap a key on the virtual keyboard.

>> **Lock Sound:** Tap this switch off to silence the sound your iPad makes when you lock and unlock it.

>> **Headphone Safety:** If you use headphones with your iPad, tap this setting, tap the Reduce Loud Sounds switch on, and then select a decibel value. iPadOS will monitor the headphones' audio and automatically turn down any sounds that are over the decibel value you selected.

Enabling dark mode and other display customizations

If you've ever used your iPad in a dark or even somewhat dark room, you no doubt noticed just how incredibly *bright* the screen is. In fact, the darker your surroundings, the more annoyingly bright the screen seems. Even turning down the screen brightness (as I discuss shortly) doesn't really help because the screen content (particularly the background) is still white or light gray (or both).

The secret to using your iPad in a dark or near-dark environment is to turn on *dark mode*, which essentially reverses the color scheme by turning the white and light gray background colors to dark gray and black, respectively. Dark mode also reduces the saturation of the rest of the screen colors. The result is that it's much easier to look at the screen. Figure 15-8 shows the Settings app's Display & Brightness page in dark mode.

To configure dark mode, tap the Settings app's Display & Brightness category, and then use the following settings in the Appearance group:

>> **Dark:** Select this option to immediately switch to dark mode. Select the Light option to return to the default light mode.

>> **Automatic:** Leave this switch on to have your iPad automatically switch between light mode and dark mode depending on the ambient light in your environment.

>> **Options:** Tap this setting to schedule when your iPad switches to dark mode. The default is Sunset to Sunrise, but you can also tap Custom Schedule and then use the time selectors to choose when your iPad switches to dark mode and back to light mode.

FIGURE 15-8:
The Settings app in dark mode.

Some apps support dynamic type, which means that if you change your iPad's default text size (say, by increasing the size to compensate for eyesight problems), those apps will honor that change by adjusting the app text accordingly. In the Display & Brightness settings, you adjust the default type size by tapping Text Size and then dragging the slider that appears. You can also ask dynamic-type apps to display all their text in bold by tapping the Bold Text switch on.

Use the Brightness slider to control how lit up your iPad's display appears. For example, you might want to increase the brightness when you're outside or in a brightly lit room; conversely, in a darker environment you might want to turn down the brightness. You can let your iPad automatically handle changes to color temperature and intensity based on ambient light conditions by leaving the True Tone switch on.

WARNING

You might be tempted to just crank up the screen brightness to the max and leave it there. Who doesn't want a bright, vibrant screen? Alas, the brightest screens exact a trade-off: Before you drag that slider all the way to the right, remember that a brighter screen saps the life from your battery more quickly.

Here's a quick look at the most important of the rest of the Display & Brightness settings (not all of which might be available on your iPad):

>> **Night Shift:** Turn this setting on (either manually or via a schedule) to shift the display colors to the warmer end of the color spectrum. Doing this at night can, at least in theory, help you get a better night's sleep.

>> **Auto-Lock:** Sets the amount of idle time that must elapse before the iPad automatically locks. The default is 2 minutes, but your other choices are 15 minutes, 10 minutes, 5 minutes, and Never.

WARNING

If you've set up your iPad with a passcode, Touch ID, or Face ID (as I describe in Chapter 17), don't choose Never for the Auto-Lock setting because if you accidentally leave your iPad unlocked and unattended, some passing snoop will have free rein with your device and what's on it.

>> **Lock/Unlock:** When on, this switch tells iPadOS to lock and unlock your iPad when you close and open a cover such as an Apple Smart Cover. (You see this switch only if you use such a cover.)

>> **Display Zoom:** Click this setting to choose a view for your iPad display. Default increases all the iPad text, while More Space creates extra space between items. Tap Done, confirm your choice, and then wait for your iPad to restart to put the new view into effect.

Customizing the Home screen and dock

In Settings, the Home Screen & App Library category has the following settings that can control various aspects of the Home screen, dock, and App Library:

>> **Use Large App Icons:** Leave this switch off to have smaller icons on each of your Home screen pages but with more space between each icon. That extra space can help prevent accidentally tapping the wrong icon. Tap this switch on to have larger icons on each Home screen page but with less space between each icon. Larger icons give you a bigger tap target for each app.

>> **Newly Downloaded Apps:** The default location for new apps is the Home screen, so in this section the Add to Home Screen option is selected; if you prefer that your new apps just go to App Library, tap App Library Only.

>> **Show App Library in Dock:** Tap this switch off to remove App Library from the dock. You can still display App Library by swiping left on the last Home screen page.

>> **Show Suggested and Recent Apps in Dock:** Display on the right side of the dock apps that Siri thinks you might want, as well as recently opened apps. Learn more about this feature in Chapter 1.

>> **Show in App Library:** Tap this switch on to configure App Library to show notification badges on app icons that have this notification type enabled.

Sprucing up your iPad with wallpaper

A *wallpaper* is a pattern, an image, or a color applied to the background of each Home screen and the background of the lock screen. The Home screen and lock screen wallpapers can be the same or different, although note that when you're specifying a lock screen wallpaper, you can also add one or more widgets that show things like the current temperature or today's calendar events.

In the Settings app's Wallpaper category, you can tap Customize to modify your current wallpaper, or you can follow these steps to create a new wallpaper:

1. **Tap Add New Wallpaper.**

   The Add New Wallpaper dialog appears, as shown in Figure 15-9.

2. **Tap a wallpaper category at the top of the dialog (Photos, Photo Shuffle, and so on), or tap an item in one of the sections (Featured, Suggested Photos, and so on).**

   A sample image fills the screen.

3. **Swipe left or right to see the available wallpapers.**

4. **When you find the wallpaper you want to use, tap Add.**

   Settings asks if you want to use the wallpaper as a pair, which means the wallpaper is applied in the same way to both your Home screen and your lock screen.

5. **Do one of the following:**

   • *To apply the same wallpaper to the Home screen and lock screen, tap Set as Wallpaper Pair.*

   • *To modify the chosen wallpaper for your Home screen, tap Customize Home Screen. Choose a customization option — Color, Gradient, Photo, or Blur — and then tap Done.*

   Your new wallpaper appears in the list, with a thumbnail of the lock screen on the left and a thumbnail of the Home screen on the right.

FIGURE 15-9: Settings offers a wide variety of wallpaper categories.

TIP

You can also customize and create wallpapers from the lock screen. With the lock screen displayed, long-press any part of the screen until you see your wallpaper collection. Tap Customize to tweak the current wallpaper, or tap + to add a new wallpaper.

Once you've created wallpapers, you can work with them as follows:

>> **Switch to another wallpaper:** Tap Settings ⇨ Wallpaper, swipe the wallpaper list horizontally until you see the wallpaper you want to use, and then tap Set as Current.

>> **Modify an existing wallpaper:** Tap Settings ⇨ Wallpaper, swipe the wallpaper list horizontally until you see the wallpaper you want to modify, and then tap Customize on the lock screen thumbnail. If you customized your Home screen wallpaper separately, you can also tap Customize on the Home screen thumbnail.

Making Your iPad More Accessible

Apple designed the iPad to be easy to use, but that doesn't mean it's easy to use for *everyone*. If you or a loved one have issues with vision, motor control, hearing, or speech, those issues can make using an iPad frustrating at best or nearly impossible at worst.

Fortunately, Apple also designed the iPad so that it can be configured to assist with or compensate for many vision, motor control, hearing, and speech issues. In Settings, the Accessibility section not only enables you to modify many aspects of the iPad to suit your needs but also offers quite a few tools that augment and enhance the iPad experience for those who require extra assistance.

There's a lot to dig into here, and space limitations mean that I can't cover every setting, so I encourage you to explore the various choices on your own, especially if you or a loved one have a particular area of need.

VoiceOver

The VoiceOver screen reader describes aloud what's on the screen. It can read email messages, web pages, and more. With VoiceOver active (in Settings, tap Accessibility ⇨ VoiceOver, and then tap the Voiceover switch on), you tap an item on the screen to select it. VoiceOver places a black rectangle around the item and either speaks the name or describes an item. For example, if you tap Display &

Brightness, the VoiceOver voice speaks the words "Display and brightness button." VoiceOver also lets you know when you rotate the iPad into landscape or portrait mode and when your screen is locked or unlocked.

Within the VoiceOver settings, you have several options. For instance, you can drag a Speaking Rate slider to speed up or slow down the speech. You can also change the default voice (tap Speech and then Voice), adjust the pitch (tap Speech and then drag the Pitch slider), and much more.

You have to know a new set of finger gestures when VoiceOver is on, which may seem difficult, especially when you first start using VoiceOver. This requirement makes a lot of sense because you want to be able to hear descriptions on the screen before you activate buttons. Different VoiceOver gestures use different numbers of fingers, and Apple recommends that you experiment with different techniques to see what works best for you. After enabling VoiceOver, you can tap and then double-tap the VoiceOver Practice button to display the VoiceOver Practice screen and practice the gestures.

I list just a few of the many available gestures here (refer to Accessibility ⇨ VoiceOver ⇨ Commands ⇨ Touch Gestures):

>> **Tap:** Speak the item.

>> **Double-tap:** Activate a selected icon or button to launch an app, turn a switch from on off, and more.

>> **Triple-tap:** Long-press a selected item.

>> **Two-finger tap:** Toggle speaking on and off.

>> **Rotate two fingers:** This gesture has multiple outcomes that depend on how you set the rotor control gesture. To select your options, head to Settings ⇨ Accessibility ⇨ VoiceOver ⇨ Rotor. The rotor control gesture is similar to turning a dial: You rotate two fingertips on the screen. The purpose is to switch to a different set of commands or features. Suppose you're reading text in an email. By alternately spinning the rotor, you can switch between hearing the body of a message read aloud word by word or character by character. After you set the parameters, flick up or down to hear stuff read back. When you type an email, the flicking up and down gestures serve a different purpose: The gestures move the cursor left or right within the text.

>> **Two-finger swipe up:** Read everything from the top of the screen.

>> **Two-finger swipe down:** Read everything from your current position on the screen.

>> **Three-finger swipe:** Scroll in the direction of the swipe.

Zoom

The Zoom feature offers a screen magnifier for those who are visually challenged. To activate Zoom, in Settings, tap Accessibility ⇨ Zoom, and then tap the Zoom switch on. You can then use the following gestures:

- **Zoom in on a region:** Double-tap the region with three fingers.
- **Move the zoom around the screen:** Drag three fingers in the direction you want to move the zoomed in area.
- **Increase the magnification:** Double-tap with three fingers and then drag up.
- **Decrease the magnification:** Double-tap with three fingers and then drag down.
- **Zoom out:** Double-tap the screen with three fingers.

You can also triple-tap the screen with three fingers to display a dialog with several zoom controls, including a slider you can drag to set the magnification.

Hover Text

If you control your iPad with a pointing device such as a mouse or trackpad, the pointer itself might be hard to find, so it might not always be clear which screen item you're about to click. You can make your pointing device easier to use by activating the Hover Text feature: In Settings, tap Accessibility ⇨ Hover Text, and then tap the Hover Text switch on. (Hover Text is available also for a second-generation Apple Pencil if you're using it with a fourth-generation or later 11-inch iPad Pro or a sixth-generation or later 12.9-inch iPad Pro.)

With Hover Text on, now when you point at some text on the screen, your iPad displays a large-text version of the text at the top of the screen. In the Hover Text settings, you can adjust the position of the hover text, the scrolling speed, and the font, size, and color of the text.

Display & Text Size

If you have trouble reading the text on your iPad screen, you can take advantage of a large number of accessibility preferences that can help. In Settings, select Accessibility ⇨ Display & Text Size. This section offers a smorgasbord of controls for messing with text, including making text bold; increasing the text size; adding shapes to text-based buttons; adding on/off labels to switches; reducing transparency; increasing contrast; and having your iPad control the screen brightness automatically.

Motion

Certain kinds of onscreen effects can be extremely annoying for people with cognitive conditions such as attention deficit hyperactivity disorder (ADHD); they can be triggering for people who have epilepsy, vestibular disorders, or migraine sensitivity; and they have been shown to cause problems such as dizziness, headaches, and nausea.

If any of these conditions applies to you, you'll want to configure your iPad to use less interface motion: select Accessibility ⇨ Motion, and then tap the Reduce Motion switch on. You might also want to turn off the following switches: Auto-Play Message Effects, Auto-Play Animated Images, and Auto-Play Video Previews. Finally, you might want to turn on the following switches: Dim Flashing Lights and Limit Frame Rate (iPad Pro only).

Spoken Content

If you have trouble reading written text, you might prefer to have it read to you. That's the idea behind the controls in the Spoken Content category (in Settings, select Accessibility ⇨ Spoken Content).

For example, if you tap the Spoken Selection switch on, the next time you select some text, the Edit menu that appears above the text will now include a Speak command (you'll need to tap > to see this command). Tap Speak and your iPad reads the selected text out loud. (If you need to stop the playback, tap the selected text, tap >, and then tap Pause.)

Similarly, if you tap the Speak Screen switch on, you can get your iPad to read aloud the entire text of a page by slowly sliding two fingers down from the top of the screen. You also see a set of playback controls that enable you to pause, play, skip forward, skip back, and choose a speaking rate.

Typing Feedback allows you to hear what you type as you type it, and there are several controls for fine-tuning this feature.

Tap Voices to change the speaking voice and use the Speaking Rate slider to adjust the speaking rate for all spoken content. And the Pronunciations section allows you to fine-tune how specific phrases and words are pronounced.

Audio Descriptions

For a video, TV show, or movie, an *audio description* is a separate audio track that describes or narrates what's currently on the screen. Not all video content provides an audio description, but for those that do, it can be a great help if you're unable to see the visual content.

To enable audio descriptions when they're available, select Accessibility ⇨ Audio Descriptions, and then tap the Audio Descriptions switch on.

Touch

If you have mobility issues, using the touchscreen can be difficult, but your iPad has a few settings that can help. Select Accessibility ⇨ Touch to find the following settings:

» **AssistiveTouch:** If you have difficulties touching the screen, tap this setting and then tap the AssistiveTouch switch on. A large dot representing the top-level menu appears; tap the dot to access several common iPad features, such as Notification Center, Control Center, and Siri. Tap Customize Top Level Menu to make this feature your own. You can also create custom gestures through AssistiveTouch.

» **Haptic Touch:** Set the length of time before your iPad recognizes a long press to Fast, Default, or Slow.

» **Touch Accommodations:** Customize the touch sensitivity of your iPad. For example, tap Hold Duration on to change the amount of time you must touch the screen before your touch is recognized. Tap Ignore Repeat on to tell your iPad to treat multiple touches as a single touch. And you can enable a Tap Assistance option to allow any single finger gesture to perform a tap before a timeout period, which you can customize, expires.

» **Tap to Wake:** When this switch is on (as it is by default), you can tap your screen to wake up your iPad. If you find that you often accidentally tap the screen, you might want to turn this switch off (which means you can now wake your iPad only by pressing the top button).

» **Shake to Undo:** When this switch is on (it is by default), you can undo your last action with a shake of your iPad. If you find that you often activate undo by accident, consider turning this switch off.

» **Prevent Lock to End Call:** Normally you can press the iPad's top button to hang up a call. If you find that you often end calls inadvertently by accidentally pressing the top button, tap this switch on to prevent that from happening.

» **Call Audio Routing:** This feature determines to which speaker or headset an incoming call is routed. When set to Automatic (the default), your iPad will send call audio to whatever speakers you're currently using. If you want, you can configure this feature to route call audio to a specific device.

Face ID & Attention

On iPad models that support Face ID, select Accessibility ⇨ Face ID & Attention to control the connection between your attention and Face ID. If you leave the Require Attention for Face ID switch on, Face ID will unlock your iPad only when you're looking directly at your iPad. If you find that difficult, consider turning off this switch. (You'll need to confirm and enter your passcode to change this setting.)

If you leave the Attention Aware Features switch on, iPadOS will check to see if you're looking at your iPad before dimming the screen or lowering the alert volume.

Voice Control

Voice Control allows you to control your iPad with your voice. Select Accessibility ⇨ Voice Control, and then tap Set Up Voice Control to run through a setup procedure for this feature. This way of interacting with and controlling your iPad is different than the usual method, so I recommend tapping Open Voice Control Guide to get familiar with the commands you can use to dictate text, navigate your iPad, edit text, and more. Use the rest of the Voice Control settings to customize this feature, including setting your language, adding new commands and vocabulary, and customizing the command feedback you prefer.

Top Button or Top Button/Touch ID

Tap the Top Button or Top Button/Touch ID section for controls that change the how your iPad's top button works:

>> **Click Speed:** Choose between Default, Slow, and Slowest to change how fast your iPad should interpret when you press the top button. This setting is relevant when you press the top button more than one time to activate a feature.

>> **Press and Hold to Speak:** On by default, press and holding down your top button will enable Siri. Tap this setting off to disable Siri when pressing and holding down the top button.

If your iPad supports Touch ID, you also see a switch named Rest Finger to Open. This setting is on by default, which means that resting your finger on the top button not only unlocks your iPad but also displays the Home screen. If you turn off this switch, once you've unlocked your iPad with Touch ID, you need to swipe up from the bottom to display the Home screen.

Sound Recognition

Tap the Sound Recognition switch on, tap Sounds, and then turn on one or more sounds that you want your iPad to recognize for you, such as a fire or smoke alarm, a cat or dog, or a doorbell.

Audio & Visual

The Audio & Visual section of Accessibility has four or five controls (depending on whether your iPad has a rear LED flash):

>> **Headphone Accommodations:** Customize audio settings for your headphones.

>> **Background Sounds:** Specify a background sound to play — such as the sound or rain or the ocean — to help you focus or relax.

>> **Mono Audio:** Combine the right and left audio channels so that both channels can be heard in each speaker of any headset you plug in. This setting is helpful if you suffer hearing loss in one ear.

>> **Balance:** Use the slider control to adjust the audio balance between the left and right output channels. This feature is helpful if you have hearing trouble that's particularly bad in one ear because you can adjust the slider to turn up the sound for your bad ear or turn down the sound for your good ear or both.

>> **LED Flash for Alerts:** Turn on this setting to have the LED on the back of your iPad flash whenever iPadOS displays an alert. You see this setting only if your iPad comes with a rear LED flash.

Subtitles and Captioning

The Subtitles and Captioning category enables you to turn on the Closed Captions + SDH (subtitles for the deaf and hard of hearing) switch to summon closed-captioning or subtitles. You can also choose and preview the subtitle style and create your own subtitle style.

Hearing Control Center

If you have an MFi (Made for iPhone) hearing device connected to your tablet, iPadOS adds a Hearing control to Control Center. (If you don't see it, tap Settings ⇨ Control Center ⇨ Hearing.) In the Accessibility settings, you use the Hearing Control Center category to customize the controls you see when you tap Hearing in Control Center.

Accessibility Shortcut

You can set up the iPad so that triple-pressing the top button turns on an accessibility feature that you specify. Tap each accessibility feature you want to turn on when you triple-press. If you turn on two or more features, triple-clicking opens the Accessibility Shortcuts dialog so that you can choose which feature to use.

Siri & Search

If you love Siri, the chatty personal digital assistant who can remind you whether to take an umbrella or clue you in on how the Giants are faring in the NFL, see Chapter 14, where I devote a good chunk of the chapter to learning more about Siri. Here in Settings, you can change its voice from female to male, choose a default language, let Siri know your name, and decide whether to summon it through the "Hey Siri" command.

You can also tell the iPad which apps you want to search for by flipping the switch for each one. There are switches here to turn on Siri Suggestions for Search, Lookup, and your lock screen.

I address Search in Chapter 2 and Siri in Chapter 14. As a reminder, you can initiate a search on the iPad by dragging down from the middle of the Home screen.

Monitoring Screen Time

Screen Time enables you to both monitor how much time you and other users are spending on your iPad and set restrictions on how much time you, your children, your employees, or your students spend on their iPad and what each person can do during that time:

>> **App & Website Activity:** Tap this setting and then tap Turn On App & Website Activity. The Screen Time page will now show a report of your screen time usage. Tap See All App & Website Activity to get a more detailed report, including how much time you've spent in individual apps. You can also see the average number of times you've picked up your iPad, as well as the average number of notifications you received. All of these tools are

designed to help you take control of your own screen time, or the screen time of your children, employees, or students.

» **Limit Usage:** This section enables you to set restrictions on how and when your iPad is used:

- *Downtime:* Set limits on when your iPad can be used. You can block your iPad from use at different times and days of the week — or at the same time every day of the week.

- *App Limits:* Choose apps you want to limit on your iPad. You can limit individual apps, a category of apps, or all apps. When you've selected the apps you want to limit, tap Next to set the number of minutes or hours (or both) that those apps can be used during a given day.

- *Always Allowed:* Choose apps that can always be accessed on your iPad, regardless of other restrictions you've set.

- *Screen Distance:* Turn this setting on to get alerts when you hold your iPad too close to your face (less than 12 inches) for an extended period. The feature works only on iPad models that support Face ID.

» **Communication:** This section enables you set limits and restrictions on communications conducted via the voice call, video call, or text:

- *Communication Limits:* Restrict who you can communicate with via the Phone, Messages, and FaceTime apps.

- *Communications Safety:* Prevent receiving or sending sensitive photos and videos.

» **Content & Privacy Restrictions:** Tap this setting and then tap the Content & Privacy Restrictions switch on to enable the restrictions, which are designed to protect your privacy or the privacy of your children, employees, or students. Quite a few restrictions are here, and I encourage you to explore them fully.

» **Lock Screen Time Settings:** Set a passcode for accessing Screen Time.

TIP

If you're setting up Screen Time for your children, employees, or students, the Screen Time passcode should be different than the passcode that unlocks your iPad to prevent them from undoing the restrictions you so carefully set.

» **Share Across Devices:** Leave this switch on if you want to copy your Screen Time settings across every device signed into your iCloud account.

If you want to turn off Screen Time, tap Settings ➪ Screen Time ➪ Turn Off App & Website Activity at the bottom of the Screen Time settings.

Exploring the General Settings

Like the junk drawer in your kitchen that holds miscellaneous items that don't fit anywhere else, the Settings app offers the General category, where you'll find quite a few settings that don't fit in any of the other categories. Ah, but there's no junk here because General is chock-full of interesting items. The next few sections take you through the most useful of the General settings.

About

The About category is where you find info about your iPad. Most of the data is spectacularly technical, meaning it can be safely ignored by the likes of you and me. There are a few useful items here, though:

» **Name:** The name of your device, which you can edit. This name will appear on your network, in the share interface when using AirDrop to transfer files, and in the name of your device backups.

» **Software version:** The version of iPadOS running on your iPad.

» **Model Name:** Apple's official name for your iPad model.

» **Model Number:** The official model number for your iPad.

» **Serial Number:** The serial number of your iPad.

» **Songs:** The number of songs stored on your iPad.

» **Videos:** The number of videos stored on your iPad.

» **Photos:** The number of photos stored on your iPad.

» **Applications:** The number of apps installed on your iPad.

» **Capacity:** The total amount of storage on your iPad.

» **Available:** The amount of storage you haven't yet used on your iPad.

Software Update

The Software Update section is for updates to iPadOS. When Apple releases an update, you can find it here. If an update is ready, tap Update Now to get things started. If you don't want your iPad to install updates automatically, tap Automatic Updates and then, in the Automatically Install section, tap the iPadOS Updates switch off. However, you should always leave the Security Responses & System Files switch on to ensure that your iPad is always patched against the latest security vulnerabilities.

AirDrop

In the AirDrop setting, you can tap Receiving Off to turn off AirDrop on your iPad. Tap Contacts Only so that only people in your Contacts list can send you an AirDrop file. Tap Everyone for 10 Minutes to allow any Tom, Dick, or Harriet to send you files for up to 10 minutes. The last option is useful for those times when AirDrop refuses to work when you have Contacts Only selected and a legit contact can't see your iPad.

AirPlay & Handoff

The AirPlay & Handoff category controls four features:

>> **Automatically AirPlay:** When this preference is set to Automatic, your iPad will automatically reconnect to devices you've used with AirPlay in the past. If you'd rather your iPad confirm before reconnecting, select Ask instead.

>> **Handoff:** When on, this setting lets you start a task on one device (such as typing an email on your iPad) and then continue the task on another device (such as your iPhone or Mac). For Handoff to work, both devices must be running iPadOS, iOS 10 or later, or macOS Yosemite (10.10) or later; be signed in to same Apple ID; have Wi-Fi, Bluetooth, and Handoff turned on; be connected to the same Wi-Fi network; and be within 33 feet (10 meters) of each other. On the tablet, you'll be able to resume with the app from your dock, as shown in Figure 15-10. On a Mac, you'll see the appropriate app on the dock.

FIGURE 15-10:
Start a task on a Handoff-compatible device, and an icon for that task appears on your iPad's dock.

Icon representing the Handoff task (email, in this case)

>> **Cursor and Keyboard:** When on, this setting enables you to use a nearby Mac's mouse and keyboard with your iPad. I show you how this feature works in Chapter 18.

>> **Continuity Camera:** When on, this setting enables you to use your iPad as a webcam for your Apple TV 4K device.

iPad Storage

The iPad Storage category gives you detailed information about how your iPad is using its built-in storage. You can see what type of files take up how much space, and even see which apps are hogging the most storage and delete those you're no longer using.

Background App Refresh

Some apps continue to run in the background even when you're not actively engaged with them. If you have a Wi-Fi iPad, flip the Background App Refresh switch on to allow such apps to update content when an active Wi-Fi connection is available. If you have a Wi-Fi + Cellular iPad, tap the Background App Refresh button, and then tap Wi-Fi to update content only over Wi-Fi, or tap Wi-Fi & Cellular Data to update content over either Wi-Fi or the cellular network.

WARNING

If you have a cellular iPad and you choose the Wi-Fi & Cellular Data option, be aware that updating app content over the cellular network can eat into your cellular data plan in a hurry.

You can also toggle Background App Refresh for any individual app listed under this setting.

Date & Time

Tap Date & Time to reveal several settings for your iPad's clock:

>> **24-Hour Time:** Display a 24-hour clock.

>> **Show AM/PM in Status Bar:** Include the AM/PM designation. This setting is visible only if you are using a 12-hour clock.

>> **Show Date in Status Bar:** Display today's date in the status bar.

>> **Set Automatically:** Set the clock to the time on Apple's servers. I strongly recommend that you use this feature.

>> **Time Zone:** Manually set your time zone. If you're using the Set Automatically feature, this option will show your current time zone, and you can't change it.

Keyboard

Tap Keyboard to see the following options covering typing on your virtual keyboard:

» **Keyboards:** Use an international keyboard (see Chapter 2). You can also choose the layout of your English keyboards in this setting, substitute the default keyboard on your iPad to, for example, Swype, SwiftKey, or Fleksy. For more on adding a third-party keyboard, consult Chapter 2.

» **Hardware Keyboard:** Tap this setting to configure an external keyboard connected to your iPad.

» **Text Replacement:** Create shortcuts that will expand into longer text. The default entry is "omw." If you leave this entry as it is, whenever you type "omw," it will automatically expand to "On my way!" Tap the + icon at the top right of the screen to add your own text replacements. Tap the Edit button at the bottom of the screen to delete text replacement entries.

» **Auto-Capitalization:** Automatically capitalize the first letter of the first word you type after ending the preceding sentence with a period, a question mark, or an exclamation point. Auto-capitalization is on by default.

» **Auto-Correction:** The iPad takes a stab at what it thinks you meant to type.

» **Check Spelling:** iPadOS checks spelling while you type.

» **Enable Caps Lock:** All letters are uppercased LIKE THIS if you double-tap the shift key. (The shift key is the one with the arrow pointing up.) Tap shift again to exit caps lock.

» **Shortcuts:** The iPad's virtual keyboard will display a shortcut bar with controls to copy and paste the text you've selected text, or to make that text bold, italic, or underline. Don't confuse this Shortcuts setting with the "." Shortcut setting described later.

» **Predictive:** The iPad keyboard suggests certain words that you might want to type next. Tap a suggested word to accept it. You can also flip the Predictive switch on or off from the keyboard itself.

» **Smart Punctuation:** Your iPad will automatically format smart quotes and smart apostrophes as you type.

» **Enable Key Flicks:** Use a downward flick to type alternate characters on your keyboard.

>> **Slide on Floating Keyboard to Type:** Slide your finger across your iPad's floating keyboard to type.

>> **Delete Slide-to-Type by Word:** Delete entire words from Slide-to-Type when you use the delete key, as opposed to deleting one letter at a time.

>> **"." Shortcut:** A period is inserted followed by a space when you double-tap the space bar. This setting is turned on by default; if you've never tried it, give it a shot.

>> **Enable Dictation:** Use your iPad's microphone — or the microphone in a connected headset — to dictate your textual input.

>> **Auto-Punctuation:** When on, your iPad will automatically enter punctuation while you dictate text. Whether this setting is on or off, you can specify the punctuation you want by saying it: "period," "exclamation point," "question mark," and so on.

>> **Stickers:** Enable memoji stickers in your keyboard. See Chapter 6 for more on memoji stickers.

Language & Region

In the Language & Region section, you can set the language in which the iPad displays text, plus the date and time format for the region in question. You can choose a Gregorian, Japanese, or Buddhist calendar, too.

Dictionary

Tap the Dictionary setting to see both the dictionaries enabled on your iPad by default and the long list of optional dictionaries you can enable. Choosing an international keyboard will often enable additional dictionaries.

Transfer or Reset iPad

If you have a new iPad, tap Get Started to prepare to transfer your old iPad's data and settings to the new iPad. I talk about resetting your iPad in Chapter 16.

Shut Down

To shut down your iPad, tap Shut Down and then slide the slide to power off slider from left to right. Your iPad will promptly shut down. Tap the Cancel (X) button at the bottom of your screen to back out of the shutdown process.

Configuring Transactional Settings

You use your iPad to shop and pay for stuff, areas where the following settings apply.

App Store

In the App Store section, you decide whether your iPad should automatically download apps and app updates. And if you give the okay, you can choose whether to tap into your cellular network (if applicable) when downloading these items.

Wallet & Apple Pay

If you have an iPad with Touch ID or Face ID and want to take advantage of Apple Pay (Apple's mobile payments system), add a new credit or debit card in the Wallet & Apple Pay section. Apple Pay lets you make secure online purchases right from your tablet.

You can also manage your Apple Cash settings, including tying in a bank for sending and receiving money through Messages using Apple Pay. For an in-depth discussion of Apple Pay and Apple Pay Cash, see Chapter 6.

IN THIS CHAPTER

» **Troubleshooting iPad woes step by step**

» **Rebooting, recharging, and resetting your iPad**

» **Fixing network and syncing issues**

» **Getting help from Apple's website and forums**

» **Restoring your stuff on a repaired iPad**

Chapter **16**

Troubleshooting Common Problems

First, the good news: Your iPad is a solid, well-made device, so it should give you years of mostly trouble-free service. Now, the bad news: that word *mostly*. iPads are fiendishly complex devices running labyrinthically intricate software, so sometimes all that convolution catches up with your iPad and things go south.

Fortunately, there's more good news: Most iPad woes are quickly and easily fixed. In this chapter, you learn the most useful troubleshooting techniques that can help remedy the majority of iPad problems. You also learn some fixes for a few specific glitches.

After all the troubleshooting, I tell you how to get even more help if nothing I suggest does the trick. Finally, if your iPad is so badly hosed it needs to go back to the mother ship for repairs, I offer ways to survive the experience with a minimum of stress or fuss, including how to restore your stuff from an iTunes, Finder, or iCloud backup.

Troubleshooting iPad Problems: A Quick Guide

If your iPad starts behaving strangely, it's tempting to assume that the device itself is broken in some way. That's not impossible, but your iPad's innards have no moving parts, so it's unlikely that some internal component has gone belly-up. Instead, you can solve almost all iPad hiccups by following this general ten-step troubleshooting procedure (each step of which is explained in more detail in the next section):

1. Shut down whatever app you're using.
2. If you recently changed a setting, restore the setting to its previous state.
3. Shut down and restart your iPad.
4. Reboot your iPad's hardware.
5. Recharge your iPad.
6. Check for and install iPadOS updates.
7. Free up some storage space on your iPad.
8. Check your Wi-Fi network connection.
9. Reset any settings that are related to the problem you're having (such as resetting network settings if you're having connection issues).
10. Erase your iPad and restore a backup.

REMEMBER

To be clear, you don't have to run through all ten steps for every problem. Start with Step 1 and, if that doesn't solve the glitch, proceed to Step 2. Continue working through the steps until you've solved the problem, and then move on to bigger and better things.

Troubleshooting iPad Problems Step-by-Step

The next few sections take you through each of the troubleshooting steps from the previous section in a bit more detail.

Shut down whatever app you're using

If your iPad is unresponsive, it usually means that the app you're using has crashed and has taken your iPad down with it. Most of the time, you can get your iPad going again by forcing the stuck app to quit. Here are the steps to follow:

1. **Display App Switcher by swiping up from the bottom of the screen, pausing when you reach the middle of the screen.**

2. **Scroll right or left as needed to bring the app's thumbnail into view.**

3. **Drag the app thumbnail up to the top of the screen.**

   iPadOS sends the thumbnail off the screen and shuts down the app.

TIP

It's perfectly okay to force-quit an app even when it's working fine. Why would you want to do that? The best reason is that it reduces clutter in App Switcher by removing apps you know you won't use for a while. Lots of iPad mavens will tell you that's a surefire way to reduce your iPad's battery life because iPadOS has to spend extra battery power the next time you start any app that you force-quit. However, the extra juice required to open an app is trivial and can be ignored.

If your iPad is unresponsive and you can't display App Switcher, you need to restart your iPad, as I describe a bit later in this chapter.

Restore a changed setting

If you make a change in the Settings app and your iPad immediately starts behaving erratically, the changed setting is most likely the culprit. If you can still get to the Settings app, open it and restore the setting to its previous state. If your iPad is unresponsive, restart it (see the next section) and then revert the change in Settings.

Shut down and then restart your iPad

If your iPad is frozen, you won't be able to access either App Switcher or the Settings app — in fact, you won't be able to do anything at all with your iPad. Anything, that is, except shut down your iPad and then restart it. What good does that do? It reloads iPadOS, which almost always solves whatever glitch was causing your tablet to go haywire.

Follow these steps to shut down and then restart your iPad:

1. **Hold down both the top button and one of the volume buttons until you see the Slide to Power Off slider, as shown in Figure 16-1.**

2. **Drag the Slide to Power Off slider to the right to start the shutdown.**

3. **Give the device a few seconds to turn everything off.**

4. **To restart, press and hold down the top button and then release the button when you see the Apple logo.**

Reboot the iPad hardware

Restarting iPadOS, as I describe in the preceding section, is usually enough to solve any iPad problem. But if the problem still exists after the iPadOS restart or your iPad won't shut down, your next step is to reboot the tablet hardware.

FIGURE 16-1:
Press and hold down the top button and a volume button until you see this screen.

Here are the steps to follow:

1. **Press and release the volume up button.**

2. **Press and release the volume down button.**

3. **Press and hold down the top button until you see the Apple logo.**

Recharge your iPad

If your iPad is unresponsive and won't turn on, the most likely reason is that the battery is completely out of juice. Connect your tablet to a power outlet and wait for a while. If after a minute or two the device turns on and you see the battery logo, you know the tablet is charging and will be back up and running in a few minutes.

Check for iPadOS updates

Many iPad problems are caused by errors — known in programming parlance as *bugs* — in iPadOS or some other piece of your iPad's system software. There's a good chance Apple knows (or will soon know) about the glitch, will (eventually) fix it, and will then make the fix available as part of an iPadOS update.

You can check for and install iPadOS updates by following these steps:

1. **Open the Settings app.**

2. **Tap General.**

   Settings displays the General screen.

3. **Tap Software Update.**

   Settings begins checking for available updates. If you see the message "iPadOS is up to date," you can move on to other things.

4. **If an update is available, tap Update Now.**

   Alternatively, if you need your iPad right now, tap Update Tonight to postpone the software upgrade until the wee hours of the morning.

   Settings downloads the update and then proceeds with the installation, which takes a few minutes.

WARNING

Your tablet will go through with the update only if it has more than 50 percent battery life through the entire update operation. To ensure that the update is a success, plug your tablet into an AC outlet or run the update when the battery is fully charged.

Free up storage space

Your iPad uses its internal storage space to hold many things, including iPadOS, preinstalled apps, the apps you install, and the content you create with those apps. However, your iPad uses its internal storage also as a kind of temporary work area. If the iPad's memory space gets full, iPadOS will offload some of the contents of memory to its internal storage to make room in memory for new apps or content.

All this happens automatically and *way* behind the scenes, so you never have to worry about any of it. Or, I should say, you never have to worry about any of it *until* your iPad's internal storage is nearly full and it becomes more difficult for iPadOS to manage memory and perform certain operations. When that happens, you start seeing error messages letting you know that some operation can't be completed because there is "No space left on device" or "There is not enough available storage."

If you see any of these low-storage messages, you need to free up some storage space on your iPad pronto. Fortunately, iPadOS gives you several ways to free up space. To see these methods, use either of the following techniques to display the iPad Storage settings:

>> If you have a storage error message onscreen, tap Settings.

>> Open the Settings app, tap General, and then tap iPad Storage.

Either way, you end up at the iPad Storage screen, shown in Figure 16-2. The chart at the top of the screen shows how much of your iPad's storage space is used by various categories of data, such as Applications, Music, Photos, and iPadOS.

You also usually see a Recommendations section that offers one or more suggestions for saving storage space. You should try these recommendations before trying anything else.

Next, take a look at the list of apps to see which ones are taking up the most storage space. Chances are you'll see one or more apps that are taking up an unreasonable amount of space. If so, you can take back some or all of that space using any of the following techniques:

FIGURE 16-2:
The iPad Storage screen shows how much storage is being used and by what.

>> **Offload the app.** Tap the app, tap Offload App, and then tap Offload App when iPadOS asks for confirmation. This method removes the app from your iPad but keeps the app's data. Use this method for large apps that aren't storing tons of data on your iPad. The Offload App command is not available for many preinstalled apps (such as Messages and Safari).

>> **Delete the app.** Tap the app, tap Delete App, and then tap Delete App when iPadOS asks you to confirm. Use this method for apps that are storing a lot of data on your iPad (assuming you no longer need that data). Note that this method is not available for many preinstalled apps (such as Photos and iCloud Drive).

>> **Delete some or all of the app's data.** Tap the app to display its data usage. If you see a Documents section, such as the one shown in Figure 16-3 for the Messages app, tap a document category, and then tap Edit to put the category in edit mode. Tap to select the check box beside each item you want to delete and then tap the trash icon.

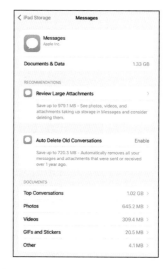

Check your Wi-Fi connection

Some apps will stop working or will act erratically if they lose access to the internet. So, if an app is acting weird — or if you can't do any internet-related chores such as view websites or check email — it could be that your iPad's Wi-Fi connection is missing in action.

FIGURE 16-3:
If an app has a Documents section, you can free up storage space by deleting individual data items from the app.

TIP

If you have an iPad that supports cellular connections and you're out of range of a Wi-Fi network, you might have problems with any app that isn't configured to use cellular data. To fix this, open Settings, tap Cellular Data, locate the app in the Cellular Data section, and then tap the app's switch on.

Checking Wi-Fi means performing two separate troubleshooting steps: Check your iPad's Wi-Fi connection and check your router's connection to the internet.

On your iPad, here are a few things to go through:

>> **Check that Wi-Fi is turned on.** Open the Settings app, tap Wi-Fi, and then, if necessary, tap the Wi-Fi switch on.

>> **Check how far your iPad is from your router.** A lack of Wi-Fi could mean your tablet is too far from the router. For most routers, the maximum range is about 230 feet, and the more obstacles between your iPad and the router, the shorter the range.

>> **Check that airplane mode is turned off.** Open Settings and then, if necessary, tap the Airplane Mode switch off. Alternatively, display Control Center and then tap to turn off the Airplane Mode icon.

- **Check that your iPad is still connected to your Wi-Fi network.** Open Settings and check the Wi-Fi setting. If you see Not Connected, tap Wi-Fi, and then tap your network to reconnect.

- **Toggle the Wi-Fi antenna:** Open Settings, tap Wi-Fi, tap the Wi-Fi switch off, and then tap the Wi-Fi switch back on again.

- **Disconnect from and then reconnect to the network.** Open Settings, tap Wi-Fi, and then tap the info icon (shown in the margin) to the right of the connected network. Tap Forget This Network to disconnect from the network and discard the network's saved login credentials. Tap your network and enter the password to reconnect.

- **Restart your iPad.** See "Shut down and then restart your iPad," earlier in this chapter.

- **Reset the network settings.** This removes all stored network data and resets everything to the factory state, which might solve the problem. See "Reset your settings," next, to learn how to do this.

On your Wi-Fi router, try these troubleshooting ideas:

- **Turn your Wi-Fi router off and then on again.** If your network accesses the internet using a separate broadband modem, turn the modem off then on again, as well.

- **Check for interference.** Many household devices — such as baby monitors and cordless phones — use the same 2.4 GHz radio frequency (RF) band as most Wi-Fi routers, which can interfere with Wi-Fi signals. If you have such a device near your Wi-Fi router, turn off the device or move it away from the router. Alternatively, set up a new Wi-Fi network using the 5 GHz band, if your router supports this. (See your router documentation.)

    You should keep your tablet and wireless access point well away from microwave ovens, which can jam wireless signals.

WARNING

- **Update the router firmware.** *Firmware* refers to the internal system software that runs the router. Router companies routinely offer firmware updates that fix device problems, so updating the router firmware might solve whatever connectivity issues you're having. (See your router documentation.)

- **Restore the router's factory settings.** If the router's settings are corrupted, you can reset the device to its original factory settings. (See the router documentation.) If you go this route, once the reset is complete, you'll need to set up your network again from scratch.

Reset your settings

A common cause of iPad wonkiness is when one or more of the tablet's settings gets corrupted. For example, if you can't connect to a known Wi-Fi network, it might mean that your iPad's network settings are broken. You can almost always work around such problems by resetting some or all of your iPad's settings. Here are the steps to follow:

1. **Open the Settings app and tap General.**

2. **Tap Transfer or Reset iPad.**

3. **Tap Reset.**

   Settings displays a list of reset options.

4. **Tap one of the following:**

   - **Reset All Settings:** Restore all settings to their factory defaults. Data and media are not deleted.

   - **Reset Network Settings:** Delete the current network settings and restore them to their factory defaults.

   - **Subscriber Services:** Reprovision (or refresh) your account and reset your authentication code. This option does not appear on all models.

   - **Reset Keyboard Dictionary:** Remove added words from the dictionary. Remember that the iPad keyboard is intelligent, and one reason why it's so smart is that it learns from you. When you reject words that the iPad keyboard suggests, it figures that the words you banged out should be added to the keyboard dictionary.

   - **Reset Home Screen Layout:** Revert all Home screen icons to the way they were at the factory.

   - **Reset Location & Privacy:** Restore your iPad's location and privacy settings to their factory defaults.

   Settings asks you to confirm that you want to perform the reset.

5. **Tap Reset.**

   Your iPad resets the selected settings.

Erase and restore your content and settings

If you have a backup of your iPad (I talk about creating iPad backups in Chapter 3), you can solve even the most recalcitrant problems by erasing all your iPad's settings and content and starting over with a fresh system. Then restore your backup and you're back in business.

Here are the steps to follow to erase your settings and contents and restore from a backup:

1. Open the Settings app, tap General, and then tap Transfer or Reset iPad.

2. Tap Erase All Content and Settings.

Settings tells you what it will erase from your iPad.

3. Tap Continue.

If you have Find My and Activation Lock turned on, Settings prompts you for your Apple ID password.

4. Type your password and then tap Turn Off.

Settings prompts you for your passcode. No passcode? Skip to Step 8.

5. Type your passcode.

Settings asks you to confirm that you want to erase your iPad.

6. Tap Erase iPad.

iPadOS erases your iPad and then restarts a few minutes later.

7. Run through the startup steps: selecting a language, country, Wi-Fi network, and so on.

If you're prompted to choose how you want to restore your iPad, tap Set Up Without Another Device. Eventually you see the Transfer Your Apps & Data dialog.

8. Tap From iCloud Backup and then sign in to your Apple ID.

Alternatively, if you used iTunes (on Mac or Windows) or Finder (on Mac) to back up your iPad, tap From Mac or PC and follow the instructions that appear.

The Choose an iCloud Backup dialog appears.

9. Tap your most recent iPad backup.

10. Continue with the rest of the setup steps.

You eventually see the Restore from iCloud screen, which shows the progress of the restore. After a few minutes, your iPad reboots, and you see your restored content and settings.

REMEMBER

iPadOS at first restores only enough to get you back up and running. The full restore from iCloud can take quite a long time, so in the interim you might find that some content, apps, or other features are temporarily unavailable.

Getting Help on the Apple Website

If you try everything I suggest earlier in this chapter and still have problems, don't give up just yet. This section describes a few more places you may find help. I recommend you check them out before you throw in the towel and smash your iPad into tiny little pieces (or ship it back to Apple for repairs, as I describe in the next section).

First, Apple offers an excellent set of support resources on its website at `https://support.apple.com/ipad`. You can browse support issues by category, search for a problem by keyword, read or download technical manuals, and scan the discussion forums.

Speaking of the discussion forums, you can go directly to them at `https://discussions.apple.com/`. They're chock-full of useful questions and answers from other iPad users. If you can't find an answer to a support question elsewhere, you can often find it in these forums. You can browse by category or search by keyword. Either way, you find thousands of discussions about almost every aspect of using your iPad.

TIP

Now for the best part: If you can't find a solution by browsing or searching, you can post your question in the appropriate Apple discussion forum. Check back in a few days (or even in a few hours), and some helpful iPad user may well have replied with the solution. If you've never tried this fabulous tool, you're missing out on one of the greatest support resources available anywhere.

Last, but certainly not least, try a carefully worded Google search. You might just find the solution.

If Nothing I Suggest Helps

If you've tried every trick in the book (this book) and still have a malfunctioning iPad, consider shipping it off to the iPad hospital (better known as Apple, Inc.). The repair is free if your iPad is still under its one-year limited warranty.

TIP

You can extend your warranty for as long as two years from the original purchase date, if you want. To do so, you need to buy AppleCare+ for your iPad. You don't have to do it when you buy your iPad, but you must buy it before your one-year limited warranty expires. AppleCare+ for iPad, iPad Air, and iPad mini is $3.49 per month for 24 months, or $69 if you pay up front. AppleCare+ for iPad Pro is $7.99 per month for 24 months or $149 if you pay up front.

Here are some things you need to know before you take your iPad in to be repaired:

>> *Your iPad may be erased during its repair,* so you should sync your iPad with iTunes, Finder, or iCloud and make a backup before you take it in, if you can. If you can't and you entered data on the iPad since your last sync, such as a contact or an appointment, the data might not be there when you restore your iPad upon its return.

>> Remove any accessories, such as a case or screen protector. If you have a cellular iPad, be sure to remove your SIM card.

TIP

Although you may be able to get your iPad serviced by Best Buy or another authorized Apple reseller, I recommend that you take it or ship it to your nearest Apple Store, for two reasons:

>> **No one knows your iPad like Apple.** One of the Geniuses at the Apple Store may be able to fix whatever is wrong without sending your iPad away for repairs.

>> **The Apple Store will, in some cases, swap out your wonky iPad for a brand-new one on the spot.** You can't win if you don't play, which is why I always visit my local Apple Store when something goes wrong (with my iPads, iPhones, iPods, and even my MacBooks and iMacs).

If you've done everything I've suggested, I'm relatively certain you're now holding an iPad that works flawlessly. Again.

That said, some or all of your stuff may not be on it. If that's the case, see the following section for a two-trick solution that usually works.

Dude, Where's My Stuff?

If you performed a restore or had your iPad replaced or repaired, you have one more task to accomplish. Your iPad may work flawlessly at this point, but some or all of your stuff — your music, movies, contacts, iMessages, or whatever — is missing. You're not sunk, at least not yet. You still have a couple of tricks up your sleeve.

>> **Trick 1: Sync your iPad with iTunes or Finder and then sync it again.** That's right — sync and sync again. Why? Because sometimes stuff doesn't get synced properly on the first try. Just do it.

>> **Trick 2: Restore from backup.** Click the General tab in Finder or the Summary tab in iTunes and then click Restore Backup. If Find My iPad (Settings ⇨ iCloud ⇨ Find My) is enabled, you'll first see a message to disable it before you restore your iPad. Then the Restore from Backup dialog appears and offers you a choice of backups. Select the one you want, click the Restore button, and let the iPad work some magic.

These backups include photos in the camera roll, text messages, notes, contact favorites, sound settings, and more, but not media you've synced, such as music, videos, or photos. If media is missing, try performing Trick 1 again.

TIP

If you have more than one backup for a device, try the most recent one first. If it doesn't work or you're still missing files, try restoring from any other backups.

If you aren't holding an iPad that works flawlessly and has most (if not all) of your stuff, it's time to make an appointment with a Genius at your local Apple Store, call the support hotline (800-275-2273), or visit the support web page at `https://support.apple.com/ipad`.

6

The Part of Tens

IN THIS CHAPTER

» Locking your iPad with a passcode, a fingerprint, or facial recognition

» Putting your iPad to sleep automatically

» Controlling app access to your location, hardware, and data

» Checking passwords for involvement in a data leak

» Setting up restrictions for a kid's iPad

Chapter **17**

Ten Ways to Beef Up Privacy and Security

Your iPad is a music and video player, a web browser and wayfinder, an email and text exchanger, a payments device, and much more. However, although you might readily see your iPad in all these different roles, there's one role you might overlook: a vault. Perhaps you dismiss the idea because, after all, a vault is a place to store valuable things. Ah, but then you've fallen right into my trap: If your iPad had seams it would be bursting at them with valuables in the form of your precious personal data. And if your iPad were to fall into the wrong hands, those hands would also have access to an uncomfortable amount of important data (important to *you*, anyway).

In this chapter, you investigate ten useful ways to turn your iPad into a vault that safeguards your sensitive (and not-all-that sensitive) personal info. From locking your iPad to backing up your stuff to setting restrictions, read on to secure your iPad and its data.

Lock Your iPad with a Passcode

No matter what model of iPad you use, your first line of defense is to set up a passcode that must be typed before iPadOS will display the Home screen. You can set a simple four- or six-digit passcode or a more complex one that uses any combination of numbers, letters, and symbols.

Here are the steps to follow to lock your iPad with a passcode:

1. **Open the Settings app.**

2. **Tap one of the following:**

- *If your iPad supports Face ID:* Tap Face ID & Passcode.

- *For all other iPad models:* Tap Touch ID & Passcode.

3. **Tap Turn Passcode On.**

The Set Passcode dialog appears.

4. **To use something other than the default six-digit passcode, tap Passcode Options and then tap the passcode type you prefer:**

- *Custom Alphanumeric Code:* A passcode of any length (minimum four characters) consisting of any combination of letters and numbers.

- *Custom Numeric Code:* A passcode of any length (minimum four characters) consisting of numbers.

- *4-Digit Numeric Code:* A passcode consisting of four numbers.

WARNING

Whatever type of passcode you use, try to avoid easily guessed codes such as the month and year of your birthday or anniversary. Also, avoid the following overly used (and therefore easily guessed) codes: 1234, 4321, 2580, 0852, 0000, 1111, 2222, 5555, 1212, 123456, 654321, 123123, 112233, 789456, 159753, 000000, 111111, 222222, and 121212.

5. **Type your passcode and, if you're entering a complex passcode, tap Next.**

Settings asks you to reenter your passcode.

6. **Type your passcode again and, if you're typing a complex passcode, tap Done.**

7. **If iPadOS prompts you for your Apple ID password, type your password and then tap Sign In.**

WARNING

Please don't forget your passcode! If you do, iPadOS will lock you out of your own device. You can still get back in, but the only route is a drastic one: You must restore the tablet's data and settings from an existing backup (which I describe in Chapter 16).

Lock Your iPad with a Fingerprint

If you have an iPad, iPad Air, or iPad mini, you can protect your tablet using Touch ID, the fingerprint sensor built into the top button. By teaching the device your unique fingerprint, you can unlock your tablet merely by leaving your finger or thumb resting on the fingerprint sensor. You can use the same fingerprint to approve purchases you make in the iTunes Store, the App Store, and with retailers who accept Apple Pay.

TIP

In the following steps, you have to enter a passcode after you add your first fingerprint. Therefore, you might as well set up a passcode now; see the preceding section for the instructions.

Here's how to set up Touch ID:

1. **Open the Settings app.**

2. **Tap Touch ID & Passcode and then type your passcode to open the Touch ID & Passcode screen.**

3. **Tap Add a Fingerprint.**

   The Touch ID screen appears.

4. **Lightly rest your thumb — or whatever finger you most often use when you're unlocking your iPad — on the fingerprint sensor (that is, the top button).**

5. **Repeatedly lift and place your finger as Touch ID learns your fingerprint pattern.**

6. **When you see the Capture All of Your Fingerprint screen, tap Continue.**

7. **Once again, repeatedly lift and place your finger, this time emphasizing the edges of the finger.**

8. **When you see the Complete screen, tap Continue.**

9. **To specify another fingerprint, repeat Steps 3–8.**

TIP

If you add multiple fingerprints, iPadOS names them "Finger 1," "Finger 2," and so on, which doesn't do much to help you tell one from the other. To give a fingerprint a more descriptive name (such as "left index finger" or "right thumb"), tap the fingerprint and then use the text box to type the new name.

Here's how you use Touch ID (for each, use the Home button instruction if your iPad has a Home button; otherwise, use the top button instruction):

>> **Unlock your iPad.** Using a fingerprint-scanned finger, either press the Home button or press, release, and then rest your finger on the top button until the Home screen appears.

>> **Make an iTunes or App Store purchase.** In the iTunes Store or the App Store, tap the price of the item you want to buy and then tap the Buy button. When the Touch ID dialog appears, rest your finger on the Home button or the top button until the purchase is approved.

>> **Make an in-app purchase.** For apps that support Apple Pay, tap the Apple Pay button in the checkout screen and then place your scanned finger over the Home button or the top button.

>> **Make an Apple Pay purchase.** You can use Touch ID to pay for goods in the real world without having to use cash or a credit card. If a merchant accepts Apple Pay, place your scanned finger over the Home button or the top button and then hold the tablet near the store's contactless reader.

Lock Your iPad with Facial Recognition

Recent versions of the iPad Pro — that is, all generations of the 11-inch iPad Pro and the third generation and later of the 12.9-inch iPad Pro — replace Touch ID with Face ID, which enables you to unlock your tablet using facial recognition. By letting your iPad learn to recognize your face, you can unlock the device just by looking at it. This works even if you are wearing sunglasses or haven't shaved for a few days.

REMEMBER

Face ID on the iPad doesn't work if you're wearing a mask, such as the cloth masks so many of us used during the COVID-19 pandemic.

You can also use facial recognition to approve purchases you make via the iTunes Store, the App Store, and Apple Pay, as well as authorize the use of AutoFill passwords.

TIP

In the following steps, you have to enter a passcode to access the Face ID settings, so you might as well set up a passcode now as I describe earlier in this chapter.

Here are the steps to follow to configure Face ID:

1. **Open the Settings app.**

2. **Tap Face ID & Passcode and then type your passcode to open the Face ID & Passcode screen.**

3. **Tap Set Up Face ID.**

   The How to Set Up Face ID screen appears.

4. **Tap Get Started.**

   Settings displays a frame on the screen.

5. **Position your face within the frame and then slowly rotate your head until you fill in the circle that appears.**

   When the circle is complete, the first Face ID scan is complete.

6. **Tap Continue.**

7. **Once again, position your face within the frame and then slowly rotate your head until you fill in the circle that appears.**

   When the circle is complete, the second Face ID scan is complete.

8. **Tap Done.**

Configure Your iPad to Sleep Automatically

You can put your iPad into standby mode at any time by tapping the top button once. However, if your tablet is on but you're not using it, the device automatically goes into standby mode after two minutes. This feature is called auto-lock, and it's handy because it saves battery power and prevents accidental taps when your iPad is just sitting there.

Auto-lock is also a crucial feature if you've protected your tablet with a passcode lock, Touch ID, or Face ID, as I describe earlier, because if your device never sleeps, it never locks either unless you shut it off manually.

To make sure that your iPad sleeps automatically or to change the default two-minute Auto-Lock interval, follow these steps:

1. **Open the Settings app.**

2. **Tap Display & Brightness.**

   The Display & Brightness settings appear.

3. **Tap Auto-Lock.**

   The Auto-Lock screen appears.

4. **Tap the interval that you want to use.**

   You have five choices: 2 Minutes, 5 Minutes, 10 Minutes, 15 Minutes, or Never.

Back Up Your iPad

The data you have on your iPad might not be vital in the overall scheme of things, but there's no doubt it's vitally important to you. Therefore, it makes sense to protect your tablet's data and settings by backing up your iPad to your iCloud account. That way, if you lose your tablet or you have to erase it because of a problem, you can at least restore your data and settings from the backup. (I show you how this is done in Chapter 16.)

Follow these steps to back up your iPad's data and settings to iCloud:

1. **Open the Settings app.**

2. **Tap your name near the top of the Settings pane.**

   The Apple ID settings appear.

3. **Tap iCloud.**

4. **Tap iCloud Backup.**

5. **If necessary, tap the Back Up This iPad switch on.**

   This configures iPadOS to make automatic backups whenever it's locked, connected to a Wi-Fi network, and plugged into a power source.

6. **Tap Back Up Now.**

   iPadOS backs up your tablet's data to your iCloud account.

Control Which Apps Can Use Your Location

When you launch an app that would like to use location data, you see a dialog similar to the one displayed in Figure 17-1. Here, the app is requesting permission to use the iPad's location tools to determine your location.

Note, however, that whichever permission you give the app, you can always change your mind later. Here are the steps to follow to control how an app can access Location Services:

1. **Open the Settings app.**

2. **Tap Privacy & Security.**

   The Privacy & Security settings appear.

3. **Tap Location Services.**

4. **Tap the app you want to work with.**

5. **Tap one of the following (note that not all apps offer all these options):**

FIGURE 17-1:
Apps that can use location data require your permission to use that data.

- *Never:* Prevents the app from using your location.

- *Ask Next Time or When I Share:* Configures the app to ask for permission to use your location the next time you run the app or use the app to share your location.

- *While Using the App:* Gives the app permission to use your location when you use the app.

- *While Using the App or Widgets:* Gives the app or its widget permission to use your location when you use the app or widget.

- *Always:* Gives the app permission to use your location even when you're not using the app. (Note that this setting is available only for certain apps.)

6. **If you don't want the app to use your exact location, tap the Precise Location switch off.**

Make Sure Apps Can't Track You

Some apps want to track your activity across the apps and websites of other companies. Why would they want to do that? Usually, they want to show you ads targeted to your activities, but sometimes they just want to sell your activity info to data brokers.

If it all sounds positively dystopian, you're right. That's why iPadOS not only requires these apps to ask for permission to track you but also denies these tracking requests by default. Thanks!

However, just to make sure, follow these steps to ensure that tracking is turned off on your iPad:

1. **Open the Settings app.**

2. **Tap Privacy & Security.**

   The Privacy & Security settings appear.

3. **Tap Tracking.**

4. **Make sure the Allow Apps to Request to Track switch is set off.**

   If it isn't, tap the switch to the off position and then say "Whew!"

Control App Access to Your iPad's Hardware and Data

Most iPad apps just go about their business and don't mess around with your privacy. However, some apps will ask your permission to use iPad data such as your contacts, calendars, and photos, and iPad hardware such as your microphone, camera, and Bluetooth radio.

If you give (or deny) permission to an app to use your iPad data or hardware, you can always change your mind and revoke (or grant) that permission. Here's how:

1. **Open the Settings app.**

2. **Tap Privacy & Security.**

   The Privacy & Security settings appear.

3. **Tap the app, data type, or hardware device that you want to work with.**

   Settings displays a list of apps that have at one time requested permission to use the resource you just tapped. If you granted permission to the app, the app appears in the list with its switch set on; otherwise, the app's switch is off.

4. **Tap the app's switch off or on to deny or grant, respectively, permission to use the resource.**

Check for Compromised Passwords

iPadOS has an autofill passwords feature that, when activated, enables web browsers to save login credentials for websites. (To activate this setting, choose Settings ⇨ Passwords ⇨ Password Options and then tap the AutoFill Passwords switch on. In some cases, the name of this switch is AutoFill Passwords and Passkeys.)

The Autofill passwords feature not only saves you time and taps but can also make your online life more secure. How? Because iPadOS has a feature that examines known data breaches. If a password you've saved via autofill has been involved in one of those data breaches, iPadOS will alert you so that you can take action (such as changing your password on the site).

Besides getting an alert for a breached password, you can also follow these steps to check for such compromised passwords:

1. **Open the Settings app.**

2. **Tap Passwords.**

   The Passwords settings appear.

3. **Tap Security Recommendations.**

   Settings displays the Security Recommendations screen, which includes a list of compromised credentials.

4. **Make sure that the Detect Compromised Passwords switch is on.**

5. **For each breach you want to fix, tap the recommendation to see its details, then tap Change Password on Website to update your password.**

Set Restrictions on a Child's iPad

If you have children with their own iPads, you probably don't want them performing certain tasks on the tablet, such as installing and deleting apps, changing account settings, and making in-app purchases. You also might be concerned about some of the content they could be exposed to on the web, on YouTube, or in iTunes, and you might not want them giving away their current location.

For all these and similar parental worries, you can sleep better at night by activating the parental controls. Follow these steps to set these controls, and restrict the content and activities that kids can see and do:

1. **Open the Settings app on your child's iPad.**

   The first time you tap Screen Time, you see an overview of the feature.

2. **Tap Screen Time, read the overview, and then tap Turn On Screen Time.**

   Screen Time asks whether this is your iPad or your child's.

3. **Tap This Is My Child's iPad.**

   The What Content Can *Name* Access? (where *Name* is your child's name).

4. **Use the slider to set your child's age.**

   Screen Time applies age-appropriate restrictions to all the categories listed below: Apps, Books, TV Shows, Movies, and so on.

5. **(Optional) Customize any category by tapping the category and then tapping an option from the pop-menu that appears.**

6. **Tap Turn On Restrictions.**

   The Set Time Away from Screens? dialog appears so that you can enable Downtime. You use Downtime to set times when the child can't use the iPad without your permission.

7. **Use the Start and End controls to set a schedule for when the child isn't allowed to use the tablet; when you're done, tap Turn On Downtime.**

   The Set App and Website Limits? dialog appears. You use App and Website Limits to set the maximum time the child is allowed to use certain app categories, such as Games.

8. **For each app category you want to limit:**

   a. *Select the check box beside an app category you want to limit.* Alternatively, select the All Apps & Categories check box to set a limit on everything at once.

b. *In the Time Amount setting, tap Set and then select the maximum number of hours and minutes the child is allowed for the selected app categories.*

c. *Tap Set App Limit.*

d. *Repeat these steps for the next app category.*

iPadOS asks you to enter a Screen Time passcode. You use this passcode to access the Screen Time settings and to override the restrictions you've set.

REMEMBER

The Screen Time passcode is not the same as the passcode used to unlock an iPad.

9. **Type the passcode you want to use, and then type the passcode again when prompted.**

iPadOS prompts you to enter Apple ID credentials.

10. **Enter your Apple ID email address and password and then tap OK.**

You can use this information to reset your Screen Time passcode if you forget it.

IN THIS CHAPTER

» **Connecting your iPad to external devices**

» **Making your iPad just a little less annoying**

» **Locating a lost iPad**

» **Making the most of your dock**

» **Taking a picture with your volume buttons**

Chapter **18**

Ten Hints, Tips, and Shortcuts

I f someone asked me to pick my ten favorite iPad features, I'd probably say something like, "How could I? It would be like picking my ten favorite children!" (Then to myself, I'd snicker and think, "Ho, ho, I don't even *have* ten children!") However, my editor just sighed and asked once again, "Could you *please* just pick your ten favorite iPad features. Thanks!" Okay, for her — and especially for *you*, dear reader — I've put together ten of my favorite hints, tips, and shortcuts. Enjoy!

Using a Mac Mouse and Keyboard with Your iPad

The iPad is a handy device, for sure, but how often have you thought to yourself, "Man, if this baby had a mouse and keyboard, I could rule the world!" What's that? You've never thought that? Really. Well, no matter, trust me when I say that if you want to do truly productive work on your iPad, an external mouse and keyboard can help, bigtime. But not just any external mouse and keyboard. No, I'm talking here about something you might already have: the mouse (or track-pad) and keyboard connected to your Mac. That's right: Why shell out big bucks for new peripherals when the ones you already have can do the job?

The secret here is a feature called Universal Control, which enables a Mac's mouse (or trackpad) and keyboard to also control a nearby iPad. To make it happen, you need the following:

» **iPad:** You're using a sixth-generation or later iPad, an iPad Pro, a third-generation or later iPad Air, or a fifth-generation or later iPad mini. You must be running iPadOS 15.4 or later.

» **Mac:** You have a relatively recent Mac running macOS 12.3 or later.

» **Apple ID:** On both your iPad and your Mac, you're signed in with the same Apple ID with two-factor authentication.

» **Settings:** On both your iPad and your Mac, you have Wi-Fi, Bluetooth, and Handoff turned on.

Bring your iPad and Mac near each other. On your Mac, click Control Center in the menu bar, click Display, and then click your iPad in the list that appears, as shown in Figure 18-1. With that done, you can control your iPad with your Mac's mouse by moving the pointer past the right edge of the Mac screen. The pointer now shows up on your iPad screen. Cool! Any typing required on your iPad you can perform also using your Mac's keyboard.

FIGURE 18-1:
Click your iPad to link your Mac's mouse and keyboard to it.

Connect Your iPad to an External Monitor

Even the big 12.9-inch screen of a top-of-the-line iPad Pro can feel cramped when you're doing certain tasks. If you have an external monitor lying around, why not take advantage of all that screen real estate and connect your iPad to the display?

Assuming your iPad has a USB-C connector or a Thunderbolt/USB-4 connector, you have two options here:

>> **If the external monitor has a compatible port:** Run your iPad's charging cable from your iPad directly to a USB-C, Thunderbolt, or USB4 port on the monitor.

>> **If the external monitor doesn't have a compatible port:** Get an adapter that converts your iPad's connector to a connector compatible with a port on your external monitor. For example, Apple offers the USB-C Digital AV Multiport Adapter, which enables a USB-C cable to connect to an HDMI (High-Definition Multimedia Interface) port on the monitor.

Note that, depending on the type of monitor you're connecting with, you might have to change the monitor input to the port to which your iPad is connected.

Turn Off Keyboard Clicks

A *keyboard click* is a brief sound effect — yep, it's a click — that fires each time you tap a key on the onscreen keyboard. For unfathomable reasons, every iPad comes with keyboard clicks turned on by default. What's the problem? Have you ever sat near someone who does a lot of typing on the iPad? If so, you know all-too-well how annoying those incessant clicks became after even just a few minutes' exposure.

Do yourself and everyone around you a huge favor and turn off keyboard clicks by choosing Settings ⇨ Sounds and tapping the Keyboard Clicks switch to off.

Locate a Lost iPad

If you lose your iPad, all might not be lost, especially if you have the Find My iPad feature turned on (as I urged in Chapter 15). Follow these steps to see whether you can locate your lost iPad:

1. **Sign in to your iCloud account at www.icloud.com from any browser on your computer.**

2. **Click the apps icon (grid of dots to the left of your profile photo in the top-right corner), click Find My, and then sign in to your Apple ID, if requested.**

   Assuming your tablet is turned on and in the coverage area, its general whereabouts turn up on a map in standard or satellite view, or a hybrid of the two.

3. **In the All Devices pane, click your lost iPad.**

   iCloud displays options for your iPad. How you proceed from here depends on where you iPad appears on the map. If the iPad is nearby, proceed to Step 4; if the iPad is far away, skip to Step 5.

4. **If your iPad is nearby, click Play Sound and then use the sound to locate your device.**

   Assuming your search was successful, tap OK on the iPad to stop the sound, and then skip the rest of these steps.

5. **Click the Mark as Lost button and then click Next.**

   If your iPad doesn't have a passcode, iCloud prompts you to enter a passcode to lock the iPad.

6. **Enter the passcode twice.**

   iCloud asks you to enter a phone number where you can be reached.

7. **Type a phone number and then click Next.**

   iCloud prompts you to enter a message that will appear on the iPad screen.

8. **Type a plea to the Good (you hope) Samaritan who picked up your iPad.**

9. **Click Activate.**

   iCloud locks your iPad and displays the message on the lost iPad's screen.

Customize Your Dock with Your Most Used Apps

The dock is one of the most used elements of iPadOS. It comes with several apps by default, as described in Chapter 2, but you can also add up to 15 apps to the dock.

To add an app to the dock, long-press the app icon on your Home screen, and then tap Edit Home Screen. With the icons now wiggling adorably, drag the icon down into the dock, drag the icon horizontally within the dock until it's in the position you prefer, and then release the icon. Done! Don't be shy — add your most commonly used apps to the dock for quick access to them from anywhere.

Type on a Floating Keyboard

Have you ever wanted the virtual keyboard in iPadOS to be smaller? Why didn't you say so? In any app that uses the virtual keyboard, just pinch the keyboard using two fingers (or a finger and a thumb), and it will shrink to less than half its normal size. The keyboard will also be set to float, so you can move it anywhere on the screen.

To move your floating keyboard, tap and drag the gray bar at the bottom of the keyboard. To expand the keyboard back to its full size and re-dock it to the bottom of your screen, either spread two fingers on it or drag it to the bottom of your screen. It will automatically expand to its normal dimensions and position.

Find Almost Anything Using Spotlight

Spotlight is a feature that can easily be overlooked. If you need to find something on your iPad or do a quick web search without opening Safari first, swipe down from the middle of your Home screen to open Spotlight. Type your search term, and you'll get relevant results from your iPad, apps on your iPad, and Siri suggestions for websites.

Long-Press Home Screen Icons

You can long-press any Home screen icon for quick access to actions specific to that app. Some apps will have more — or fewer — actions available. For instance, long-pressing the News app icon will give you quick access to some of the news sites you follow. Tapping and holding down on the Maps app gives you quick access to marking your location, sharing your location, and searching nearby. Apple's Measure app, on the other hand, has no special actions available, but every app will give you the option to Edit Home Screen or Remove App.

Lock Your Screen's Rotation

You can unlock and lock your iPad's screen rotation when needed. This feature is handy; I use it frequently. For instance, when lying down and reading, I lock my screen because I don't want my iPad rotating the screen every time I move. But when I'm doing many other activities, I usually want to be free to rotate the screen at any time. To lock or unlock your screen rotation, swipe down from the upper-right corner to open Control Center and tap the screen rotation lock icon.

Use a Volume Button as a Camera Shutter

When taking photographs with your iPad, you can use either the volume up or volume down button as a camera shutter button. Many times, I just can't reach the onscreen shutter button, and this handy trick has really helped me out. If you want to shoot a burst of photos, press and hold down either button for as long as you need.

Index

About the Author

Paul McFedries has been a technical writer for 30 years (nope, not a typo) and owns more than 1,000 iPads (definitely a typo). He has written more than 100 books that have sold more than 4 million copies throughout the known universe. Paul's books include the Wiley titles *iPad Portable Genius,* Fourth Edition, *iPhone Portable Genius,* Sixth Edition, *Macs All-in-One For Dummies,* Sixth Edition, *HTML, CSS, & JavaScript All-in-One For Dummies,* and *Teach Yourself VISUALLY Windows 11.* Paul invites everyone to drop by his personal website (https://paulmcfedries.com) and to follow him on X, formerly Twitter (@paulmcf) and Facebook (www.facebook.com/PaulMcFedries/).

Dedication

For Karen and Chase

Author's Acknowledgments

The American journalist and essayist Pete Hamill once said that "Everyone needs an editor." I believe that to be true and that it gives me carte blanche to act, however briefly, as Mr. Hamill's editor. So, allow me to amend his words slightly: Everyone doesn't just need an editor, they need an editor as good as Susan Pink, who was this book's project editor and copy editor. If this book reads well (and I happen to think it does), that's courtesy of the just-so editorial ministrations of Susan. Thanks for making me look so good in print, Susan! And if this book is accurate (and I happen to think it is), that's courtesy of the keen eye and unmatched technical know-how of technical editor Guy Hart-Davis. Thanks for having my back, Guy! I'd also like to thank acquisitions editor Elizabeth Stilwell for all her hard work getting this project off the ground and executive editor Steve Hayes for asking me to writing this book in the first place.

Publisher's Acknowledgments

Acquisitions Editor: Elizabeth Stilwell

Project Editor: Susan Pink

Copy Editor: Susan Pink

Technical Editor: Guy Hart-Davis

Proofreader: Debbye Butler

Production Editor: Saikarthick kumarasamy

Cover Image: © anand purohit/Getty Images; © Farknot_Architect/Getty Images

PERSONAL ENRICHMENT

9781119187790	9781119179030	9781119293354	9781119293347	9781119310068	9781119235606
USA $26.00	USA $21.99	USA $24.99	USA $22.99	USA $22.99	USA $24.99
CAN $31.99	CAN $25.99	CAN $29.99	CAN $27.99	CAN $27.99	CAN $29.99
UK £19.99	UK £16.99	UK £17.99	UK £16.99	UK £16.99	UK £17.99

9781119251163	9781119235491	9781119279952	9781119283133	9781119287117	9781119130246
USA $24.99	USA $26.99	USA $24.99	USA $24.99	USA $24.99	USA $22.99
CAN $29.99	CAN $31.99	CAN $29.99	CAN $29.99	CAN $29.99	CAN $27.99
UK £17.99	UK £19.99	UK £17.99	UK £17.99	UK £16.99	UK £16.99

PROFESSIONAL DEVELOPMENT

 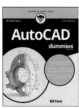     

9781119311041	9781119255796	9781119293439	9781119281467	9781119280651	9781119251132	9781119310563
USA $24.99	USA $39.99	USA $26.99	USA $26.99	USA $29.99	USA $24.99	USA $34.00
CAN $29.99	CAN $47.99	CAN $31.99	CAN $31.99	CAN $35.99	CAN $29.99	CAN $41.99
UK £17.99	UK £27.99	UK £19.99	UK £19.99	UK £21.99	UK £17.99	UK £24.99

9781119181705	9781119263593	9781119257769	9781119293477	9781119265313	9781119239314	9781119293323
USA $29.99	USA $26.99	USA $29.99	USA $26.99	USA $24.99	USA $29.99	USA $29.99
CAN $35.99	CAN $31.99	CAN $35.99	CAN $31.99	CAN $29.99	CAN $35.99	CAN $35.99
UK £21.99	UK £19.99	UK £21.99	UK £19.99	UK £17.99	UK £21.99	UK £21.99

dummies.com

dummies®
A Wiley Brand